The Concept of Environment in Judaism, Christianity and Islam

Key Concepts in
Interreligious Discourses

Edited by
Georges Tamer

Volume 10

The Concept of Environment in Judaism, Christianity and Islam

Edited by
Christoph Böttigheimer and
Wenzel Maximilian Widenka

DE GRUYTER

KCID Editorial Advisory Board:
Prof. Dr. Asma Afsaruddin; Prof. Dr. Nader El-Bizri; Prof. Dr. Christoph Böttigheimer;
Prof. Dr. Patrice Brodeur; Prof. Dr. Elisabeth Gräb-Schmidt; Prof. Dr. Assaad Elias Kattan;
Dr. Ghassan el Masri; PD Dr. Elke Morlok; Prof. Dr. Manfred Pirner; Prof. Dr. Kenneth Seeskin

ISBN 978-3-11-078231-8
e-ISBN (PDF) 978-3-11-078245-5
e-ISBN (EPUB) 978-3-11-078269-1
ISSN 2513-1117

Library of Congress Control Number: 2022948643

Bibliographic information published by the Deutsche Nationalbibliothek
The Deutsche Nationalbibliothek lists this publication in the Deutsche Nationalbibliografie;
detailed bibliographic data are available on the Internet at http://dnb.dnb.de.

© 2023 Walter de Gruyter GmbH, Berlin/Boston
Printing and binding: CPI books GmbH, Leck

www.degruyter.com

Preface

The present volume of the book series "Key Concepts in Interreligious Discourses" (KCID) documents the results of a conference which dealt with the concept of "Environment" in Judaism, Christianity and Islam and was held at the Catholic University of Eichstätt-Ingolstadt. The conference was organised by the research unit "Key Concepts in Interreligious Discourses" and held online on June 17 and 18, 2020, due to the then ongoing pandemic of COVID-19.

The research unit "Key Concepts in Interreligious Discourses" was jointly run by the Friedrich-Alexander-University Erlangen-Nuremberg and the Catholic University Eichstätt-Ingolstadt between June 2018 and June 2021. As the title already implies, the joint project focused on interreligious discourse. Its aim was to reflect upon and thereby facilitate a theologically well founded interreligious dialogue. For only if every partner in a conversation has a clear notion of what is discussed, the dialogue can be conducted reasonably. It was the project's ambition to provide such clarification by examining concepts that are of central importance for Judaism, Christianity and Islam, both, historically in terms of their interdependencies, and by setting them in a relation to one another. Common values and origins, but also differences and contradictions between the three monotheistic religions shall be clearly elaborated, by reflecting on and comparing central ideas and beliefs in their historic contexts. By disclosing key concepts of the three closely interconnected religions: Judaism, Christianity and Islam, a deeper mutual understanding is fostered, prejudices and misunderstandings are counteracted and thus a contribution is made to peaceful interaction based on respect and recognition.

Only through precise knowledge of the central ideas of the foreign as well as of one's own religion a well-founded, objective and constructive interreligious understanding can prevail. Conferences at which international experts from the fields of theology, religious studies and philosophy of religion intensively discussed and clarified core religious ideas from the perspective of the three religions served this purpose. Developments within religious history never proceed in isolation; rather, they interpenetrate each other and are mutually dependent. Thus, the research unit "Key Concepts in Interreligious Discourses" pursued fundamental research and aimed at an "archaeology of knowledge" with its comparative conceptual-historical investigations.

Inasmuch as world peace cannot be obtained without religious peace, the project contributed importantly to a peaceful social coexistence and thus corresponds to the obligation that has been newly assigned to the universities in recent decades, namely, to engage in social concerns in addition to teaching and research. This is expressed by the term "third mission".

I wish to thank Dr. Wenzel Maximilian Widenka, who not only organised the conference but also edited this volume. In addition to the cooperation partners of the Friedrich-Alexander-University Erlangen-Nuremberg and the De Gruyter publishing house for including this volume in the book series "Key Concepts in Interreligious Discourses", we would like to express our sincere thanks to the third-party funders, the Karpos Foundation of the Diocese Eichstätt, Maximilian Bickhoff Foundation and the ProFor Program of the Catholic University Eichstätt-Ingolstadt. Without their support, neither the conference nor the present volume would have been brought into being.

Christoph Böttigheimer

Table of Contents

Rabbi Yonatan Neril and Rabbi Leo Dee
The Concept of Environment in Judaism —— 1

Kerstin Schlögl-Flierl
The Concept of Environment in Christianity —— 77

Yasin Dutton
The Concept of Environment in Islam —— 135

Christoph Böttigheimer and Wenzel M. Widenka
Epilogue —— 161

List of Contributors and Editors —— 171

Index of Persons —— 173

Index of Subjects —— 177

Rabbi Yonatan Neril and Rabbi Leo Dee
The Concept of Environment in Judaism
An Ecological Perspective Based on Jewish Tradition

1 Introduction

"Rabbi Amorai asked: 'Where is the Garden of Eden?' He replied: 'It is on earth.'"[1]

Rabbi Jonathan Sacks writes, "Hope is a human virtue, but one with religious underpinnings. At its ultimate it is the belief...[that God] is mindful of our aspirations, with us in our fumbling efforts, that He has given us the means to save us from ourselves; that we are not wrong to dream, wish and work for a better world. Hope is the knowledge that we can choose; that we can learn from our mistakes and act differently next time."[2]

Many people fear that humans have irrevocably destroyed the ecology of "Eden" on earth. But God created the world out of love for life on earth. This chapter, adapted from Eco Bible volume 1: An Ecological Commentary on Genesis and Exodus, explores the deep inspiration we can find in the Hebrew Bible for fulfilling the blessing of all life, for changing course to preserve God's creation, and for sustaining human life in harmony with nature and all of God's creatures.

The Hebrew Bible is also called the Torah, the Five Books of Moses, or the Pentateuch (and also refers to the Prophets and Writings, which are not addressed in this commentary). How does the Hebrew Bible relate deeply to living in balance with God's creation, through a lifestyle that is not only aware of but protects the natural world? Is concern for environmental stewardship external to the Hebrew Bible, or a central message embedded within it? This chapter reveals a spiritually grounded vision for both long-term sustainability and immediate environmental mindfulness and action.

Some people believe religion is separate and distinct from ecology or care for God's creation. Most Hebrew Bible study, teaching, and preaching occur without addressing the ecological crisis, the greatest crisis facing humanity. This chapter

---
1 Sefer HaBahir 31.
2 Sacks, Jonathan, *The Dignity of Difference: How to Avoid the Clash of Civilizations*, London: Continuum, 2003, 207.

applies an ecological perspective to reveal how the Hebrew Bible itself, and thousands of years of Biblical teaching by Jewish rabbis, indeed *embrace* care for God's creation as a fundamental message. An ancient Jewish commentary on the Hebrew Bible, the Midrash, teaches that "God gazed into the Hebrew Bible and created the world."[3] The Divine teaching is a blueprint for all of creation and instructs us about living sustainably in the world God created.

Were it not for the receiving of the Hebrew Bible on Mt. Sinai, the Midrash teaches, God would have returned the world to chaos and void.[4] Rabbi Samson Raphael Hirsch writes that the ideal of the Hebrew Bible "awaits the generation which will finally have become matured for its ideals to be made into a reality."[5] Applying the teachings of the Hebrew Bible to stewardship of God's creation is not just an idea for today, but essential for a future in which we achieve a balanced, worldwide ecosystem and thrive on a planet viable for all life.

This chapter quotes scores of rabbis and other Jewish thinkers commenting on verses from the Hebrew Bible. *Eco Bible*, including Volume I, Genesis and Exodus, and Volume II, Leviticus, Numbers, and Deuteronomy, was published during a time of accelerating environmental challenges, a worldwide coronavirus pandemic, and widespread protests for racial justice. Ecological disasters and COVID-19's devastating spread are causing the tragic loss of so many lives as well as a profound disruption of natural ecosystems, families, communities, cultures, and the populations of entire nations. Pollution disproportionately impacts people of color and calls for environmental justice are growing.

These interconnected crises are signals to humanity of the need for restoring balance between people and nature. The Hebrew Bible's Divine wisdom can provide important messages for striving to find this balance. Some of the Hebrew Bible's verses – which first "spoke" to people in ancient times when the Bible was given – may seem cryptic, obscure, or irrelevant to our modern times or lives. The chief function of contemporary commentaries like *Eco Bible*, as with all rabbinic commentaries that have strived to enlighten, is to make the holy book relevant in our own generation and those to come.

This chapter explores how the Hebrew Bible and traditional commentaries relate to a range of critical, contemporary ecological challenges, such as preserving animal and plant biodiversity, ensuring clean air, land, and water, and showing compassion to both domestic and wild animals. Each of us can take many

---

[3] Midrash Genesis Rabbah 1:1.
[4] Midrash Exodus Rabbah 47:4.
[5] Hirsch, Samson Raphael, commentary to Numbers 8:11, in: *The Pentateuch*, vol. 4: Numbers, Gateshead, England: Judaica Press, 1989.

different kinds of actions that sustain the world and sustain our souls. "Study is not the most important thing, but action,"[6] Rabbi Shimon ben Gamliel says.

1.1 The Need for Jewish Ecological Ethics

The Ark, which held the Tablets God gave Moses on Mt. Sinai, physically moved with the Israelites during their 40 years in the desert.[7] The word of God contained in the Ark is a revolutionary teaching; to remain dynamic and alive, it has to keep moving with human concerns or it will become reactionary, static, fixed. Commentaries on the Bible must move forward too. This new *Eco Bible* commentary is extremely timely – both grounded in millennia of rabbinic thought and speaking to the greatest challenges facing humanity in the twenty-first century.

Rabbi Abraham Isaac Kook, the first chief rabbi of Israel before its statehood in 1948, spoke of learning the Hebrew Bible "for its sake," where the teachings "become more and more expansive."[8] Rabbi Daniel Kohn understands this to mean that the Hebrew Bible becomes ever more multifaceted, expressive, variegated, and beautified.[9] *Eco Bible* attempts to unfold and reveal the profound Divine teachings of the Hebrew Bible from an ecological perspective, among what Rabbi Shlomo ben Aderet recognizes as "the ever-increasing number of fresh understandings of the Bible's verses."[10]

Religion has been a channel for moral and ethical instruction across the ages and the world. Faith can and should help us to address the roots of our planet's ecological crisis. Rabbi Dov Berkowitz says in regard to the Hebrew Bible, "How do we utilize 3,500 years of spiritual consciousness for the betterment of our contemporary society?"[11] When we are faced with the compelling, sustained insights of religious thought and tradition, we can come to see our current life choices in a different and more ecological light.

---

6 Ethics of the Fathers 1:17.
7 Numbers 10:35.
8 Kook, Abraham Isaac, "On Torah for its Own Sake," *Orot HaTorah II*, Jerusalem: Sifriat Hava, 2005, §1.
9 Kohn, Daniel, oral teaching, Yeshivat Sulam Yaakov, Jerusalem, May 2011.
10 Rashbam, commentary to Genesis 37:2.
11 Talk at Vayehi Ohr Conference, Hebrew University of Jerusalem, April 5, 2009.

1.2 Addressing the Spiritual Roots of the Ecological Crisis

What on earth are we doing to creation? We have disrupted the ecological balance of all God created on earth, and we owe it to God, to each other, and to all species to restore the balance. This is the greatest physical and spiritual challenge humanity has ever faced together. Caring for creation is key to receiving the full blessings of the Creator. Awareness of the Infinite opens us up to protecting the immediate – the very planet on which we live.

As a fundamental part of many people's lives, religion can be a key motivator by shaping values. Religion appeals not just to our intellect but to our soul – and this is where change is most needed. When God is at the center of our environmental awareness, it becomes much more powerful. At this moment in history, we need a major infusion of energy specifically to help faith groups inspire behavioral change for sustainable living.

We offer this chapter to accelerate the awakening religious and spiritual process, so humanity can keep moving fast enough to avert irreversible environmental deterioration of our only home. The environmental movement has failed to effect transformational change in the past 50 years partly because fear of the darkness of ecological collapse has driven the movement. The light of spirituality can spark a more hopeful approach with deeper and broader effect. Here are three reasons why.

First, religion can persuade people to consume in moderation as they find true satisfaction in spirituality, community, and family. Spiritual living should bring consciousness to our consumption. To rise to this ultimate challenge for human civilization, we have to raise our spiritual awareness and maturity. A person can exist at varying levels of soul awareness, but a sustainable planet will require that we learn to live and thrive at higher levels of spiritual consciousness.

Second, religious teachings help instill foresight and long-term thinking. The rabbis of the Talmud taught about 1,500 years ago: "Who is the wise person? The person who can see the effect of their actions."[12] We must put both the present and future of our children and grandchildren first, above expanding our own standard of living. Spiritual awareness can help us recognize the link between our actions and the larger problem, while cultivating foresight, concern, and change.

Finally, and perhaps most importantly, religion embodies hope. Some people – out of terror, anger, or depression – despair of our ever returning to personal and

---

12 Babylonian Talmud, Tamid 32a.

planetary balance and sustainability. Yet, to reiterate Rabbi Sacks' words, "Hope is a human virtue, but one with religious underpinnings."[13]

Billions of people equally respect the scientific view of the universe and the spiritual view. This chapter draws on the wisdom of many generations of Jewish sages, contemporary rabbis, and scientific sources to connect religion and science. E.O. Wilson, famed biological scientist and educator, writes in his book *The Creation: An Appeal to Save Life on Earth*, "Religion and science are the two most powerful forces in the world today... If there is any moral precept shared by people of all beliefs, it is that we owe ourselves – and future generations – a beautiful, rich and healthful environment."[14]

1.3 Drilling On Ships

According to a 1,800-year-old Jewish commentary on the Hebrew Bible, Rabbi Shimon bar Yochai describes a group of people traveling in a boat. One of them takes a drill and begins to bore a hole. The others ask, "Why are you doing this?" The person replies, "Why are you concerned? Am I not drilling under my own place?" The rest reply, "But you will flood the boat for all of us!"[15]

Imagine being a passenger on this boat. One person, without concern for others, jeopardizes your safety and security. The person drilling may have compelling reasons. Perhaps they are hungry and want to drop a fishing line, or hot and want to cool their feet in the water. Maybe the boat is on fresh water, and they are thirsty. But no matter how compelling the reason, drilling a hole in a boat to fulfill one person's desires threatens everyone.

Rabbi Shimon's story warns us of the destructive power of letting our selfish desires overtake all other considerations. Today's environmental challenges are *not* about "whatever floats your boat." Everyone on the boat (or planet) needs to work together to ensure such behavior doesn't continue. The person drilling is dangerous, but the rest of us ignoring the threat they pose is equally dangerous. If the boat sinks, the fault is both the driller's and those who stood idly by.

---

13 Sacks, Jonathan, *The Dignity of Difference: How to Avoid the Clash of Civilizations*, London: Continuum, 2003, 207.
14 Wilson, Edward O., *The Creation: An Appeal to Save Life on Earth*, New York: W.W. Norton & Company, 2006, 3–5.
15 Midrash Leviticus Rabbah 4:6.

1.4 The Earth Is Our Collective Ship

We have one home. With close to eight billion people and around eight million species, the earth is our collective ship. Jumping ship is out of the question. Some of the most profound ecological lessons come from people on a ship, from Noah to today's polar researchers, on a ship trapped in Arctic ice to study climate change. Something about being surrounded by water heightens our awareness of vulnerability, and of personal and collective safety. People on a ship can feel more compelled to act when someone behaves recklessly, because they see how directly another's damage can endanger their and others' lives. The ship metaphor sharply conveys the paradigm of responsibility, stewardship, and respect that we need for sharing and steering our planet.

In our times, the indirectness and "invisibility" of the planetary damage we cause poses a major challenge. Even when we are very aware of our role in the problem, we don't see the effect of our actions on a daily basis. The earth is so big and complex. Turning on a car engine, a light switch, or an air-conditioner doesn't suddenly raise the outside temperature or trigger an extreme storm. But we are essentially drilling holes without fully grasping the consequences of our action. If we did fully grasp them, could we look our children in the eye and admit to them that our lifestyle will jeopardize their future?

Perhaps we are ecologically passive because our current lifestyle gives us so much pleasure and comfort. We are bombarded, tantalized, and too often influenced toward increased consumption by advertising mottoes like "Makes me happy" and "I'm lovin' it!" The Ba'al Shem Tov teaches that when the soul lacks spiritual pleasure, it compensates by pursuing the pleasures of this world and its excesses.[16] What do we truly care about most? We must face the collective reality that we cannot simultaneously expand our consumer behaviors and live sustainably.

Our actions are the true indication of our commitments. In 1992, the world's governments committed to curbing climate change and reducing emissions of greenhouse gases, yet every year since, humanity's emissions have risen. Emissions of CO_2 in 2020 have doubled since 1990. Clearly, we are not sufficiently committed to the announced goal. Since 1992, billions of people have continued to source their food unsustainably from across the planet, collectively taken millions of plane flights and driven billions of miles, and eaten a tremendous amount of food cultivated through unsustainable and even dangerous processes. These trends show no sign of reversing. What can shift our direction, to care and

---

16 As quoted by Rabbi Moshe Luria, Bahir Beit Ganzei, *Pitchei Tefillah*, part 2, 15.

work more diligently toward what is most important – a thriving, spiritually aware, and sustainable humanity – and to live in ways that can actually achieve this?

1.5 Noah's Ark and the Titanic[17]

According to Jewish oral tradition, God gave humans 120 years before unleashing the Flood. God chose Noah as a messenger to build the Ark as a sign to the people that the flood would come unless they changed their actions.[18] Noah said to the people, "Return from your evil ways and deeds."[19] They did not. What led God ultimately to carry out the most serious environmental catastrophe in human history and, through flood, wipe away virtually all living creatures?

The judgment was sealed because of the sin of lawlessness, robbery, or wrongdoing (ḥamas). The rabbis of the Talmud teach that "a person would put out a market stall full of beans, and each person would come and take less than a penny's worth so that they could not be prosecuted by the law."[20] Rabbi Samson Raphael Hirsch teaches that "ḥamas is a wrong that is too petty to be caught by human justice, but if committed continuously can gradually ruin your fellow person."[21]

God said, "You are not playing by the book, so I too will not play by the book."[22] God responded by bringing a single drop of rain and then another. Just as the people took one bean and then another, without looking at the consequences of their combined actions, so God punished them drop by drop, culminating in the Flood.

We can see parallels in our modern times. In 1896, Swedish Nobel chemist Svante Arrhenius was recognized for his theory of climate change.[23] Nearly a century later, the UN created the 1988 Intergovernmental Panel on Climate Change "to provide the governments of the world with a clear scientific view of what is

---

17 Part of this section on Noah is from Neril, Yonatan, "*Countering Destruction: Lessons from Noach*," Canfei Nesharim, a branch of Grow Torah, February 19, 2004, http://canfeinesharim.org/countering-destruction-lessons-from-noach-longer-article/

18 *Eitz Yosef* commentary to Midrash Tanchuma, Parshat Noach, §5.

19 Pirkei d'Rabbi Eliezer, ch. 22.

20 Midrash Genesis Rabbah 31:5.

21 Hirsch, Samson Raphael, commentary to Genesis 6:11, in: *The Pentateuch*, vol. 1: Genesis, Gateshead, England: Judaica Press, 1989, 138.

22 Midrash Genesis Rabbah 31.

23 Maslin, Mark, *Global Warming, A Very Short Introduction*, Oxford: Oxford University Press, 2004.

happening to the world's climate."[24] The world has largely ignored the panel's warnings. Even concerned nations struggle to significantly change the actions of their governments and populations.

It has been 120 years since Arrhenius' climate change theory, and massive floods now repeatedly threaten even the most developed countries. After Hurricane Harvey in 2017, *The New York Times* quoted Maya Wadler, a teenager in Houston, Texas, as she recalled the moments her family's home flooded. "I usually just trust my parents that everything is going to be okay. But I looked up, and I saw that my dad was closing his eyes, the water was getting in his eyes. And I just thought: He has absolutely no idea where we are going to go."[25] In 2019, Houston flooded for the third time in three years.

Many such devastating events have arrived sooner and more intensely than predicted.[26] We are ill-prepared. With eight billion people sharing our planet, the greatest risk again comes from seemingly inconsequential actions of individuals, combining in their impact. This age is even called the Anthropocene, including the human-caused sixth great extinction event on earth.[27] *For the first time, humans can now destroy or radically alter virtually all life on earth – a power so great it could once only be ascribed to God.*

Our current reality has striking similarities to the Titanic, whose captain received many warnings of icebergs from other ships but chose to ignore them. He believed that his ship – the largest ever built – was stronger than nature, unsinkable. By the time the crew spotted the fatal iceberg, it was too late to turn the ship away from its cataclysmic collision course.

Today, we are on an ecological collision course of our own making and are bearing full steam ahead. But there is still time to act like Noah instead of the Titanic's captain. Our ship carries all of humanity and all species. By uniting and striving to live in balance with creation, and with God's help, we can steer toward a future that ensures the survival and thriving of everyone and everything on board.

---

24 "History of the IPCC," Intergovernmental Panel on Climate Change, accessed March 1, 2020, https://www.ipcc.ch/about/history/
25 Turkewitz, Julie / Fernandez, Manny / Blinder, Alan, "In Houston, Anxiety and Frantic Rescues as Floodwaters Rise," *The New York Times*, August 27, 2017, https://www.nytimes.com/2017/08/27/us/hurricane-harvey-texas.html?_r=0
26 Linden, Eugene, "How Scientists Got Climate Change So Wrong," *The New York Times*, November 8, 2019, https://www.nytimes.com/2019/11/08/opinion/sunday/science-climate-change.html
27 Ceballos, Gerardo / Ehrlich, Paul R. / Raven, Peter H., "Vertebrates on the Brink as Indicators of Biological Annihilation and the Sixth Mass Extinction," *Proceedings of the National Academy of Sciences*, June 2020, 201922686, https://www.pnas.org/doi/10.1073/pnas.1922686117

1.6 Key Jewish Ecological Principles

Traditional Jewish views towards the land, animal life and the environment come from a number of explicit sources in the Torah dealing with:
- the commandment not to waste or destroy;
- the Oneness of God's creation, and importance of protecting it and maintaining biodiversity;
- commandments to rest from creating and altering the environment (the weekly sabbath, and the sabbatical year);
- commandments regarding the ethical treatment of animals.

These Biblical commandments have had a profound impact on Jews and their approach to the environment and animal life.

1.7 Historical Development of Jewish Ecology

The concept of Jewish ecology has developed over the millennia, and a full reckoning of this history is beyond the scope of this chapter. Since the beginning of the modern environmental movement in the 1960s, the Jewish ecology movement has grown, and hundreds of books have been published that relate to Jewish ecological teachings. Indeed, while there are only fifteen million Jews in the world, the Jewish ecological movement has been robust to a much greater extent than the number of Jews might indicate. Jewish ecologists have also taken prominent roles in the global religion and ecology movement.

1.8 Jewish Communities in Israel on Environmental Sustainability

Israel has become a key provider of clean technology and a role model for many other nations in the fields of water recycling, solar power and forestry with its constant flow of new technologies aimed at solving the world's greatest sustainability problems. However, Israel's domestic ecological issues have only recently started to hit the Nation's radar. Part of this stems from the fact that most Jewish educational institutions do not emphasize Jewish ecological teachings as part of their educational programs.

Whilst Israel is undeniably a "light unto the Nations" in the field of Clean Technology, it has yet to demonstrate that it is a "light unto itself", applying its own environmental saving technologies nationally, but one can only pray that that will come, in time.

With all the positive signs from the Jewish state (investment in Clean Technology, planting of trees, wide adoption of solar panels by household, etc), there are some clear challenges ahead for Israel.

- The discovery of huge Natural Gas resources off the coast of Tel Aviv means that substantial investment in renewable energy within the State of Israel is likely to be delayed, and Israel is likely to become a major exporter of fossil fuels.
- Israel holds the unenviable title of the greatest consumer of single-use plastics (SUP) per capita in the world. This is partly due to the convenience factor of SUP with large families (Israel has an over 80 % greater fertility rate of the OECD average[28]) and partly due to the kashrut issues of separating milk and meat, where SUP use avoids the problems of eating milk-based foods on plates previously used for meats. Since this text was first written, the Israeli government has enacted a 100 % tax on single use plastics and the authors hope that this will see a substantial decline in use over the coming years.
- Recycling in Israel is still in its infancy. Whilst most municipalities have the facility to recycle paper, plastic and glass, there is still a lack of organic recycling or composting.
- Whilst recent regulations to charge minimally for plastic bags in supermarkets has dramatically reduced plastic bag usage, these rules still do not apply in many shops, noticeably local grocers, and packaging of products within the supermarkets has yet to be addressed in any significant way.

May it be God's will, that with the abundant information available to us in this connected world, we increasingly understand the benefits that caring for our planet has on ourselves, our communities, humanity, and all of God's creations.

2 Jewish Ecology in the Creation Narrative

2.1 Caring for Creation

The first quote we'll look at is the very first line of the Bible: *Genesis 1:1 – In the beginning, God created the heavens and the earth.*

---

[28] Cf. OECD Data, 2018, which reveals Israel has a fertility rate of 3.1 versus an OECD average of 1.7.

Rabbi Samson Raphael Hirsch makes the first verse in Genesis personal and proactive. He writes that the words teach us "to think of the world as God's world and ourselves as creatures of God... We must not destroy the world, but preserve it – every single creature, every insect, every plant is part of God's world. Woe to those that disturb His world! Hail to those that preserve His world!"[29]

Rabbis throughout the ages make clear that God tasks humanity with caring for creation. "When God created Adam, He took him and showed him all the trees of the Garden of Eden and said to him... Be careful not to spoil or destroy my world – for if you do, there will be nobody after you to repair it,"[30] teaches the Midrash, a major rabbinic commentary on the Hebrew Bible.

Rabbi Shlomo Eiger, a distinguished intellectual who became a Hasid (spiritual and pious person), was asked what he learned from his first visit with the hasidic Rabbi Menachem Mendel of Kotzk. Rabbi Eiger answered simply, "In the beginning, God created." The questioner pressed him: "Did a renowned scholar have to travel to a hasidic rabbi to learn the first verse of the Bible?" Rabbi Eiger responded: "I learned that God created only the beginning; everything else is up to human beings."[31]

Rabbi David Rosen explains the ecological impact of the Bible's opening verse: "If you believe that this world is the creation of a Divine Power, therefore creation itself manifests the Divine Presence, as it says in Psalms, 'The heavens declare the glory of God and the firmament declares the work of His hands.'[32] If you are a Divinely sensitive person, whether you want to define that as religious or spiritual, then the wellbeing, the health of the environment, and of creation, is a religious imperative."[33]

2.2 Sustainability and Spiritual Awareness

We are given reason to understand how sustainability is woven into the essence of the beginning. Genesis 1:3 states "God said, 'Let there be light'; and there was

---

[29] Hirsch, Samson Raphael, commentary to Genesis 1:1.
[30] Midrash Ecclesiastes Rabbah 7:13.
[31] As cited in Lamm, Norman, *Derashot Ledorot: A Commentary for the Ages – Genesis,* Jerusalem: OU Press and Maggid Books, 2012, and Lamm, Rabbi Norman, *Faith and Doubt,* Brooklyn: KTAV Publishing House, 1986, 175.
[32] Psalms 19:1.
[33] Rosen, David, *"Jewish Ethics, Animal Welfare, and Veganism: A Panel of Rabbis and Experts,"* interview, Jewish Eco Seminars Productions, January 2018, https://www.youtube.com/watch?v=UHIyXrN1JAI

light." Since the sun was not created until the fourth day (see Genesis 1:16), the light God created on the first day of creation was not a physical light but a spiritual one. Rabbi Sholom Berezovsky teaches that "without this holy light there is no merit in sustaining creation."[34] Those who seek God perceive this spiritual light. The sustainability of creation therefore depends on the spiritual awareness of humanity.

2.3 Previous and Current Extinction Events

There's a hint that unimaginable catastrophes are built into the fabric of creation in Genesis 1:5: "God called the light Day, and the darkness He called Night. And there was evening and there was morning, a first day." The Midrash asks why this verse reads *"And* there was evening" rather than just "There was evening" – implying that there was something else before. The Midrash answers, "…time existed before this…God created and destroyed worlds until this one…when it says, 'God saw everything He had made and behold it was very good,'[35] that teaches us that the previous ones were not."[36]

This explanation suggests that cataclysmic extinction events once occurred, and that sustained existence on this planet is not guaranteed. Scientists understand that five extinction events occurred in the last 500 million years, and humans are causing a sixth one at the current time.[37] The previous extinction events were caused by "acts of God," like comets and massive volcanic eruptions. But the current one is caused by people on a creation that God declared "very good."

2.4 Water and Dry Land

We learn something interesting from Genesis 1:9, which says "God said, 'Let the water below the sky be gathered into one area, that the dry land may appear.' And it was so." The Midrash about this verse states: "In human experience, a person empties a full vessel into an empty one; does one ever empty a full vessel

---

34 Berezovsky, Shalom, *Netivot Shalom*, Jerusalem: Yeshivat Beit Avra-ham Slonim, 2000, Numbers 41.
35 Genesis 1:31.
36 Midrash Genesis Rabbah 3:7.
37 Greshko, Michael, "What Are Mass Extinctions, and What Causes Them?", *National Geographic*, https://www.nationalgeographic.com/science/prehistoric-world/mass-extinction/

into a full vessel? Now the world was full of water, yet it says [that God gathered the water], 'into one area'! From this we learn that the little held a lot."[38]

Water separated from the earth by draining into the seas and by forming ice on the land. For most people who do not live near a glacier, the amount of earth's water held as ice may seem small compared to all the water in lakes and oceans. In fact, roughly 68 percent of the world's freshwater is locked in ice caps, glaciers, and permanent snow.[39] Due to human-caused climate change, however, ice melting of Antarctica has increased from 40 gigatons per year in the 1980s to 252 gigatons per year over the 2010s. All that ice melting into the ocean has raised global sea levels.[40] In some coastal areas, sea level rise is beginning to regularly flood whole towns and low-lying parts of major cities. God said that dry land should appear from the water, yet by humanity's actions, more and more water is covering land.

2.5 Edible Trees

Let's take a look at Genesis 1:11–12, which says: "And God said, 'Let the earth sprout vegetation: seed-bearing plants, fruit trees of every kind on earth that bear fruit with the seed in it.' And it was so. The earth brought forth vegetation: seed-bearing plants of every kind, and trees of every kind bearing fruit with the seed in it. And God saw that this was good." As Rabbi Jacob ben Asher points out, God commanded the earth to produce "fruit trees that bear fruit," meaning trees whose bark could be eaten as well as their fruit. However, he notes that the earth produced trees (whose bark is not eaten) that produce fruit in order that the trees themselves would not be devoured.[41]

Long ago, and today, we have come to understand that trees – in addition to the fruit they produce – have broader value including providing homes for animals large and small, and retaining soil to prevent erosion and catastrophic mudslides.

---

[38] Midrash Genesis Rabbah 5:7.
[39] "Ice, Snow, and Glaciers and the Water Cycle," Water Science School, US Geological Survey, accessed February 18, 2020, www.usgs.gov/special-topic/water-science-school/science/ice-snow-and-glaciers-and-water-cycle?qt-science_center_objects=0#qt-science_center_objects
[40] Rignot, Eric et al., "Four Decades of Antarctic Ice Sheet Mass Balance from 1979–2017," *Proceedings of the National Academy of Sciences* 116, 4 (2019), 1095–1103, https://doi.org/10.1073/pnas.1812883116
[41] Tur Ha'Arokh on Genesis 1:11.

2.6 God Blesses Fish and Birds

There's abundance built into God's creation, as we see in Genesis 1:22: "God blessed them [fish and birds], saying, 'Be fertile and increase, fill the waters in the seas, and let the birds increase on the earth.'" Radak (Rabbi David Kimchi) explains that God's blessing to fish to "be fertile" is to have the potential to create new generations, while the blessing to "increase" is to thrive in numbers.[42]

Worldwide, humans are now depleting the planet's fish stocks through overfishing and plastic use. A UN report indicates that one-third of marine fish stocks were being harvested at unsustainable levels in 2015.[43] Extensive plastic pollution kills fish, marine mammals, seabirds, and other wildlife, and reduces their ability to give birth, rear their young, and sustain their species.[44] In regard to birds, a 2019 Cornell University study "finds steep, long-term losses across virtually all groups of birds in the US and Canada. It reveals across-the-board declines that scientists call 'staggering.' All told, the North American bird population is down by 2.9 billion breeding adults."[45]

God desires abundant sea life to fill the ocean and healthy bird populations. Should we not, therefore, be strong advocates for sustainable fishing, ending ocean pollution, and protecting both land birds and sea birds?

2.7 On Eating Animals

The verse Genesis 1:26 states God intends for people to rule over fish, birds, and animals: "And God said, 'Let Us make man in Our image, after Our likeness. They shall rule the fish of the sea, the birds of the sky, the cattle, the whole earth, and all the creeping things that creep on earth.'" Yet in Genesis 1:29, God states that human beings are only permitted a plant-based diet. Rabbi

---

[42] Radak on Genesis 1:22. See also Midrash Genesis Rabbah 97:3 and Baby-lonian Talmud, Berakhot 20a which relate to Genesis 48:16 on the use of the Hebrew root containing fish, *dag*, as meaning "to reproduce and proliferate."

[43] "UN Report: Nature's Dangerous Decline 'Unprecedented'", United Nations, May 6, 2019, https://www.un.org/sustainabledevelopment/blog/2019/05/nature-decline-unprecedented-report/ citing IPBES Global Assessment Report on Biodiversity and Ecosystem Services.

[44] Acevedo-Whitehouse, Karina / Duffus, Amanda L. J., "Effects of Environmental Change on Wildlife Health," *Philosophical Transactions of the Royal Society B, Biological Sciences* 364, 1534 (2009), 3429–3438, https://doi.org/10.1098/rstb.2009.0128

[45] Rosenberg, Kenneth et al., "Decline of the North American Avifauna," *Science*, 2019, https://www.birds.cornell.edu/home/wp-content/uploads/2019/09/DECLINE-OF-NORTH-AMERICAN-AVIFAUNA-SCIENCE-2019.pdf

Isaac Karo explains that "ruling" over creatures mentioned in the verse clearly does not involve killing them for human food.⁴⁶ Rabbi Gil Marks notes:

> ...historically, meat, when consumed, was usually a flavoring agent and, as a rule, a component in a dish reserved for special occasions. Only in the past century has animal flesh assumed such a prominent role in the diet, with meat frequently being served once, sometimes twice, or even three times, a day. On the contrary, throughout most of history, cattle and sheep were not regarded as sources of food, but rather sheep were prized for their milk and wool, and cows were valued for plowing, turning the wheels that drew water from rivers and canals, hauling heavy materials, trodding grain for winnowing, powering the millstones for grinding grain, and turning the stone wheel for pressing olives. Flocks and herds served as the principal source of clothing, wealth, and security for our ancestors, something that would have been squandered if eaten. Meat was the exception, not the rule.⁴⁷

2.8 Will Humans Rule, or Animals?⁴⁸

On the surface, the words of Genesis 1:28 appear to give people license to degrade and subdue the earth: "God blessed them and God said to them, 'Be fertile and increase, fill the earth and master it; and rule the fish of the sea, the birds of the sky, and all the living things that creep on earth.'" However, the rabbis over the millennia for the most part do not read them this way. The rabbinic commentaries reveal much about these verses beyond the simple reading and make clear that a wholly different message is being conveyed.

Verse 26 states, God said, "Let Us make man in Our image, after Our likeness. They shall rule (*e-yir-du*) the fish of the sea, the birds of the sky, the cattle, the whole earth, and all the creeping things that creep on earth."⁴⁹ Verse 28 uses a command verb form, with God saying, "Rule (*u-re-du*) the fish of the sea, the birds of the sky, and all the living things that creep on earth.'"⁵⁰

The Midrash commentary here is based on a play on words in Hebrew, in which the root of the word "to rule" is the same root as the word "to be taken down." Rabbi Chanina interpreted the Midrash to say: "If humankind is worthy,

---

46 Karo, Isaac, Toldot Yitzchak commentary to Genesis 1:28.
47 Marks, Gil, *Olive Trees and Honey*. Hoboken, NJ: Wiley Publishing Co., 2005, viii.
48 This is adapted from Neril, Yonatan, "Genesis and Human Stewardship of the Earth," February 24, 2014, content produced by Canfei Nesharim, a branch of Grow Torah. It is available at http://canfeinesharim.org/genesis-and-human-stewardship-of-the-earth/
49 Genesis 1:26.
50 Genesis 1:28.

God says '*u-re-du*' [you rule!]; while if humankind is not worthy, God says, '*yé-ra-du*' – he will be taken down (or let others [the animals] rule over him)."[51]

Based on the Midrash, Rashi agrees that if we are not worthy, we will be ruled by animals.[52] In this vein, Harry Freedman and Maurice Simon comment, "Man is entitled to pre-eminence only as long as he cultivates his God-like qualities; when he voluntarily abandons them he is even lower than the brute creation."[53]

Can humans be ruled by animals today? At first, we may think human beings are so powerful, we are immune to these predictions. Yet, for example, insect infestations around the world have caused tremendous havoc in human life, from grasshoppers in Africa to bed bugs in North America. Insect-borne diseases such as malaria, dengue fever, West Nile virus, and Zika virus have spread to more northern latitudes, as human-induced climate change expands the range of certain mosquito species.[54] The most recent case of tiny organisms antagonizing people is the coronavirus pandemic. Some research indicates that the virus likely spread from bats to pangolins (a spiny anteater) to people.[55]

One key message from the Midrash is that God's blessing to rule over other creatures depends on our living as righteous people. If humanity becomes worthy by living in a righteous way, then humans shall rule over nature. But if humans do not merit dominion, because they do not act in an upright fashion, then humanity will descend and not be granted rulership over nature. The rabbis learn this from the juxtaposition of God saying that humans will be created in

---

51 Midrash Genesis Rabbah (Vilna Edition), 8:12. Artscroll Rashi to Genesis 1:26 notes, "The Maharal explains in Gur Aryeh to Genesis 1:26 that 'the verse uses *veyirdu* for "ruling," from the root *resh-dalet-heh*, rather than the more common *mashal*, so that it can be expounded as if it were from the root *yud-resh-dalet*, "declining, degenerating," as well.'"
52 Rashi on Genesis 1:26.
53 *Midrash Rabbah: Genesis,* trans. Dr. Harry Freedman and Maurice Simon, London: Soncino Press, 1983.
54 Pachauri, Rajendra K. / Meyer, Leo (eds.), *Climate Change 2014: Synthesis Report. Contribution of Working Groups I, II and III to the Fifth Assessment, A Report of the Intergovernmental Panel on Climate Change,* IPPC, 2014, https://www.ipcc.ch/site/assets/uploads/2018/05/SYR_AR5_FINAL_full_wcover.pdf
55 "Missing Link in Coronavirus Jump from Bats to Humans Could Be Pangolins, Not Snakes," American Chemical Society, March 26, 2020, https://www.acs.org/content/acs/en/pressroom/newsreleases/2020/march/missing-link-in-coronavirus-jump-from-bats-to-humans-could-be-pangolins-not-snakes.html

God's image immediately before saying that humans will rule over other creatures.[56]

Rabbi David Sears writes that ruling "comprises a form of stewardship for which humanity is answerable to God. Both Talmudic and kabbalistic sources state that it is forbidden to kill any creature unnecessarily, or to engage in wanton destruction of the earth's resources. All forms of life are precious by virtue of the Divine wisdom that brings them into existence, whatever rung they may occupy in the hierarchy of creation... The Divine mandate for man to dominate the natural world is a sacred trust, not a carte blanche for destructiveness."[57]

2.9 A Plant-Based Diet for People

One of the only statements God made to people when they were created is to eat a plant-based diet, in Genesis 1:29: "God said, 'See, I give you every seed-bearing plant that is upon all the earth, and every tree that has seed-bearing fruit; they shall be yours for food.'" About this, Rabbi Abraham Isaac Kook writes: "It is altogether impossible to conceive of the Blessed Ruler of all creation... imposing upon this most excellent creation an eternal decree such as this: that the human race would maintain its existence by going against its moral sensibilities through the shedding of blood, albeit the blood of animals. Is it possible to conceive that a highly valued moral virtue, which had already existed as a part of the human legacy, should be lost forever?"[58]

---

[56] Rabbi Zev Wolf Einhorn in his commentary (Perush Maharzav) to the Midrash explains that this midrash is explaining the different grammatical uses of the verb "to rule" in verses 26 and 28. In verse 26, before the human being has been created, God says about them, *"veyirdu,"* in the future tense, meaning "and they shall rule over." Verse 27 reads "And God created Man..." Verse 28 contains God's blessing to people, in the imperative form *"urdu,"* meaning "rule over." The Midrash, however, reads the latter verse differently. The lettering can also be read *"veyeiradu,"* in the passive form meaning "they [people] will be ruled over [by animals]."

[57] Sears, David, "Selections From 'A Vision of Vegetarianism and Peace'," in: *The Vision of Eden: Animal Welfare and Vegetarianism in Jewish Law and Mysticism*, trans. David Sears, David Cohen (ed.), https://www.jewishveg.org/DSvision.html

[58] Kook, Abraham Isaac, "Selections From 'A Vision of Vegetarianism and Peace'," in: Cohen, David / Rubenstein, Jonathan (eds.), *The Vision of Eden: Animal Welfare and Vegetarianism in Jewish Law and Mysticism*, California: CreateSpace Independent Publishing Platform, 2nd edition, 2014, 246.

Rabbi Kook wrote in the early 1900s that in a "brighter era," people will return to a plant-based diet and "God shall cause us to make great spiritual strides, and thus extricate us from this complex question."[59]

Rabbi Elchanan Samet teaches: "What is the content of God's first statements to man? They do not contain commandments and prohibitions related to man's relationship to God. Rather, these initial statements are intended to mold people's relationship with creation. In current times, this question has become crucial, owing to the ecological crisis threatening the world and all its inhabitants. Human beings, having 'filled the world and conquered it, and ruling' over all its elements (animal, vegetable, mineral), have brought our generation to this crisis, which already threatens our world and places a question mark over the future of the generations to come."[60] Indeed, our own survival depends on the health and thriving of creation.

2.10 Vegan Crocodiles

Contemporary science researchers have discovered that the early ancestors of crocodiles, for example, had herbivore teeth, suggesting that they were vegan at some point early in their evolution.[61] We see a hint of this in Genesis 1:30: "'And to all the animals on land, to all the birds of the sky, and to everything that creeps on earth, in which there is the breath of life, [I give] all the green plants for food.' And it was so." Rashi teaches us about this line: "God equated cattle and the animals to them [to people] regarding the food [that they were permitted to eat]. God did not permit Adam and his wife to kill a creature and to eat its flesh; only every green vegetation they were all permitted to eat equally."[62] Animals were also created to be vegan.

2.11 Creation Was "Very Good"

In Genesis 1:31 it states: "And God saw all that He had made and found it very good. And there was evening and there was morning, the sixth day." Nachma-

---

59 Ibid., §§1–7.
60 Samet, Elchanan, "The Story of Creation and Our Ecological Crisis," Yeshivat Har Etzion VBM, 2002, https://www.etzion.org.il/en/story-creation-and-our-ecological-crisis
61 Giaimo, Cara, "Crocodiles Went Through a Vegetarian Phase, Too," *The New York Times*, June 27, 2019, https://www.nytimes.com/2019/06/27/science/crocodiles-vegetarian-teeth.html
62 Rashi on Genesis 1:30.

nides asks what was very good on the sixth day and suggests that it was the wholeness of creation, not any individual piece of it.[63]

From an ecological standpoint, the sixth day was "very good" because people and animals were eating a plant-based diet, and there was no killing of sentient beings in order for other creatures to survive. There was to be no violence by humans toward animals, animals toward animals, or animals toward people on planet earth. In the words of the prophet Isaiah, "the wolf will dwell with the lamb."[64]

2.12 Praying for Creation

It says in Genesis 2:5: "When no shrub of the field was yet on earth and no grasses of the field had yet sprouted, because the Lord God had not sent rain upon the earth and there was no man to till the soil." Rashi asks about this line, based on the Midrash, "And what is the reason that God had not caused it to rain? Because there was no person to till the ground and no one to recognize the utility of rain. When Adam came, however, and realized that rain was necessary for the world, he prayed for it and it fell, so that trees and plants sprang forth."[65]

Based on this, Rabbi Daniel Kohn explains that the human being's first appearance was as one who cared about creation – the person is that same earth, made of dust and water, a clod of dirt with a soul that prays. The Midrash teaches that plants did not grow until the first human showed concern for creation, and the prayer for rain and plant growth is what makes plants grow. Hence the primary role of a person is to recognize God and to pray. "Adam" is from the Hebrew word *adama*, meaning earth. This suggests that to pray is to summon the essential "clod of dirt" within us, to pray on behalf of the entire planet.[66]

2.13 Re-creating Paradise

It's hard to overstate how important the concept of Paradise is to humanity. It says in Genesis 2:8: "The Lord God planted a garden in Eden, in the east, and placed there the man whom He had formed."

---

63 Nachmanides on Genesis 1:4.
64 Isaiah 11:2.
65 Rashi on Genesis 2:5.
66 Rabbi Daniel Kohn, Jerusalem, 2012.

Rabbi Kook says about this: "Our sense is yearning to re-create Eden: the social and environmental harmony, peace, absence of conflict, absence of competition, absence of environmental problems. Our purpose on earth is to re-create paradise."[67]

2.14 The Stewardship Paradigm (*by* Rabbi Jonathan Sacks)[68]

Genesis chapter 1 is only one side of the complex Biblical equation. It is balanced by the narrative of Genesis chapter 2, which features a second creation narrative that focuses on humans and their place in the Garden of Eden. Genesis 2:15: "The Lord God took the man and placed him in the garden of Eden, to till it and tend it."

The first person is set in the Garden "to work it and take care of it."[69] The two Hebrew verbs used here are significant. The first – *le'ovdah* – literally means "to serve it." The human being is thus both master and servant of nature. The second – *le'shomrah* – means "to guard it." This is the verb used in later Biblical legislation to describe the responsibilities of a guardian of property that belongs to someone else. This guardian must exercise vigilance while protecting and is personally liable for losses that occur through negligence. This is perhaps the best short definition of humanity's responsibility for nature as the Bible conceives it.

We do not own nature. "The earth is the Lord's and the fullness thereof."[70] We are its stewards on behalf of God, who created and owns everything, and we are duty-bound to respect its integrity. The mid-nineteenth-century commentator Rabbi Samson Raphael Hirsch put this rather well in an original interpretation of Genesis 1:26, which reads, "Let Us make the human in Our image after Our own likeness."[71] The verse has always been puzzling, since the hallmark of the Torah is the singularity of God. Who would God consult in the process of creating humans? Hirsch says the "us" refers to the rest of creation. Before creating the

---

67 Kook, Abraham Isaac, *Gold from the Land of Israel*, Chanan Morrison (ed.), California: CreateSpace Independent Publishing Platform, 2017, 216–217. Adapted from Kook, Rabbi Abraham Isaac, *Orot HaKodesh, Volume II*, Jerusalem: Mosad HaRav Kook, 1937. 563–564.
68 Quoted (with permission) in its entirety from Sacks, Jonathan, The Stewardship Paradigm, January 14, 2014, http://rabbisacks.org/tubshvat/
69 Genesis 2:15.
70 Psalms 24:1.
71 Hirsch, Samson Raphael, commentary on Genesis 1:26. The commentaries on this verse by Radak, Nachmanides, and Ralbag also shed light on this point.

human, a being destined to develop the capacity to alter and possibly endanger the natural world, God sought the approval of nature itself. This interpretation implies that we would use nature only in such a way that is faithful to the purposes of its Creator and acknowledges nature's consenting to humanity's existence.

The mandate in Genesis 1 to exercise dominion is, therefore, not technical but moral: humanity would control, within our means, the use of nature toward the service of God. This mandate is limited by the requirement to serve and guard as seen in Genesis 2. The famous story of Genesis 2–3 – the eating of the forbidden fruit, leading to Adam and Eve's exile from Eden – supports this point. God does not permit everything. God provides limits on how we interact with the earth. The Torah has many commandments relating to the earth, from how to sow crops, to how to collect eggs, to how to preserve trees in a time of war, just to name a few.[72]

When we do not protect creation according to God's will, disaster can follow. We see this today as more and more cities sit under a cloud of smog and as mercury poisons large sectors of our fishing waters.[73] Deforestation of the rainforests, largely a result of humanity's growing demand for timber and beef, has brought on irrevocable destruction of plant and animal species.[74] We can no longer ignore the massive negative impact that our global industrial society is having on the ecosystems of the earth. Our unbounded use of fossil fuels to stoke our energy-intensive lifestyles is causing global climate change. An international consensus of scientists predicts more intense and destructive storms, floods, and droughts resulting from human-induced changes in the atmosphere.[75] If we do not take action now, we risk the very survival of civilization as we know it.

The Midrash says that God showed Adam around the Garden of Eden and said, "Look at My works! See how beautiful they are – how excellent! For your sake I created them all. See to it that you do not spoil and destroy My world; for if you do, there will be no one else to repair it."[76] Creation has its own dignity

---

[72] Leviticus 19:19, Deuteronomy 22:6–7, and 20:19–20.
[73] "Mercury and Air Toxics Standards," US Environmental Protection Agency, accessed June 7, 2020, https://www.epa.gov/mats
[74] University of California – San Diego, "Climate Change and Deforestation Will Lead to Declines in Global Bird Diversity, Study Warns," *ScienceDaily*, June 5, 2007, www.sciencedaily.com/releases/2007/06/070604205627.htm
[75] *Climate Change 2014: Synthesis Report Summary for Policymakers,* Rajendra K. Pachauri / Leo Meyer (eds.), Geneva, IPCC, 2014, https://www.ipcc.ch/site/assets/uploads/2018/02/AR5_SYR_FINAL_SPM.pdf
[76] Midrash Ecclesiastes Rabbah 7:13.

as God's masterpiece, and though we have the mandate to use it, we have none to destroy or despoil it. Rabbi Hirsch says that Shabbat was given to humanity "in order that one should not grow overbearing in his dominion" of God's creation. On the Day of Rest, "he must, as it were, return the borrowed world to its Divine Owner in order to realize that it is but lent to him."[77] Ingrained in the process of creation is a weekly reminder that our dominion of earth must be for the sake of Heaven.

The choice is ours. If we continue to live as though God had only commanded us to subdue the earth, we must be prepared for our children to inherit a seriously degraded planet, with the future of human civilization at risk. If we see in our role as masters of the earth a unique opportunity to truly serve and care for the planet, its creatures and its resources, then we can reclaim our status as stewards of the world, and raise our new and future generations in an environment much closer to that of Eden.

2.15 Forbidden Fruit and Self-Control

The need for human self-control is a central message of God telling Adam and Eve not to eat from the Tree of Knowledge of good and evil. It sets us up with Genesis 2:17: "But as for the tree of knowledge of good and bad, you must not eat of it; for as soon as you eat of it, you shall die." As the story plays out, human lack of restraint clearly leads God to expel people from the Garden of Eden, Rabbi Arthur Waskow teaches. Today, lack of moderation and excessive consumerism are driving the widespread degradation of our planet.[78] We are on the verge of self-induced expulsion.

2.16 Learning from Animals

God created animals after people in the second creation story, with the purpose of Adam naming the animals. As it says in Genesis 2:19: "And the Lord God formed out of the earth all the wild beasts and all the birds of the sky, and brought them to the man to see what he would call them; and whatever the man called each living creature, that would be its name." Adam was engaged

---

[77] Hirsch, Samson Raphael, *The Nineteen Letters of Ben Uziel*, New York: BN Publishing, 2011, 30.
[78] Waskow, Rabbi Arthur, "Torah and the Climate Crisis", webinar, May 2019.

in a relationship of recognition and non-violent interaction: I-Thou, not I-It. Today, encountering meat in a supermarket is an I-It relationship, but encountering animals directly – from a bird nesting in a nearby tree, to an eagle soaring high overhead – can be I-Thou.[79] The language the Torah uses for insects, animals, and people is *nefesh ḥaya*, literally "a soul of life."

According to one midrash, God paraded the various animals before Adam to name them after he studied their respective characteristics.[80] In light of this midrash, the specific names Adam gave to animals reflected his wisdom, each name capturing the outstanding characteristic which made one animal species distinct from the others.

Every letter Adam chose in naming reflected a special meaning. When the Midrash said, "Due to his wisdom, Adam recognized the nature of the lion, *aryeh*," this means he was aware that the lion was the king of the animals due to its fearless posture. The Hebrew letters that make up the word *aryeh* – alef, resh, yud, heh – are letters that also appear in the various names of God. As the prophet Hosiah wrote, using imagery from the natural world, "They will follow the Lord because He roars like a lion."[81]

The lion's name in Hebrew reflects its role in the animal kingdom and its behavior. This is true for the other animals as well. The original human was granted dominion because of his ability to respect and learn about the animal kingdom in this manner. As Midrash Pirkei D'Rabbi Eliezer notes regarding Adam and Eve's burial of their son Abel: "Adam and his partner came and cried [over Abel], and they didn't know what to do... One raven whose companion died said, 'I will teach Adam this is what to do.' The raven set down his friend and dug in the earth before their eyes and buried him. Adam said, 'Like the raven, this is what we will do.'"[82]

Rabbi David Seidenberg writes, "The rabbis that told these stories clearly thought that we could learn God's ways by observing the other animals. The thread that unites these midrashim is that the animals come to us as teachers, providing moral examples for us; they are not just presented as vassals or objects to be taken care of. We can learn from them only by humbly standing in relation to them, i.e., by 'under-standing,' in the truest and deepest sense of the word."[83] As the rabbis said, "Even if the Torah had not been given we would have been

---

[79] Buber, Martin, *I and Thou*, London: A&C Black, 1937.
[80] Genesis Rabbah 17:4.
[81] Hoseah 11:10.
[82] Pirkei d'Rabbi Eliezer 21.
[83] Seidenberg, David, *Crossing the Threshold: God's Image in the More-Than-Human World*, PhD thesis, Jewish Theological Seminary, 2004, 164.

able to learn modesty from the cat and an aversion to theft from the ant."[84] Indeed, the Book of Proverbs states, "Lazybones, go to the ant; study its ways and learn."[85]

2.17 Holy Eating

To get a sense of how important eating is, let's take a look at Genesis 3:6: "When the woman saw that the tree was good for eating and a delight to the eyes, and that the tree was desirable as a source of wisdom, she took of its fruit and ate. She also gave some to her husband, and he ate." The Torah makes it clear that eating is central to human existence: "And God commanded man saying, 'Of every tree of the garden you may freely eat. But of the Tree of Knowledge of good and evil you shall not eat of it, for on the day that you eat thereof, you shall surely die.'"[86]

Adam and Eve broke this commandment with the first sin – eating from the Tree. The Tree of Life represents holy eating, Rabbi Tzadok HaKohen teaches, while the Tree of Knowledge of Good and Evil represents eating suffused with craving for physical pleasure.[87] Based on this teaching, Sarah Yehudit Schneider writes that "humanity's first sin was not Adam and Eve's eating of forbidden fruit, but rather the way they ate it. The Tree of Knowledge... was not a tree or a food or a thing at all. Rather it was a way of eating. Whenever a person grabs self-conscious pleasure from the world, he falls, at that moment, from God consciousness ... Whenever we eat without proper *kavanna* [intention] we repeat this original sin. The primary fixing of human civilization is to learn to eat in holiness."[88]

In a somewhat different vein, Or HaChayim (Rabbi Chayim ben Moshe ibn Attar) says Adam did not know he was eating from the forbidden fruit, and his sin was in not trying to find out where Eve got the fruit she gave him.[89] The premodern reality was that most people grew some of the food they ate. How much effort do we make today to find out where our food comes from? Do we know if it was sourced locally or from abroad? Do we know if the farm

---

84 Babylonian Talmud, Eruvin 100b.
85 Proverbs 6:6.
86 Genesis 2:16–17.
87 Rabbi Tzadok HaKohen Rabinowitz of Lublin, "Section 8: Genesis," in *Pri Tzadik*.
88 Schneider, Susan (Sarah Yehudit), *Eating as Tikun*, Jerusalem: A Still Small Voice, 1996, 18.
89 Or HaChayim commentary to Genesis 3:17.

workers were paid a fair wage? Do we know what potentially harmful toxins were used in its growing? Do we grow any of our food ourselves?

2.18 All Creations Are Connected

Why did Adam and Eve not previously realize they were naked? We see in Genesis 3:11: "Then He [God] asked, 'Who told you that you were naked? Did you eat of the tree from which I had forbidden you to eat?'" The Midrash explains that initially Adam and Eve were created with translucent suits, like fingernails. This is one reason why many Jews look at their fingernails in the flame light of the candle used at the end of Shabbat each week. This tradition is to remember their God-given state before the sin of the fruit.[90] After Adam and Eve ate the forbidden fruit, the translucent coverings became opaque, and the first man and woman realized they were naked.

Rashi states that before Eve was removed from Adam, the original human was both male and female together.[91] When you look through an infrared (heat imaging) camera at two people standing close together, you see them merge into a single heat unit. Life before the forbidden fruit may have been like that – all of creation merged together without opaque boundaries. There was no "you" and no "me," just "us." When humankind today, or in the future, returns to the understanding that all God's creations are inseparably linked, we will truly have returned to the Garden of Eden.

Indeed, we must learn to view our planet through a lens of inter-connected ecosystems, not just individual species. Modern science has only scraped the surface of understanding how intricately all biological species interrelate – for example how a hummingbird's beak fits so well for collecting nectar from a particular flower species. Therefore, we must preserve the entire web of life around us as much as possible. We can compare our ecosystem to a line of dominoes: If we push down a single species, others will follow. Through our lack or ignoring of deep ecological understanding, we have caused great damage to God's creation. Our challenge is to see life more holistically, just as Adam and Eve saw life before the forbidden fruit.

---

90 Pirkei d'Rabbi Eliezer 14.
91 Rashi on Genesis 2:21 and Midrash Genesis Rabbah 8:1.

2.19 Eating the Forbidden Fruit

Few lines in the Bible – or in history – have as much import as Genesis 3:17, which states: "To Adam He [God] said, 'Because you did as your wife said and ate of the tree about which I commanded you, 'You shall not eat of it,' cursed be the ground because of you; by toil shall you eat of it all the days of your life.'"

For the developed world, agricultural technology removes much of the curse of the Biblical expulsion. In material terms, we have all but re-created the abundance of Garden of Eden, with the comfort and assurance of plentiful food. We have re-created the choice that Adam and Eve faced as well – whether or not to eat from the tree. Today, that means whether or not to choose to gratify ourselves without regard to our impact on the sustainability of the planet. If we keep eating from the tree, we will be expelled again from the abundance of the Garden. And this time, it is not clear we will be able to repair the environmental damage we have wrought.

2.20 Edible Weeds

The extent of the curse is terrifying, as we learn in Genesis 3:18: "Thorns and thistles shall it sprout for you. But your food shall be the grasses of the field."

Rashi asks, "What sort of curse is this? Didn't God just bless him with every seed-bearing herb?" Rashi explains, "When you sow the ground with beans or garden vegetables, the ground will cause thorns and thistles and other grasses of the field to grow and you shall have no choice but to eat them."[92]

In the twenty-first century, invasive weed species cost the Chinese more than $14.5 billion per year[93] to remove and pose one of the greatest challenges to local grain farmers. Removal can often involve use of dangerous chemical weed killers. Perhaps, as some researchers suggest, we can transform "some 'neglected' species, sometimes considered as weeds in extensive major crop cultivation, into 'new functional crops.'"[94] In other words, we could recognize "weeds" as

---

[92] Rashi on Genesis 3:18.
[93] Xu, Haigen et al., "The Distribution and Economic Losses of Alien Species Invasion to China," *Biological Invasions* 8, October 2006, 1495–1500, https://doi.org/10.1007/s10530-005-5841-2
[94] Ceccanti, Costanza et al., "Mediterranean Wild Edible Plants: Weeds or 'New Functional Crops'?" *Molecules* 23, 9 (2018), 2299, https://dx.doi.org/10.3390%2Fmolecules23092299

natural food resources and spend less effort, cost, and contamination than in trying to eliminate them.[95]

2.21 Connected to the Earth

The Torah reminds us that we are made up, ultimately, of stardust, as is the rest of creation. It tells us in Genesis 3:19, "By the sweat of your brow shall you get bread to eat, until you return to the ground – for from it you were taken. For dust you are, and to dust you shall return." We share that origin with every substance in the universe. Terrestrial life on our planet absorbs most of its vitality from a six-inch layer of topsoil. Even though we operate daily on the assumption that we are separate from the earth, this verse reminds us in fact we are intricately connected: "For dust you are, and to dust you shall return."

2.22 Taking Responsibility for Others

Rabbi Shlomo Riskin teaches that to be a protector means to be responsible. He finds a root of this in Genesis 4:9: "The Lord said to Cain, 'Where is your brother Abel?' And he said, 'I do not know. Am I my brother's keeper?'"

Rabbi Riskin's teacher, Rabbi Joseph Ber Soloveitchik, taught this as a core Jewish value: "I am responsible, therefore I am." Being responsible and taking responsibility is core to being human. This is very clear from Cain's response to God when asked of Abel's whereabouts: "Am I my brother's keeper?" The actual term used is not "keeper" here but "protector" in the same sense of "protection" mentioned in the Garden of Eden. To Cain's question, the Bible surely implies, "Yes!"[96]

Sustainable living involves being attentive to and taking responsibility for the effects of our actions. In a globally and environmentally connected world, today our failure to take responsibility for our actions on a planet of almost eight billion people has major, detrimental consequences. We use the resources of the world – trees, mineral ores, petroleum – without sufficient attention to how these resources are gathered or mined, refined, transported, and disposed of. We often fail to see, or ignore, the consequences to air and water where we

---

[95] Clearly this must be subject to a full toxin analysis to ensure that they are nutritious and not harmful.
[96] Riskin, Rabbi Shlomo, oral teaching, Yeshivat Hamivtar, Migdal Oz, November 2009.

live and far beyond, as well as to our own health and other people's health. Studies in the US indicate that minority, especially African-American, communities suffer disproportionately from living near factories that emit high levels of air pollutants.[97] Exposure results in more cases of asthma and other lung diseases, which in turn make people more susceptible to the most severe incidence of diseases like COVID-19.

2.23 From Farmer to Refugee

Cain, the farmer, polluted the earth with Abel's blood, and God cursed Cain that the earth would no longer produce for him. There is an ecological warning built into this human story: Cain worked the ground but cared little about others, and asked, "Am I my brother's keeper?" meaning, "Am I a steward?" God consequently made him a wanderer, disconnecting him from the land he knew and, in effect, giving him permanent refugee status – no longer a steward over nature. And so in Genesis 4:13, we see the consequence: "Cain said to the Lord, 'My punishment is too great to bear!'"

Refugees today are often fleeing from hunger caused by climate change and environmental degradation. The World Bank estimated in 2018 that by 2050, Latin America, sub-Saharan Africa, and Southeast Asia will generate 143 million more climate migrants.[98] As a Brookings Institution report notes, "In 2017, 68.5 million people were forcibly displaced, more than at any point in human history. While it is difficult to estimate, approximately one-third of these (22.5 million to 24 million people) were forced to move by 'sudden onset' weather events – flooding, forest fires after droughts, and intensified storms."[99]

2.24 The Ark and Green Building

There's a suggestive hint about building sustainably in Genesis 6:16, where it says: "Make an opening [tsohar] for daylight in the Ark and terminate it within

---

[97] Mikati, Ihab et al., "Disparities in Distribution of Particulate Matter Emission Sources by Race and Poverty Status," *American Journal of Public Health* 108, 4 (2018), 480–485, https://doi.org/10.2105/AJPH.2017.304297

[98] Rigaud, Kanta Kumari et al., "Groundswell: Preparing for Internal Climate Migration," World Bank Group, 2018, https://openknowledge.worldbank.org/handle/10986/29461

[99] Podesta, John, "The Climate Crisis, Migration, and Refugees," The Brookings Institution, July 25, 2019, https://www.brookings.edu/research/the-climate-crisis-migration-and-refugees/

a cubit of the top. Put the entrance to the Ark in its side; make it with bottom, second, and third decks."

Rashi offers two possible meanings of *tsohar*, an "opening" or a "stone that emits light."[100] The Ark was a "green building," with a window for natural lighting from the sun, a whole floor dedicated to composting of animal waste, and wood from forests Noah planted, according to the Midrash. Studying the design of the first Divine-commanded building could teach us about Divine green building standards.

The end of this verse states that God commanded Noah to build the Ark with three levels. The Talmud explains why. Humans were to be on the top deck, the animals in the middle deck, and their manure stored at the bottom. Why store the manure? After all, it could have just been thrown into the sea! As farmers in the Midwestern United States learned after the 2019 floods, "Flooding drains nutrients out of the soil that are necessary for plant growth as well as reducing oxygen needed for plant roots to breathe and gather water and nutrients."[101] So perhaps it was not just the vine branches that Noah took out of the Ark after the floodwater receded, but also the wisely-accumulated manure stored on the bottom level of the vessel.[102] This may be the first Biblical reference to organic fertilizer.

Recent years have seen multiple unintended explosions of ammonium nitrate (used as both a chemical, non-organic fertilizer and an explosive). In August 2020, 2,750 metric tons of ammonium nitrate exploded in Beirut, killing 157 people, wounding 5,000, and causing 300,000 to be homeless. Large explosions also occurred in Tianjin, China (2015) and Texas (2013).[103] These disasters reveal another impact of the widespread use of ammonium nitrate.

The Ark was a "green" project in Biblical times. Today, about one third of US building projects are considered "green," saving an average of 15 percent on water and electricity costs compared to conventional buildings. Natural lighting, solar power, and water recycling (such as diverting sink waste to water external

---

100 Rashi on Genesis 6:16.
101 Ippolito, Jim / Al-Kaisi, Mahdi, "The Dirt on Soil Loss from the Midwest Floods," Colorado State University, April 16, 2019, https://source.colostate.edu/the-dirt-on-soil-loss-from-the-midwest-floods/.
102 Babylonian Talmud, Sanhedrin 108b.
103 https://en.wikipedia.org/wiki/List_of_ammonium_nitrate_disasters

gardens) are just some of the many architectural and design features that ensure buildings will consume less of nature's resources.[104]

2.25 Population and Restraint

God makes a provocative statement to Noah in Genesis 6:18: "But I will establish My covenant with you, and you shall enter the Ark, with your sons, your wife, and your sons' wives." Radak explains that God's statement to Noah does not mention husbands and wives together, but intentionally separates them. This signifies to Noah that in a time of limited resources, human energies should go into surviving and not procreating.[105]

The world population has grown from around two billion in 1950 to an expected 9.8 billion in 2050. However, these numbers disguise the fact that almost all of this growth has occurred in developing nations, where resources are most limited, with an anticipated increase of over seven billion people in just 100 years.[106] Population concerns have complex causes, and often controversial solutions, but the needs of our planet's ever-growing population must be addressed in the context not just of development but of environmental preservation. The most immediate impact of so many people is the astonishing 60 percent drop in total wildlife globally.[107]

2.26 Noah as Earth Steward (*by* Shimshon Stüart Siegel)[108]

Take a deeper look at Genesis 6:19, where it says: "And of all that lives, of all flesh, you shall take two of each into the Ark to keep alive with you; they shall be male and female". We are seeing Noah through the eyes of the rabbinic commentaries, discovering a man who spent his life caring for nature and

---

104 *World Green Building Trends 2018: Smart Market Report*, Steven A. Jones ed., Bedford: Dodge Data Analytics, 2018, https://www.worldgbc.org/sites/default/files/World%20Green%20Building%20Trends%202018%20SMR%20FINAL%2010-11.pdf
105 Radak on Genesis 6:18.
106 US Census Bureau. World Population 1950–2050. https://www.census.gov/library/visualizations/2011/demo/world-population-1950-2050.html
107 Grooten, M. / Almond, R.E.A. (eds.), "Living Planet Report–2018: Aiming Higher,"., WWF, Gland, Switzerland, https://www.wwf.org.uk/sites/default/files/2018-10/wwfintl_livingplanet_full.pdf
108 This content was produced by Canfei Nesharim, a branch of Grow Torah. It is available at http://canfeinesharim.org/noach-a-paradigm-for-environmental-consciousness/

spreading Divine awareness. This fresh look can provide us many lessons as we strive to bring our world back to a state of holy balance. What can we learn from Noah's efforts?

We can learn that caring about the environment requires patience and forethought. The Midrash says that 120 years before the Flood, Noah actually planted the trees from which he would take the wood for the Ark.[109] (No old-growth logging here!) Aware of the massive resources that his project would demand, Noah tried to be as self-sustaining as possible.

The Talmud explains why the Ark had three levels: one for Noah and his family, one for the animals, and one for the waste – tons upon tons of animal droppings.[110] Noah's family spent a lot of their time shoveling manure. Whether they systematically removed it from the Ark, stored it in a designated waste facility, or found a practical use for it, we see that Noah toiled to maintain the cleanliness of the Ark. Noah's lesson teaches us today that the benefits of a clean, healthy living space – clean of both natural and industrially created waste – are worth the effort for humans and animals coexisting on earth.

Another lesson we can learn from Noah is that it helps to see the world as a "closed," integrated system. Noah and his seven-person crew maintained a sort of proto-Biodome inside the Ark, struggling to preserve a functional level of ecological balance in the most challenging of situations. Within such a system, every action has a significant impact and ramifications, and individual elements can be aligned to strengthen and assist one another.

In modern times, this ecological balance is demonstrated by walking, riding bikes, and using public transportation in congested areas. These individual decisions collectively reduce pollution while easing traffic jams. Partly as a result of the coronavirus pandemic, cities are exploring how to permanently block off more areas for walkers and bikers traveling to work or getting outdoors after work and on weekends. Less traffic and cleaner air reduce many kinds of human health risk from both accidents, pollution, and communicable disease. Individually, these very same choices can reduce personal stress and keep us more fit as well.

After the flood, Noah reinvented himself as an agricultural pioneer. The Midrash explains that Noah revolutionized farming techniques to soften the backbreaking toil that had been the way of the land since the sin of Adam and

---

109 Midrash Genesis Rabbah 30:7.
110 Babylonian Talmud, Sanhedrin 108b based on Genesis 6:16.

Eve. By easing the burdens on people and the soil, he truly earned the meaning of his name, "rest."[111]

Overall, Noah's relationship with the land was harmonious and productive, not adversarial or injurious to the planet for his own well-being. Like Noah, modern farmers can promote agricultural techniques, such as organic farming, that keep consumers healthier and keep the land fruitful, both literally and figuratively, for future generations. Also we must not fill our breadbasket at the expense of suffering by farmworkers – such as their exposure in the fields to toxic pesticides.

For Noah, the Ark was an unfortunate but necessary solution to a global crisis. Even when all signs were grim, he maintained his faith, greeting every challenge with further innovation. So, too, must we continue to strive for a better tomorrow, educate others about environmental issues, and ensure that our actions on every level make a difference. When we step outside after a rainstorm and see the rainbow in the sky, we remember God's promise to Noah, and we can believe and know that we are not alone in our efforts.

2.27 Caring for Creatures

Malbim (Rabbi Meir Leibush ben Yechiel Michel) looks at Genesis 6:21 – "For your part, take of everything that is eaten and store it away, to serve as food for you and for them." He explains that God is telling Noah, "Don't expect that each animal will bring food for itself in the same way that it hides away food during the summer for the winter months, but rather, make sure that you bring all the necessary provisions with you on to the Ark."[112] In other words, due to the disruption of animals' usual behavior in their ecosystems, Noah becomes responsible not just to bring the animals onto the Ark, but to guarantee their survival by supplying appropriate food for all of the animals, birds, and insects. In our times, ecological devastation has a similar impact and puts similar demands on humans. After catastrophic fires in Australia wiped out eucalyptus forests, leaving any surviving koalas without their only food source, human rescuers are relocating koalas to other eucalyptus areas that were not burned.

---

111 Midrash Aggadah, v. 29.
112 Malbim on Genesis 6:21.

2.28 Plastic, Fish, and People

There is a notable omission in Genesis 7:23, "All existence on earth was blotted out – people, cattle, creeping things, and birds of the sky; they were blotted out from the earth. Only Noah was left, and those with him in the Ark." Nachmanides asks, "What happened to the fish?!" He suggests that they escaped to the depths of the oceans where they survived, while the floodwaters over the earth were boiling and thus unsuitable even for fish life.[113] Sadly, fish today are not safe even in great ocean depths.

Contemporary researchers investigating nonbiodegradable plastics in our planet's ocean find that they "are ubiquitous even at depths of more than 6,000 meters and 92 percent are single-use products and that these plastics are harmful to sea life and ultimately to us as they are accumulated in our food chain.[114] Single-use plastic has even reached the world's deepest ocean trench at 10,898 meters."[115] By 2050, some analysts believe there will be more plastic (by weight) in the oceans than fish.[116] Much of this plastic breaks down into tinier pieces, which are then eaten by fish and make their way into both the wild and human food chain. So, in a sense, we are experiencing a flood of plastics that threatens to blot out sea life, and we must transform our planet into an Ark to preserve God's creation.

2.29 Saving the Raven

In the Talmud, Reish Lakish (Rabbi Shimon ben Lakish) describes a fascinating conversation between the raven and Noah, basing it on Genesis 8:6–7 – "At the end of forty days, Noah opened the window of the Ark that he had made and sent out the raven; it went to and fro until the waters had dried up from the earth." The raven (a non-kosher bird) said, "Your Boss [i.e., God] hates me, and YOU hate me. Your Boss hates me because He said that there should be

---

[113] Nachmanides on Genesis 7:23.
[114] Savoca, Matthew, "The Bad News Is That Fish Are Eating Lots of Plastic. Even Worse, They May Like It," *The Washington Post*, April 9, 2017, https://www.washingtonpost.com/national/health-science/the-bad-news-is-that-fish-are-eating-lots-of-plastic-even-worse-they-may-like-it/2017/09/01/54159ee8-8cc6-11e7-91d5-ab4e4b76a3a_story.html
[115] Chiba, Sanae et al., "Human Footprint in the Abyss: 30 Year Records of Deep-Sea Plastic Debris," *Marine Policy* 96 (2018), 204–212, https://doi.org/10.1016/j.marpol.2018.03.022
[116] "The New Plastics Economy: Rethinking the Future of Plastics," World Economic Forum, 2016, http://www3.weforum.org/docs/WEF_The_New_Plastics_Economy.pdf

seven pairs of each kosher animal and only one pair of each non-kosher animal. And you hate me because, despite there only being one breeding pair on board, you sent me out to scout the land, risking the extinction of my whole species!"[117] In response, God told Noah to take the raven back into the Ark. Noah then sent the dove, of which seven pairs were in the Ark. Noah is thus seen as preserving the diversity of life on earth.

We would be wise to learn from Noah's example in a century known as the Anthropocene, or great human-caused extinction era.[118] According to recent research on local and regional species loss in China, the estimated proportion of species loss, out of 252 key protected vertebrate species, during the past half-century was 47.7 percent for mammals, 28.8 percent for amphibians and reptiles, and 19.8 percent for birds.[119] Scientists recognize human-induced environmental impacts and climate change as the greatest threats to all species' survival.

2.30 Rainbows and Responsibility[120]

Rabbi Samson Raphael Hirsch explains that the symbolism of the rainbow is its multiple colors in one cohesive structure.[121] He starts from Genesis 9:13 – "I have set My bow in the clouds, and it shall serve as a sign of the covenant between Me and the earth." God's pact of peace with humankind and all of creation is represented by this eternal symbol of diversity. Today we know that our global ecosystem is extremely complex and interlinked, even beyond what humans can currently comprehend. Our actions in diverting a single river or allowing the use of a single refrigerant chemical can have devastating effects on aspects of the planet we don't even know about – including even species not yet identified – that could affect us for generations to come.

Nachmanides teaches that the rainbow signifies an upside-down bow and serves as "a reminder of peace." The feet of the rainbow are bent downward

---

117 Babylonian Talmud, Sanhedrin 108b and Midrash Genesis Rabbah 38:4.
118 Ceballos, Gerardo / Ehrlich, Paul R. / Raven, Peter H., "Vertebrates on the Brink as Indicators of Biological Annihilation and the Sixth Mass Extinction," *Proceedings of the National Academy of Sciences*, June 16, 2020, 117 (24) 13596–13602, https://doi.org/10.1073/pnas.1922686117
119 He, Jinxing et al., "Quantifying the Effects of Climate and Anthropogenic Change on Regional Species Loss in China," *PLOS One* 13, 7 (2018), https://doi.org/10.1371/journal.pone.0199735
120 Part of this section is from Neril, Yonatan, "Countering Destruction: Lessons from Noach," Canfei Nesharim, a branch of Grow Torah, February 19, 2004, http://canfeinesharim.org/countering-destruction-lessons-from-noach-longer-article/.
121 Samson Raphael Hirsch on Genesis 9:13.

to show that the Heavenly "shooting" (the torrential rains) has ceased.[122] Rabbi Shlomo Riskin explains the meaning of Nachmanides' teaching: "Ancient cultures fought their wars with the bow and arrow, and the side which surrendered, pursuing peace instead of war, would express their will to do so by raising an inverted bow that the enemy could see. Similarly, God places an inverted bow in the heavens as a sign that He is no longer warring against humanity."[123] The rainbow testifies to the Creator's intention for life on our planet to continue to exist. It is a sign that God desires the existence of the world and not its destruction.

Rabbi Riskin continues that the symbolism of the rainbow extends beyond God's commitment – to encompass humans: "The rainbow is a half-picture, lacking a second half to complete the circle of wholeness. God can pledge not to destroy humanity, but since He created humanity with freedom of choice, He cannot guarantee that humanity will not destroy itself."[124] Yet the rabbis make clear that God does not want us to destroy creation either.

At present, humanity is emitting over 36 billion tons of CO_2 per year into the atmosphere. In the past 800,000 years, atmospheric concentrations of CO_2 did not exceed 300 parts per million (ppm).[125] Yet people have dramatically increased the concentration of CO_2 in the atmosphere in the past 200 years, to 417 parts per million and rising every year.[126] A consensus of climate scientists understands that humans are directly causing climate change.[127] Through our consumption, it is as if we are shooting carbon arrows into the atmosphere, inadvertently waging war on God's creation.

In Israel, one first sees rainbows after the Jewish New Year and Day of Atonement, when the winter rains begin to fall in October. According to the Ziv HaZohar commentary, the rainbow as a whole reminds us to turn our hearts to improve our actions.[128] Perhaps the timing of the rainbow's appearance, soon after the period of repentance, can motivate each of us to keep improving our-

---

122 Nachmanides on Genesis 9:12.
123 Riskin, Rabbi Shlomo, "The 'Noah Covenant' with Mankind," *Arutz Sheva*, October 31, 2018, http://www.israelnationalnews.com/Articles/Article.aspx/8340
124 Ibid.
125 Ritchie, Hannah / Roser, Max, "CO2 and Greenhouse Gas Emissions," Our World in Data, revised December 2019, https://ourworldindata.org/co2-and-other-greenhouse-gas-emissions#co2-in-the-atmosphere
126 CO2 Earth, accessed June 21, 2020, https://www.co2.earth/
127 Hausfather, Zeke, "Analysis: Why Scientists Think 100% of Global Warming Is Due to Humans," Carbon Brief, December 13, 2017, https://www.carbonbrief.org/analysis-why-scientists-think-100-of-global-warming-is-due-to-humans
128 Footnote 43 to Zohar, Noah 72b.

selves and become better servants of the Creator and collective stewards of creation.

2.31 Floods and Fairtrade

Rashi was a vintner, and he cites the Midrash[129]: "When he [Noah] entered the Ark, he brought with him vine branches and shoots of fig trees." When he left the Ark, he planted them, as we saw in Genesis 9:20 – "Noah, the tiller of the soil, was the first to plant a vineyard." Yet the Midrash states that about a foot of soil, "the depth [that the blade of a] plow [digs into], was washed away in the flood."[130] How did Noah succeed in growing a vineyard? Noah may have used the massive stores of dung on the Ark to compost and revitalize the land.

In Kerala, India, during the heavy monsoons of 2018, rainfall was so heavy that more than 450 people died and over two million took shelter in camps – yet the topsoil remained. In the aftermath, the Fairtrade Foundation was able to utilize this topsoil and wisely supported farmers with 200,000 seedlings to replant crops lost in the floods.[131]

2.32 Lording Over Nature

Evan Eisenberg writes that the Tower of Babel, in the Mesopotamian kingdom of Sumeria, represents the arrogance of the world's early farmers who thought their own work cultivated their prosperity. We're introduced to the Tower in Genesis 11:1–3 – "Everyone on earth had the same language and the same words. And as they migrated from the east, they came upon a valley in the land of Shinar and settled there. They said to one another, 'Come, let us make bricks and burn them hard.' Brick served them as stone, and bitumen served them as mortar."

Eisenberg notes that the Mesopotamians embraced a type of thinking where "the man-made order is so firmly established that it seems God-made. All is stripped from nature and affixed to the social and technical order." They saw themselves as a source of bounty and power, not as recipients of God's blessing.

---

[129] Rashi on Genesis 9:20, citing Genesis Rabbah 26:3.
[130] Rashi on Genesis 6:13, citing Genesis Rabbah 31:7.
[131] Kurian, Bijumon, "Farmers Plant 200,000 Seedlings to Replace Lost Crops after Kerala Floods," Fairtrade Foundation, November 27, 2018, https://www.fairtrade.org.uk/Media-Centre/Blog/2018/November/Farmers-become-earth-builders-after-Kerala-floods

In spite of all their efforts and mastery, Eisenberg notes, Sumerian society declined due to unsustainable agricultural practices, which created rising salt content in the soil of the agricultural fields.

By contrast, the Israelites "were neither desert nomads mistrustful of nature nor proud hydraulic despots lording it over nature. They were good farmers living frugally on the margins and using the best stewardship they knew. They were dependent on rain and groundwater, neither of which was overabundant, and on thin and rock-strewn soil, and had to use their wits to conserve both."[132]

2.33 The Limits of Technology

We can discover technological arrogance in Genesis 11:4 – "And they said, 'Come, let us build us a city, and a tower with its top in the sky, to make a name for ourselves; else we shall be scattered all over the world.'" Dr. Manfred Gerstenfeld states, "Often, the negative effects of uncontrolled technological development are one of the reasons for the deterioration of the environment... The roots of the limitations of technology are stated in the Bible. This is made clear in the story of the Tower of Babel."[133] Ultimately, God does scatter the people who build the Tower of Babel – and whose names are now only remembered in the context of failure, both ecological and social, and disarray.

Dr. Jeremy Benstein writes:

> The Tower was not only a vertical reality, but a virtual one as well, perhaps the first in history. Ancient Mesopotamians built those ziggurats – cultic towers – on the flat floodplain, as a replacement for an actual mountain of God. Even their building materials were artificial substitutes for more natural stones and mortar (see Genesis 11:3). Today's towers, and all that they represent, dwarf those of antiquity. Alienation from the earth, each other, and the divine too often typifies our society. Recent trends of corporate globalization, pointing to a world monoculture – unity through uniformity – threaten that delicate fabric of diversity, of cultures and their habitats. This can serve as a warning to us, like the builders of Babel, not to put our faith in technology for our salvation, especially when it clouds our trust in the Creator.
>
> Real mountains and vast natural phenomena deeply remind us we should feel humble in the face of the cosmos and even in local representations of it, like mountains. Perhaps there is a built-in humility "gene," evolutionarily acquired to engender wonder, to give us a healthy respect for things which we cannot fathom much less control. But when artificial

---

[132] Eisenberg, Evan, "The Mountain & the Tower," *Torah of the Earth*, vol. 1, Arthur Waskow (ed.), 30–33.
[133] Gerstenfeld, Manfred, *The Quality of the Environment,* Israel: The Jerusalem Institute for Research, 2002, 48.

towers like skyscrapers – or technology, or other products of human ingenuity – begin to mimic that effect, to co-opt that feeling, we begin to lose sight of reality, subjugate ourselves to our own tools, and limit our ability to experience wonderment at anything but the work of our own hands.[134]

Technology can be a blessing and a curse. Used well, it can bring peace, progress, and prosperity. Yet it often causes discord and even violence, pollution and environmental degradation.

2.34 Diversity Sustains Life

Shadal (Rabbi Samuel David Luzzatto) explains, "They were one people, with one society and one opinion."[135] In other words, they were a society with no diversity whatsoever as we saw in Genesis 11:6 – "And the Lord said, 'If, as one people with one language for all, this is how they have begun to act, then nothing that they may propose to do will be out of their reach.'"

We need diversity for sustainability, both in the animal kingdom and in the human world. While every society must have its own customs and constraints, survival in times of disaster may ultimately depend on learning from outsiders.

Greenland in the Middle Ages was inhabited by two peoples – the Norse from Scandinavia and the native Inuit. According to historical records, the two peoples met on a very occasional basis but never cooperated. In the words of Pulitzer Prize winner and anthropologist Jared Diamond, "If only the Norse, besides eating many of the wild foods used by Native American societies in Greenland (especially caribou, migratory seals, and harbor seals), had also taken advantage of other wild foods that Native Americans used but the Norse did not (especially fish, ringed seals, and whales other than beached whales), the Norse might have survived. That they did not…was their own decision. The Norse starved in the presence of unutilized food resources."[136]

God sees the people of Babel becoming too uniform and determines to break them up into more diverse groups, each with their own language and ideas. With this, God lays the foundations for sustainable diversity within humanity. Yet human diversity has declined significantly in the past century, including in diet. McDonald's, Subway, Kentucky Fried Chicken, Burger King, and Pizza

---

[134] Benstein, Jeremy, *The Way Into Judaism and the Environment*, Vermont: Jewish Lights Publishing, 2008, 64–66.
[135] Shadal on Genesis 11:6.
[136] Diamond, Jared, *Collapse*, London: Penguin, 2005, 274.

Hut have 116,000 stores, in a majority of countries around the world.[137] The majority of people in the world eat these chains' food each year, with common ingredients being meat, cheese, wheat, corn, oil, and sugar. The homogeneity in diet worldwide has contributed to a dramatic decline in the biodiversity of food crops, which the UN cites as a threat to global food security. A UN report notes that "the lack of variety and increasing uniformity of crops may render them unsuitable for the changing conditions under which they grow."[138]

With regard to biodiversity, Jared Diamond notes how destroying a lot of little species matters to the same extent that taking out a lot of little screws holding together an airplane matters.[139] The extinction of a single species, the destruction of large tracts of rainforest, ocean pollution, and poisoning of billions of sea animals with plastic – these acts equally diminish the holiness of creation.

3 Jewish Ecology in the Lives of Abraham, Isaac and Jacob

3.1 Palace on Fire

Let's take a look at Genesis 12:1 – "The Lord said to Abram, 'Go forth from your native land and from your father's house to the land that I will show you.'" The Midrash explains how Abram (whose name becomes Abraham) discovered God. It describes Abraham passing by a palace that is on fire. He wonders aloud, "Is it possible that the palace doesn't have an owner? Who is the owner of this palace?" The owner hears him and says, "It is Me!"[140]

In the words of Rabbi Yosef Y. Jacobson: "Abraham's bewilderment is clear. This sensitive human being gazes at a brilliantly structured universe, a splendid piece of art. He is overwhelmed by the grandeur of a sunset and by the miracle of childbirth; he marvels at the roaring ocean waves and at the silent, steady beat

---

[137] "Top Chain Restaurants Worldwide," Restaurant Engine, accessed June 17, 2020, https://restaurantengine.com/top-chain-restaurants-worldwide/
[138] "UN Agency Sounds Alarm: Dwindling Agrobiodiversity 'Severe Threat' to Food Security," UN News, November 14, 2019, https://news.un.org/en/story/2019/11/1051411
[139] Diamond, Jared, *Collapse: How Societies Choose to Fail or Succeed*, New York: Viking, 2009, 489.
[140] Midrash Genesis Rabbah 39:1.

of the human heart. The world is indeed a palace. But the palace is in flames. The world is full of … pain."[141]

Rabbi Jonathan Sacks explains that the question, "Is it possible that the palace doesn't have an owner?" speaks to the responsibility of humanity to put out the fire that we have started. The palace is a metaphor for nature.[142] Today with global warming, the world's great rainforests and boreal forests are burning as never before.[143] One could look at the planet and legitimately ask, "Who is in charge of this problem?" And God's response may be to us, just as it was to Abraham, "Go forth," or "Reach into yourself." In other words, we all share responsibility for our common home.

3.2 Famine in Genesis

The verse in Genesis 12:10 reads: "There was a famine in the land, and Abram went down to Egypt to sojourn there, for the famine was severe in the land." It emphasizes that Abraham and his family had to migrate due to the famine. In the Land of Israel, the crops that depend on rainfall, like wheat, barley, olives, and grapes, produce little or no grain or fruit during a drought. Fig trees, pomegranate trees, and vegetables that depend on water produce even less. In a sustained drought, even the springs dry up, which prevents irrigation.

According to Rabbeinu Bachaya (Bachaya ben Asher ibn Halawa), citing the rabbis of the Talmud, there were ten famines from Adam to the end of Genesis.[144] The Midrash states that the Torah explicitly mentions only three famines, one each during the lifetimes of Abraham, Isaac, and Jacob.[145] These three famines occur in a period of about 200 years.[146]

Ten extreme famines occurred in the twentieth century. They killed over 70 million people, predominantly in China, the Soviet Union, and India, and also

---

141 Jacobson, Yosef Y., "The Burning Palace," Chabad, September 11, 2002, www.chabad.org/library/article_cdo/aid/59473/jewish/The-Burning-Palace.htm
142 Sacks, Jonathan, *Radical Then, Radical Now*, London: Continuum, 2000, 49–53.
143 Symonds, Alexandria, "Amazon Rainforest Fires: Here's What's Really Happening," *The New York Times*, August 28, 2019, https://www.nytimes.com/2019/08/23/world/americas/amazon-fire-brazil-bolsonaro.html
144 Rabbeinu Bachaya on Genesis 26:1.
145 Midrash Genesis Rabbah 64:2. Famine occurs in the time of Isaac in Genesis 26:12, and in the time of Jacob in Genesis 41:56.
146 See Seder Olam for the dates that Abraham went to Egypt and the date that Jacob left for Egypt.

drove migration of millions more to new regions.¹⁴⁷ This suggests an average of ten years between major world famines. While the immediate and deeper causes of famines are complex, unsustainable agricultural practices contributing to salinity, loss of natural water bodies, or soil erosion can play a role.¹⁴⁸ A 2019 United Nations Climate Change report highlights the increased likelihood of future, major global famine due to climate change, stressing the world's major breadbaskets.¹⁴⁹ Abraham and Sarah had no choice but to become famine refugees. Today, the individual and collective actions of people could reduce the frequency and severity of famines in our times and in the future.

3.3 Sustainable Coexistence (*by* Rabbi Tuvia Aronson)[150]

Abraham and Lot's inability to coexist on one piece of land leaps out at us in Genesis 13:6 – "So that the land could not support them staying together; for their possessions were so great that they could not remain together." In our era, when environmental issues such as population, food, and land distribution divide communities and nations, we can look to this text for guidance. Rabbi Samson Raphael Hirsch and Netziv (Rabbi Naftali Tzvi Yehuda Berlin) explain this verse to show that divisiveness put an extra burden on the land and the people.[151]

It was not because they had too many herds or because there was insufficient pasture for both of them. If they had combined their herds into one, the land would have been sufficient. But if two people cannot agree, separate tents are needed – boxes, crates, everything separate for each of the two parties. Had their personalities been compatible, there would have been no need for sep-

---

[147] Devereux, Stephen, "Famine in the Twentieth Century," *IDS Working Papers*, 105, January 2000.
[148] IPCC, "Climate Change and Land, An IPCC Special Report on Climate Change, Desertification, Land Degradation, Sustainable Land Management, Food Security, and Greenhouse Gas Fluxes in Terrestrial Ecosystems," Summary for Policymakers, IPCC, 2019, https://www.ipcc.ch/site/assets/uploads/2019/08/4.-SPM_Approved_Microsite_FINAL.pdf
[149] Borenstein, Seth / Keaten, Jamey, "UN Climate Report: Change Land Use to Avoid a Hungry Future," Phys.org, August 8, 2019, https://phys.org/news/2019-08-climate-hungry-future.html
[150] This content was produced by Canfei Nesharim, a branch of Grow Torah. It is available at http://canfeinesharim.org/lech-lecha-joining-together-for-justice-in-the-land/
[151] Ha'amek Davar on 13:6 and Rabbi Samson Raphael Hirsch on Genesis 13:6 in Oratz, Efraim (ed.), *The Pentateuch*, trans. Gertrude Hirschler, New York: Judaica Press, 1986. This idea has a precedent in Pesikta Rabati 83.

arate pastures. Only profits counted in Lot's enterprise, while Abraham's household gave attention to higher interests.

Abraham and Lot's attitudes were incompatible; therefore they could not cooperate. This is why the verse stresses "together" – *yaḥday*. Interestingly, the second-century translator Onkelos translates *yaḥday* using the wording "as one," connoting the need for a deep interconnection that ultimately enables living in harmony with the Land.[152] The Abrahamic tradition demands that we make our personal and societal decisions based on both environmental and social considerations.

Religious environmental education stresses the importance of togetherness. Community gardens are flourishing, and consumer-assisted farming projects are enhancing life in ways that promote both communal unity and harmony with nature. Hazon's Adamah program in Connecticut is one such example. Intentional ecological communities are gaining momentum. Concern for the environment crosses denominational and philosophical divides. Working as one to take care of our precious resources is incredibly powerful.

3.4 The Dead Sea Is Dying

In Biblical times, the Dead Sea region was lush and fertile, like the Garden of Eden, as it tells us in Genesis 13:10 – "Lot looked about him and saw how well watered was the whole plain of the Jordan, all of it – this was before the Lord had destroyed Sodom and Gomorrah – all the way to Zoar, like the garden of the Lord, like the land of Egypt." Ralbag (Rabbi Levi ben Gershon) explains that the Dead Sea valley had many fields, suggesting that there was ample water for irrigation at that time.[153] Rashi teaches that it had streams, trees, and crops.[154]

Over the past 60 years, modern irrigation techniques have significantly expanded agriculture in Israel, Jordan, Syria, and Lebanon. In addition, many millions of people now live in the Dead Sea drainage basin. They use water for domestic and industrial uses, including the extraction of Dead Sea minerals. This has threatened the region's ecology, with significant lowering of the Dead Sea's water level and formation of sinkholes around the sea. The diversion of tributary rivers and streams for human use has significantly reduced the annual flow to

---

[152] Onkelos on Genesis 13:6. Ibn Ezra also translates *yachdav* as *yachid* – united, and not *yachad* – together.
[153] Ralbag on Genesis 14:3.
[154] Rashi on Genesis 13:10.

the Dead Sea, just as climate change has made rainfall in the Dead Sea watershed scarcer.[155] Dead Sea water levels continue to decline at a rate of about 3.4 feet (1.1 meter) per year.[156] Without significant collaborative action, the Dead Sea may suffer a similar fate as two of the world's great lakes – Lake Baikal in Russia, and Lake Mali in Africa, which have shriveled in recent decades. That the Torah describes the Dead Sea valley as comparable to the Garden of Eden should motivate us to stop and reverse the damage we have already done.

3.5 Hiking the Land

Abraham connected to God by being alone in nature. Abraham was commanded to walk the width and breadth of Israel: Genesis 13:17 – "Get up, walk about the land, through its length and its breadth, for I give it to you." Why is this one of very few commands given specifically to him? Abraham traveled throughout the Middle East by foot and by donkey – from present-day Iraq, crossing through Turkey, Syria, and Egypt, before returning to Israel. His travels and time in nature created a foundation for his spiritual growth and awareness. He also kept himself in good physical shape. At the age of 127, the Bible says, he hiked for three days and climbed Mount Moriah for the binding of Isaac.

Isaac also connected to God through nature when he went out into the fields. So did Jacob when he slept and dreamt of the ladder, alone outdoors. How many city dwellers today have ever slept alone in nature? How can we bridge the ecological gap between our lifestyle and that of our forefathers?

3.6 Stuck in Crude Oil

The kings of Sodom and Gomorrah fell into pits of "black gold" or bitumen, also known as asphalt (in Hebrew, ḥemar).[157] Genesis 14:10 – "Now the Valley of Sid-

---

[155] Pe'er, Guy / Safriel, Uriel N., *Climate Change Israel National Report: Impact, Vulnerability and Adaptation* Israel: Blaustein Institute for Desert Research, Ben-Gurion University of the Negev, October 2000.

[156] Israel Water Authority, "Saving the Dead Sea," accessed June 18, 2020, http://www.water.gov.il/Hebrew/Water-Environment/Dead-Sea/DocLib1/saving-dead-sea-eng.pdf

[157] This is distinct from clay, which is referred to as ḥomer. Onkelos translates ḥemar into Aramaic as ḥemra, which is understood by language scholars to refer to bitumen or asphalt. See Jastrow, Marcus, *Dictionary of the Targumim*, 1926, accessed January 3, 2020, https://www.se

dim was dotted with bitumen pits; and the kings of Sodom and Gomorrah, in their flight, threw themselves into them, while the rest escaped to the hill country."

In ancient times as today, surface seepages of this thick, sticky form of crude oil[158] occurred and still occur in a limited number of places in the world, including Azerbaijan, Iran, Pennsylvania, Alberta, and the Dead Sea.[159] People used and still use the natural tar for its waterproofing qualities[160] and for roads.

Why does the Torah mention this geological detail in relation to the leaders of these ultimately decimated societies? The Torah continues, "The invaders [four Middle Eastern kings] seized all the wealth of Sodom and Gomorrah and all their provisions, and went their way."[161] Once the kings of Sodom and Gomorrah fell into the bitumen pits, they got trapped and lost all of their wickedly gained wealth.

The story of the kings stuck in bitumen relates deeply to our world today. Canada is the planet's fourth-largest oil producer, and 60 percent of its oil comes from the bitumen of oil sands.[162] The Canadian province of Alberta has most of the world's reserves of natural bitumen in the Athabasca oil sands, an area larger than England.[163] Bitumen is considered the dirtiest and most polluting fossil fuel, due to the energy required to separate the crude oil from the sand and the carcinogenic chemicals used to thin it for pipeline transport.[164] In July 2010, the largest oil pipeline spill in US history occurred, spilling over a million

---

faria.org.il/Jastrow%2C_%D7%97%D6%B5%D7%99%D7%9E%D6%B8%D7%A8%D6%B8%D7%90?lang=he

See also Safa Ivrit, "Chimer and Chomer." https://www.safa-ivrit.org/form/khomer.php

158 "Bitumen," Energy Education, University of Calgary, last modified June 25, 2018, https://energyeducation.ca/encyclopedia/Bitumen

159 Rabbi Aryeh Kaplan writes, "Even now asphalt is found in the Dead Sea region. The Romans referred to it as Mer Asphaltitus, the Asphalt Sea, as it was known to cast up lumps of asphalt. Rabbi Aryeh Kaplan, *The Living Torah*, commentary to Genesis 14:10, 65. Josephus, *The Wars of the Jews* 4:8:4; Tacitus, *Histories* 5:6.

160 Asaf, Oron et al., "Early Maritime Activity on the Dead Sea: Bitumen Harvesting and the Possible Use of Reed Watercraft," *Journal of Maritime Archaeology* 10, 1 (2015), 65–88, https://doi.org/10.1007/s11457-015-9135-2

161 Genesis 14:11.

162 "What Are the Oil Sands?", Canadian Association of Petroleum Producers, accessed March 1, 2020, https://www.capp.ca/oil/what-are-the-oil-sands/

163 Leahy, Stephen, "This Is the World's Most Destructive Oil Operation – and It's Growing," *National Geographic*, April 11, 2019, https://www.nationalgeographic.com/environment/2019/04/alberta-canadas-tar-sands-is-growing-but-indigenous-people-fight-back/

164 Song, Lisa, "Why Tar Sands Oil Is More Polluting and Why It Matters," *Reuters*, May 22, 2012, https://www.reuters.com/article/idUS201043482520120522

gallons of Canadian diluted bitumen (dilbit) into Michigan's Kalamazoo River. As Inside Climate News reported, "The spill triggered the most expensive clean-up in US history – more than ¾ of a billion dollars – and it lingered on for years."[165] Today, we and our leaders are trapped by economic inertia and political resistance. Oil remains our fuel of choice to make gasoline for cars and trucks, jet fuel for airplanes, tar and asphalt for paving the roads, and even plastic which is filling our oceans with trash that never fully breaks down.

The Midrash teaches that Abraham, the prophet of light, pulled the kings out of the bitumen pits.[166] Abraham provides an example of lifting people from being trapped in fossil fuels. Comparatively, scientists published a 2017 study and environmental roadmap on how most countries in the world could transition to 100 percent wind, water, and solar energy by 2050.[167] We do not need to wait until someone rescues us – or until we run out of all fossil fuels – but can now take steps as individuals, communities, and nations to free ourselves from devastating fossil-fuel use.

3.7 Abraham and Self-Satisfaction

Abraham recognizes where wealth and abundance ultimately come from – God. We learn this from Genesis 14:22–23 – "But Abram said to the king of Sodom, 'I swear to the Lord, God Most High, Creator of heaven and earth: I will not take so much as a thread or a sandal strap of what is yours; you shall not say, 'It is I who made Abram rich.'" The Maharal of Prague (Rabbi Judah Loew ben Betzalel) taught that Abraham epitomizes "satisfaction with what one has" and being content with what arrives in one's hand based on a normal amount of work.[168] Rashi points out that Abraham made sure to earn his living through honest means, by only grazing his flocks on ownerless land.[169] The trait of being satisfied with what one has flows from an awareness that God provides each person based

---

[165] Mcgowan, Elizabeth / Song, Lisa, "The Dilbit Disaster: Inside the Biggest Oil Spill You've Never Heard Of," InsideClimate News, Jun 26, 2012, https://insideclimatenews.org/news/26062012/dilbit-diluted-bitumen-enbridge-kalamazoo-river-marshall-michigan-oil-spill-6b-pipeline-epa/

[166] Genesis Rabbah 42:7, quoted by Rashi on Genesis 14:10.

[167] Jacobson et al., "100% Clean and Renewable Wind, Water, and Sunlight All-Sector Energy Roadmaps for 139 Countries of the World," *Joule 1*, 108–121 (2017), Elsevier Inc., http://dx.doi.org/10.1016/j.joule.2017.07.005

[168] Maharal, Netivot Olam, Netiv HaOsher 1:4.

[169] Cf. Rashi on Genesis 13:7.

on their merit. Abraham appreciates the gift of being fully alive through meeting his needs through his own efforts and has no need of gifts from the king of Sodom.

In modern consumer society, we would be wise to learn from Abraham. Being satisfied with what we have, instead of constantly seeking more things, is a root solution for ecological sustainability.

3.8 Finding God Outdoors

Why did God take Abraham outside? Genesis 15:5 – "He took him outside and said, 'Look toward heaven and count the stars, if you are able to count them.' And He added, 'So shall your offspring be.'"

Ibn Ezra writes poetically of finding God, "Wherever I turn my eyes, around on earth or to the heavens, I see You in the field of stars, I see You in the yield of the land, in every breath and sound, a blade of grass, a simple flower, an echo of Your holy name."[170] Elie Wiesel relates:

> When the Holy Seer of Lublin was a little boy, he was known to skip school for hours or even days. Once, his teacher followed the young boy to see what became of these free moments. The Seer walked to the edge of the town, into deep woods, and there, in a small, green circle of trees, he began to pray. The next day the teacher asked the boy what drew him to those woods. The Seer of Lublin replied, "I can find God there." "But," said the teacher, "surely God is the same in the town as in the woods." "That's true," replied the Seer, "but I am not the same!"[171]

3.9 The Cure Before the Sickness

Rabbi Mordechai Hochman addresses Genesis 15:13–14 – "Know well that your offspring shall be strangers in a land not theirs and they shall be enslaved and oppressed four hundred years; but I will execute judgment on the nation they shall serve, and in the end they shall go free with great wealth." He explains that these verses encapsulate the rabbinical dictum that "God gives us the cure

---

[170] ibn Ezra, Abraham, "God Everywhere" (1089–1164).
[171] Benstein, Jeremy, *The Way Into Judaism and the Environment,* Vermont: Jewish Lights Publishing, 2006, 142, citing Elie Wiesel.

before the sickness." In other words, God tells Abraham that his descendants will suffer but emerge much stronger from it.[172]

With regard to sustainability, it is easy to think that the world is doomed to destruction. However, God has given us the cure before the sickness. There have never been so many possible solutions available for reducing carbon emissions (solar panels are cheaper than ever), for conserving water, and for replacing single-use plastics. Our challenge as humankind is in deciding to embrace them.

3.10 Resilience of Trees

Rabbeinu Chananel asked why the angels revealed themselves to Abraham under a tree[173]: Genesis 18:4 – "Let a little water be brought; bathe your feet and recline under the tree." He answered that in doing so they revealed a message to Abraham: "You, like a tree, will flourish even in your old age," as it says in the book of Job, "For a tree has hope; if it is cut it will again renew itself, and its trunk will never cease,"[174] and in the words of the Psalmist, "He shall be as a tree planted beside streams of water, which brings forth its fruit in its season. Its leaves do not wilt; and whatever it does prospers."[175]

Abraham's resilience and prosperity are compared to a tree. Indeed, trees are one of the most resilient organisms, specifically against drought. This is increasingly important in light of climate change causing unpredictable rainfall, extreme weather events, and stronger pests that threaten forests.[176] Contemporary researchers have discovered that diverse "forests with trees that employ a high diversity of traits related to water use suffer less of an impact from drought."[177] They are also more resilient to forest fires.

---

172 Hochman, Mordechai, "Footnote 1 based on the Midrash," in "The Bird That Brings Life to the Carcasses," Yeshiva Beit El, published Kislev 5, 5770, https://www.yeshiva.org.il/midrash/12714
173 Rabbeinu Chananel on Genesis 18:4.
174 Job 14:7–9.
175 Psalms 1:3.
176 Velasquez-Manoff, Moises, "Can Humans Help Trees Outrun Climate Change?" *The New York Times*, April 25, 2019, https://www.nytimes.com/2019/04/25/climate/trees-climate-change.html?searchResultPosition=7
177 Anderegg, William R.L. et al., "Hydraulic Diversity of Forests Regulates Ecosystem Resilience during Drought," *Nature* 561, 7724 (2018), https://doi.org/10.1038/s41586-018-0539-7

3.11 Veal Then and Now

What is happening with the choice of a calf in Genesis 18:7? "Then Abraham ran to the herd, took a calf, tender and choice, and gave it to a servant-boy, who hastened to prepare it."

Radak explains that the calf was "fatty."[178] A Biblical fatty calf would have been naturally well fed by its mother and not overworked, so that it could put on weight. Today, however, calves are raised unnaturally for veal, kept in cramped conditions, and fed artificial fluids.

Regarding the permissibility of this modern way of raising calves, Rabbi Moshe Feinstein, one of the greatest twentieth-century authorities on Jewish law, writes, "Regarding the new method of fattening calves in special, narrow stalls where they don't even have enough room to take a few steps, and they are not fed any normal animal feed nor are they allowed to suckle at all but instead are fed with fatty liquids from which they derive no pleasure at all and they are also frequently ill because of this and require all kinds of medication: Those who perform this (the fattening) are surely guilty of the prohibition of causing pain to animals. For even though it (pain) is permitted when there is a purpose, for example to slaughter them for food or to use them for plowing or transport, etc. but not for senseless pain, which is forbidden even if someone makes monetary gain from it...In any case, it is forbidden to cause pain to an animal, to feed it food which it doesn't enjoy, which causes pain, or which causes it to be ill."[179]

3.12 Sodom and Acid Rain

How should we understand what is happening in Genesis 19:24? "The Lord rained upon Sodom and Gomorrah sulfurous fire from the Lord out of heaven." According to the Midrash[180], nothing that descended from heaven was bad, in and of itself. Only when this rain reached the earth's atmosphere did it receive the additive of sulfur and fire.

Acid rain can be seen as a modern-day equivalent. As water evaporates, it combines with the acidic and often sulfurous emissions from cars, factories, and coal-generating plants to form acid rain. In recent years, Taoyuan's Zhongli

---

[178] Radak on Genesis 18:7.
[179] Responsa Igrot Moshe, Even Ha'Ezer, vol. iv 92. Quoted in: Stokar, Saul, "The Environment in Jewish Thought and Law," *Sviva Israel* (2018), 28.
[180] Midrash Tanchuma Vayeira 23:1.

District in Taiwan measured rain acidity levels equivalent to that of lemon juice (pH of 3.8).[181] Acid rain has been successfully reduced in most Western countries where it was once prevalent. In the US, the EPA emissions trading program "helped deliver annual sulfur dioxide (SO2) reductions of over 93 percent and annual nitrogen oxides (NOX) emissions reductions of over 86 percent...from fossil fuel–fired power plants, extensive environmental and human health benefits, and far lower-than-expected costs."[182]

The success in the US and Europe in dramatically reducing acid rain shows how government environmental policies can rein in high pollution and the ensuing effects on human health and nature. With regard to acid rain, we have a choice about whether or not to experience some of what God rained down on the selfish people of Sodom.

3.13 Morality and Ecology (*by* Rabbi Yuval Cherlow)[183]

Two cosmic catastrophes unfold in the book of Genesis. In the flood, God brings waters down from the Heavens to destroy almost all life. We see the second, in Genesis 19:24 – "The Lord rained upon Sodom and Gomorrah sulfurous fire from the Lord out of heaven." By the utter devastation of Sodom and Gomorrah, an area previously known as a fertile and lush "Garden of God,"[184] becomes a desolate land "that cannot be sown, nor sprout, and no grass shall rise up upon it, like the upheaval of Sodom and Gomorrah...which God overturned in His anger, and His wrath."[185]

One of the connections we see between these two events is the word that the Torah employs in both cases – to destroy. When God relates to Noah that He will bring the flood, He says, "I am about to destroy [*mashḥitam*] them from the earth."[186] In the case of Sodom we see the same word applied: "When God destroyed [*beshaḥet*] the cities of the plain [...]"[187]

---

181 Everington, Keoni, "Taoyuan's Zhongli District Has Worst Acid Rain in Taiwan," *Taiwan News*, August 19, 2019, https://www.taiwannews.com.tw/en/news/3764930
182 "Acid Rain Program," US EPA, accessed June 22, 2020, https://www.epa.gov/acidrain/acid-rain-program
183 This content was produced by Canfei Nesharim, a branch of Grow Torah. It is available at http://canfeinesharim.org/wp-content/uploads/2014/05/Parsha-vayera-sin-of-sedom-Rabbi-Cherlow-sourcesheet.pdf
184 Genesis 13:10.
185 Deuteronomy 29:22.
186 Genesis 6:13.

The Torah does not elaborate on the sin of Sodom, but the underpinnings are expressed later in the prophecy of Ezekiel: Sodom "[...] had pride, excess bread, and peaceful serenity, but did not strengthen the hand of the poor and the needy."[188] The prophet's description, combined with what the Torah reveals to us, gives us the following picture: The people of Sodom insisted on preserving their high quality of living to such an extent that they established a principle not to let the poor and homeless reside in their city.

Consequently, when a destitute person would come seeking help, they would revoke their right to any welfare, public or private! In this rule, the Sodomites figured they would preserve an elite upper class community that could monopolize the profits that the bountiful land offered, without having to distribute any revenues to a "lower class" of people.

An opinion in the Mishnah further strengthens this picture of moral depravity when it defines the Sodomite as one who says, "What's mine is mine and what's yours is yours."[189] The Mishnah decries a man who wishes to remove himself from the social responsibility of welfare by closing himself and his wealth from others, even if he makes the claim that he is not taking away from anyone else.

But the Torah also uses the verb "to destroy" in relation to the environment, regarding the prohibition of wanton destruction during a military siege: "Do not destroy [*tashḥit*] the trees."[190]

What could be the connection between the corruption of the generation of the flood, the people of Sodom, and environmental sins? Humanity itself is part and parcel of its environment and is not separate from it. Having been created in the image of God, we may think that we are detached from creation.

The central point in the connection between moral behavior and environmental behavior comes from the understanding that both behaviors go hand in hand. One without the other corrupts the Divine vision for human action. That is, a society may be passionate about preserving its natural environment while maintaining a complete disregard for the welfare of its citizens. Sodom is a perfect example of this, where they cared so much for their "garden of God" that they refused to aid anyone in need.

In effect, the people of Sodom's perverted ways were extremely unsustainable – causing God to turn one of the most fertile and lush ecosystems on earth into what today is infamous for its barrenness and desolation. From the mistakes

---

187 Ibid., 19:29.
188 Ezekiel 16:49.
189 Mishnah Avot 5:10.
190 Deuteronomy 20:19.

of the people of Sodom, we can learn the essential character traits that allow one to live in balance with the Creator and creation.

The moral human being is devoted to the holiness and purity of life, refrains from harming others, and sacrifices some personal pleasure for an ethical and upright path. When we are capable of fulfilling this ideal, we will naturally be triumphant in attaining the great spiritual task of infusing our religious/moral lifestyle with one that is also environmentally sustainable.

3.14 Abraham and the Burning Kiln

We see the extent of the devastation in Genesis 19:25: "He annihilated those cities and the entire Plain, and all the inhabitants of the cities and the vegetation of the ground." Rashi comments on the verse, "He [Abraham] saw the smoke of the land rising like the smoke of a kiln,"[191] saying this was like the smoke rising from a kiln burning limestone to create lime used for bricks.[192] Today, burning of tropical rainforests not only devastates the region where the burning occurs, but puts pollution in the air that is carried far beyond a nation's borders. Burning of the environment is an international ecological threat.

Chizkuni (Rabbi Chizkiyahu ben Rabbi Mano'ach) explains why vegetation is also mentioned in this verse: It teaches that anyone who takes a handful of earth from Sodom, even to this day, and transfers it to a garden, will make the garden infertile.[193]

Today, scientists teach us, "When acid rain [from pollution] falls, it can affect forests as well as lakes and rivers. To grow, trees need healthy soil in which to develop. Acid rain is absorbed into the soil, making it more difficult for trees to survive. As a result, trees are more susceptible to viruses, fungi and insect pests."[194]

The acid rain effect is reversible with the addition of large quantities of alkaline lime to the soil. In Sweden, the cost of such treatment is over $50 million per year.[195] This is an example of an "externality," a cost of operating our cars

---

[191] Genesis 19:28.
[192] Rashi on Genesis 19:28.
[193] Chizkuni on Genesis 19:25.
[194] "Impacts of Acid Rain on Soils," *Air Pollution UK*, accessed May 16, 2019, http://www.airquality.org.uk/16.php
[195] Stevens, William K., "To Treat the Attack of Acid Rain, Add Limestone to Water and Wait," *The New York Times*, January 31, 1989, https://www.nytimes.com/1989/01/31/science/to-treat-the-attack-of-acid-rain-add-limestone-to-water-and-wait.html

and factories that is paid by taxpayers instead of by polluters. If such treatment costs were included in the costs of fossil fuels, according to some analysts, fuel prices would rise by up to 50 percent.[196]

3.15 Sustainable Peace

The theme of regeneration is displayed in Genesis 21:33: "[Abraham] planted a tamarisk [eshel] at Beersheba, and invoked there the name of the Lord, the Everlasting God." Malbim explains that the *eshel* was an orchard.[197] The peace pact made with Abimelech, king of Gerar (today's Gaza), is concluded with the planting of fruit trees, representing the importance of sustaining longterm and environmental prosperity for all, and demonstrating that true peace is based upon a joint hope for a better future. This is comparable to modern Israel and Jordan basing a 1994 peace pact on sharing water resources.[198] The Israeli-Palestinian-Jordanian NGO Eco Peace has proposed a shared, cross-border nature park as a way to promote peace.

3.16 Sarah and Sustainable Burial

Abraham seeks to buy land to bury Sarah, with a particular emphasis on ownership, in Genesis 23:4 – "I am a resident alien among you; sell me a burial site among you, that I may remove my dead for burial." While he purchases both a field and cave in Hebron, Sarah was buried in a cave. Rabbeinu Bachaya explains that there was a custom for every family to have their own burial area.[199] Contemporary scholar Eldad Keynan explains the Biblical method of burial: "The body was not laid and covered with dust for eternity, like the trench graves practices. Instead, it was laid in a shallow pit or on a shelf for the first year, during which the flesh decayed, while the soul underwent the purifying process. A year after the burial, the relatives returned to the tomb, collected the bones, and put them in stone boxes: ossuaries...Now, they moved the

---

[196] Tirole, Jean, "Some Economics of Global Warming," *Rivista di Politica Economica* 98, 6 (2008), 9–42.
[197] Malbim on Genesis 21:33.
[198] "Article 6" in "Treaty of Peace between the State of Israel and the Hashemite Kingdom of Jordan," Israel Ministry of Foreign Affairs, October 26, 1994, https://mfa.gov.il/mfa/foreign policy/peace/guide/pages/israel-jordan%20peace%20treaty.aspx
[199] Rabbeinu Bachaya on Genesis 23:4.

bones to the ossuary, and put the ossuary in a niche, carved into the tomb wall."[200]

Contemporary researchers have identified two major ecological risks posed by modern cemeteries: contamination of local water sources and of the soil.[201] Traditional Jewish burial practices in Israel overcame these two issues through burial in a rock cave to minimize water contamination, and through burial in simple cloth, without a coffin or other non-decomposable objects.

Modern Jerusalem, a society that lives mostly in urban space and spends most of its time in buildings, now buries many of its dead in multistory structures that resemble parking lots. The main cemetery is next to an urban area and expanded highway, which is common in many cities. A different recent burial design in West Jerusalem's main Har HaMenuchot cemetery is based on the Biblical method of burying in a cave, but creates crypts that are up to 160 feet underground in order to leave space above ground for the living.[202] This may be needed since Israel faces a shortage of 1.5 million burial plots in the coming decades, according to a report from the State Comptroller.[203]

3.17 Relationship With Earth

The specific connection of people to the earth itself is raised in Genesis 23:13: "And [Abraham] spoke to Ephron in the hearing of the people of the land, saying, 'If only you would hear me out! Let me pay the price of the land; accept it from me, that I may bury my dead there.'"

Rabbi Matis Weinberg explains:

> God tells humankind in the Creation story that we "will return to the earth for you were taken from it. For you are dust, and to dust you will return."[204] God does not inform people

---

[200] Keynan, Eldad, "Private vs. Public Burials: Differences and Time Span," The Bible and Interpretation, The University of Arizona, October 2010, http://www.bibleinterp.com/articles/burial357907.shtml#sdfootnote9sym. Citing Jerusalem Talmud, Mo'ed Katan 1:5, 80d; Sanhedrin 6:10, 23d.
[201] Uslu, Aysel / Barış, Emin / Erdoğan, Elmas, "Ecological Concerns over Cemeteries," *African Journal of Agricultural Research* 4, 13 (2009), 1505–1511.
[202] Sokol, Sam, "Squeezed for Burial Space, Jerusalem Prepares an Underground City of the Dead," *The Times of Israel*, October 26, 2019, https://www.timesofisrael.com/squeezed-for-burial-space-jerusalem-prepares-an-underground-city-of-the-dead/
[203] Altman, Yair, "Shortage of 1.5 Million Graves in the Center of Israel" (in Hebrew), *Israel Hayom*, March 23, 2020, https://www.israelhayom.co.il/article/744597
[204] Genesis 3:19.

of mortality per se, but of burial: to dust you will return. It is the underlying relationship with the earth that needs to be restored. That relationship, as with a spouse, is not like the use of an object, but rather through the deep connection we make with the other party.

It is because we were "taken from the earth" in the first place, that we are able to "return to it" and ultimately to find peace. The Midrash teaches that "God collected the dust for man's creation from the four corners of the earth, so that wherever he would die he would find his place for burial."[205] The earth, *adama*, is the name of our species humankind *adam*, just as "human" is drawn from the Latin "humus" meaning "earth." If we lose sight of that connection, we lose all connection to ourselves and to life. Burial is a restoration of that connection.[206]

To invoke the philosopher Martin Buber, our connection to the earth should not be an I–It relationship, but rather an I–Thou relationship, much like an ideal marriage.[207]

3.18 Sarah and Trees

The Torah tells us about the eternal transfer of the cave of the Patriarchs to the seed of Abraham in Genesis 23:17–18 – "The field with its cave and all the trees anywhere within the confines of that field – passed to Abraham as his possession in the presence of the Hittites, of all who entered the gate of his town." But why does the Torah need to tell us that the trees were also sold? In ancient societies, trees next to burial sites were protected from being cut down.[208] Near Jerusalem today, at Sataf, one of the only old-growth oak groves in the Judaean hills is adjacent to a Muslim sheik's burial site. In downtown Jerusalem, a Sufi sheik's tomb is surrounded by mature trees.

The Talmud tells the story of Choni HaMe'agel: "One day he was journeying on the road and saw a man planting a carob tree. He asked, 'How long will it take [for this tree] to bear fruit?' The man replied, 'Seventy years.' He then asked the man, 'Are you so certain that you will live another seventy years?' The man replied, 'I found carob trees in the world that my ancestors planted for me, so I am planting these trees for my children.'"[209]

---

[205] Tanchuma, Pekudei 3.
[206] Weinberg, Matis, *Frameworks: Genesis*, Boston: Foundation for Jewish Publications, 1st edition, 1998, 100–101.
[207] Buber, Martin, *I and Thou*, London: A&C Black, 1937.
[208] Hughes, J. Donald / Thirgood, J.V., "Deforestation, Erosion, and Forest Management in Ancient Greece and Rome," *Journal of Forest History* 26, 2 (1982), 60–75, https://doi.org/10.2307/4004530
[209] Babylonian Talmud, Ta'anit 23a.

Trees represent continuity and sustainability, producing fruit for many decades. The Torah makes the connection between the death of Sarah and the purchase of the trees to stress that just as the trees will benefit future generations who will eat their fruit and breathe their oxygen, so, too, will Sarah's life continue to have meaning for future generations.

In the time of Choni HaMe'agel, the old man advocated sustainable agriculture, planting a tree for his grandchildren to enjoy. Today, we see youth increasingly engaging with environmental causes and even influencing policy at the UN.[210] Nowadays, children are more likely to be convincing their parents of the importance of sustainability than the other way around.[211] The most visible face of the global climate movement has been a Swedish teenager, Greta Thunberg. In August 2018, at age 15, she began a strike for climate action outside of the Swedish Parliament, following the heat waves and wildfires during Sweden's hottest summer in at least 262 years.[212]

3.19 Rebecca's Kindness to Camels

Kli Yakar (Rabbi Shlomo Luntschitz) suggests that just as the Talmud explains why the heron is called *ḥasidah* in Hebrew – because it does *ḥesed* (kindness) with others of its species – so too the camel is called *gamal* because it does acts (*gemilut*) of kindness with other camels.[213] The Bible encourages us to learn from animals and birds, as the Book of Job states, "God teaches us by the animals of the earth, and makes us wiser by the birds of the sky."[214]

It is significant that the one test for the appropriate wife for Isaac was whether the woman would not only show kindness to people, but also to animals. We see this in Genesis 24:14 – "Let the maiden to whom I say, 'Please, lower your jar that I may drink,' and who replies, 'Drink, and I will also water your camels' – let her be the one whom You have decreed for Your servant Isaac. Thereby shall I

---

210 "Dreams to Action: Beginning a Meaningful Conversation with Young Leaders," UN Environment Programme, published April 23, 2019, https://www.unenvironment.org/news-and-stories/story/dreams-action-beginning-meaningful-conversation-young-leaders
211 Denworth, Lydia, "Children Change Their Parents' Minds about Climate Change," *Scientific American*, May 6, 2019, https://www.scientificamerican.com/article/children-change-their-parents-minds-about-climate-change/?redirect=1
212 Crouch, David, "The Swedish 15-Year-Old Who's Cutting Class to Fight the Climate Crisis," *The Guardian*, September 1, 2018, https://www.theguardian.com/science/2018/sep/01/swedish-15-year-old-cutting-class-to-fight-the-climate-crisis
213 Babylonian Talmud, Chulin 63a.
214 Job 35:11.

know that You have dealt graciously with my master." Rebecca is selected to be one of the four matriarchs because of her compassion, giving water to animals.

Rebbetzin Chana Bracha Siegelbaum explains that Rebecca's kindness is revealed by the challenging work she is prepared to perform for Eliezer and his camels: "How much water would that take? There are different opinions of how long a camel can go without drinking, but at the very least for six to eight days under desert conditions. Thereafter, a camel must drink to replenish its body water, and when water is available, it may drink more than a third of its body weight.[215] When a camel has become dehydrated and then suddenly has access to water, it is capable of drinking up to 35 gallons (135 liters) of water in thirteen minutes.[216] Keep in mind, we have to multiply this number by ten for all of the camels that Rebecca watered in her incredible act of kindness!"[217]

3.20 Praying in the Fields (*by* Drew Kaplan)[218]

There may have been an agricultural element to Isaac's outing in the field, in Genesis 24:63 – "And Isaac went out walking in the field toward evening and, looking up, he saw camels approaching." Rashbam (Rabbi Shmuel ben Meir) suggests that Isaac was planting trees as well as checking his agricultural efforts.[219]

This verse is understood in the Talmud to refer to Isaac praying outdoors, in the field.[220] In line with this, Rabbi Yochanan in the Talmud said that one may not pray in a house without windows.[221] Rashi explained that this is because looking outside causes one to focus toward heaven and one's heart will be hum-

---

[215] Schmidt Nielsen, Knut, *Animal Physiology: Adaptation and Environment* Cambridge: Cambridge University Press, 5th ed., 1997.
[216] Kingdon, Jonathan, *East African Mammals: An Atlas of Evolution in Africa, Volume 1*, Chicago: University of Chicago Press, 1984.
[217] Siegelbaum, Rebbetzin Chana Bracha, "Discovering the Camel Connection: Nature in the Parasha: Parashat Chayei Sarah," *Women on the Land*, November 11, 2014, http://rebbetzinchanabracha.blogspot.com/2014/11/discovering-camel-connection.html
[218] This content was produced by Canfei Nesharim, a branch of Grow Torah. It is available at http://canfeinesharim.org/parshat-chayei-sarah-praying-in-the-fields/
[219] Genesis 24:63.
[220] Babylonian Talmud, Berakhot 26b, citing use of the same Hebrew root word in Psalms 102:1.
[221] Ibid., 34b.

bled.²²² In contrast, when praying in a house without windows, one is surrounded by human handiwork, with far less power to inspire awe and appreciation for God.

Rebbe Nachman of Breslov instructed his followers to engage in meditation, or to speak with God in nature for an hour every day.²²³ In explaining Rebbe Nachman's teachings, Rabbi Natan Greenberg states that real prayer involves conversation with the surrounding natural world. Indeed, the strength of prayer comes from the Divine, spiritual energy flowing from nature. He explains that we need the spiritual energy of the earth to give strength to our prayers. Isaac first manifests this type of prayer through his connection to nature. He comes to it because he finds it difficult to relate to the world around him. He wants to be in a simple world, God's world, so he walks and prays in the field.²²⁴

For Isaac, praying to God in nature was a central part of his Divine service, and it can be for us as well. Our ability to connect to our Creator in the world He created is an indicator of our ability to live in balance with that natural world. However, a primarily urban, post-industrial generation that is alienated from God's Oneness as manifested in the natural world will certainly misuse that which God has given us.

The litany of ecological problems we face – from air and water pollution to species extinction and urban sprawl – testify to our disconnect from the natural environment which God gave us. Reconnecting to the inspired outdoor prayers of our forefathers can help us regain a sense of the grandeur of God's world and of our responsibility to live in balance with it.

3.21 Sustainable Luxuries

We are told Esau and Jacob will become two nations, in Genesis 25:23 – "And the Lord answered her, 'Two nations are in your womb, two separate peoples shall issue from your body; one people shall be mightier than the other, and the older shall serve the younger.'"

Rashi comments: "These [two nations] are Antoninus and Rabbi, for neither radish nor lettuce ceased [to be found] on their tables neither during the sunny season nor during the rainy season."²²⁵ The Talmud states: "They [Antoninus

---

222 Ibid.
223 Rabbi Nachman of Breslov, Likutei Moharan I:52.
224 Shiur on Likutei Moharan, part 2, teaching 11. Rabbi Greenberg is the Rosh Yeshiva of the Bat Ayin Yeshiva. This shiur is available in audio form at www.bat-ayin.org
225 Citing Babylonian Talmud, Avodah Zarah 11a.

and Rabbi] were 'proud ones' in that they were so wealthy that they could afford to have seasonal products all year round."[226] Antoninus was the Roman emperor, and Rabbi (Judah the Prince) was a key Jewish leader in Roman Judaea.

This Talmudic teaching reveals how food availability has changed dramatically in the transition from pre-modern, pre-industrial society to modern industrial society. Today most Westerners take for granted the availability of seasonal produce all year. Ironically, Israel exports significant amounts of "summer produce" grown in greenhouses in the winter to Europe, including Rome. This does not just include radish and lettuce but an array of tropical fruits, including mango, which was unheard of in the time of Rabbi and Antoninus. While the amounts of vegetables exported have declined somewhat in the last decade, exports of avocados and dates have increased.[227]

This can help us gain perspective on how we define need versus luxury. What were considered luxuries for our parents and grandparents are now essential items to our generation. Yet choosing to live with fewer material products and favoring local produce is a critical part of sustainable living. It becomes much easier when religious communities encourage and exemplify sustainability. In this regard, the emergence of "green teams" at houses of worship is an encouraging development. These green places of worship champion sustainability, often by using solar power, composting, and maximizing the use of locally grown fruit and vegetables in their events.

3.22 The Conflict of Jacob and Esau (*by* Rabbi Shaul David Judelman)[228]

A verse describes the growth of the two children, in Genesis 25:27 – "When the boys grew up, Esau became a skillful hunter, a man of the outdoors; but Jacob was a mild man who stayed in camp." We can interpret this as saying Esau lives his life in the field, a place of open uncertainty, while Jacob is of the tent and the home, a place of stability and conviction. Esau and Jacob are destined for conflict, as prophetically related to Rebecca when she inquired of the unrest she felt in her womb. The dichotomy here is between the driving force of Esau's unbri-

---

226 Babylonian Talmud, Avodah Zarah 11a.
227 Israel Central Bureau of Statistics, "Agricultural Statistics Quarterly July–September 2019," https://www.cbs.gov.il/en/publications/Pages/2020/Agricultural-Statistics-Quarterly-July-September-2019.aspx
228 This content was produced by Canfei Nesharim, a branch of Grow Torah. It is available at http://canfeinesharim.org/the-conflict-of-yaakov-and-esav/

dled desire and Jacob's *tikkun*, or repair, of this urge. Resulting tension pervades their interactions.

Kabbalistic interpretations teach that Esau's soul came from the world of *tohu* (chaotic and wild).[229] This phrase refers to the story of creation and the status of the world before light and the beginning of order.[230] *Tohu* is a spiritual state with recognizable manifestations in this world. In environmental terms, this state would be deemed unsustainable, though it is far more than this. Often, *tohu* is dominated by urge over thought, the moment over the future. In this aspect, Esau's actions represent much of what we see in the world today.

Esau returns from a day of hunting while Jacob has been cooking soup. Incidentally, these verses seem to tell us that Esau is also called Edom (red) because of his desire to pour the "red, red soup" down his throat upon his coming home tired. Esau offers a phenomenal reason for selling his birthright to Jacob for the soup: "I am at the point of death, so of what use is my birthright to me?"[231]

The Torah's description of Esau's decision offers deep insights for any society that so readily swallows the values of Esau. The culture that wants things now has given us fast food, fast cars, and quickly melting polar ice caps. This culture is out of balance. What does balance mean? Balance means that my own physical needs are balanced against a nexus of relationships. These might include other people's needs, my future needs, or the availability of resources. There is a strong critique within environmental discourse against the nature of the society that developed modern technology. However, this is not a diatribe against technology or modernity, but rather a strong statement about the manner in which we pour things down our throat. This analysis occurs both on the personal level of our private consumption habits and on the societal level of manufacturing and pursuing lifestyles that have not yet proven their balance.

Esau and the energies of *tohu* have a tendency toward destruction. The Kabbalah refers to the doomed Kings of Esau as the unsustainable elements of the creation process.[232] They are the destroyed worlds. The lights broke the vessels. Their desires and abilities shattered the physical world's capacity to contain them.

The Kings of Esau are still alive (though maybe not for long!) in our day. Consider the following statistic: If the whole world lived with the same consumption

---

[229] Etz Chayim, Heikhal HaNikudim (Sha'ar 8, ff.).
[230] Genesis 1:2.
[231] Ibid., 25:32.
[232] Arizal, Likutei Torah on Parshat Vayishlach.

pattern as the average American, it would take 5.3 earths to support everyone.[233] The Esau of today is living as if he's going to die tomorrow. That is not without a kernel of truth. He will.

The crucial question is will we leave a livable earth for our children to inherit? Will there be fresh drinking water, fish in the seas, and birds in the trees? Will our children be able to run freely and breathe fresh air?

3.23 Love of Meat

The Torah emphasizes that Isaac preferred Esau because of Isaac's love of meat and Esau's ability to bring him roasted meat: Genesis 25:28 – "And Isaac loved Esau, because venison was in his mouth." The Torah uses the word "love" three times in relation to Isaac and food and in particular a meat dish: "'Then prepare a dish for me such as I love, and bring it to me to eat, so that I may give you my innermost blessing before I die.' ... Rebecca said to her son Jacob, 'Go to the flock and fetch me two choice kids, and I will make of them a dish for your father, such as he loves'... He got them and brought them to his mother, and his mother prepared a dish such as his father loved."[234]

Of all the things that the Torah could describe Isaac "loving," it refers to meat. According to Rabbi Raphael Zarum, Isaac's love of meat caused him to pass over his relationship with Jacob.[235] A desire for meat can cause a person to overlook negative practices by those who produce the meat; in this Biblical case it is Esau. These days, people's love of meat causes them to overlook and tolerate inhumane treatment of most of the 80 billion factory-farmed animals. Too many people ignore that meat production processes and facilities are a leading driver of the climate crisis, and a contributor to the spread of diseases, including those caused by pathogens in the animals and meat, and among the meat plant workers.

---

[233] "U.S. Environmental Footprint Factsheet," Center for Sustainable Systems, University of Michigan, accessed December 12, 2019, http://css.umich.edu/factsheets/us-environmental-footprint-factsheet

[234] Genesis 27:4–14.

[235] Zarum, Rabbi Raphael, oral class, Limmud Festival UK, December 26, 2019, based on Rabbi Henau, *Nechmad Lemareh*, commentary on Genesis Rabbah 63:10.

3.24 Holy Eating (*by* Rabbi Yonatan Neril)[236]

We learn a powerful lesson about eating in Genesis 25:30 – "And Esau said to Jacob, 'Pour into [me] some of this red, red [pottage], for I am faint'; he was therefore named Edom." Esau's consumption represents a classic case in the Torah of a human being eating in an unrefined, base way. The Midrash links Esau to a camel through the word *hal'iteini* – a word used to describe pouring food down a camel's throat into its stomach, so it will walk on a long journey without needing to stop to eat.[237] Based on this, Rabbi Samson Raphael Hirsch explains *hal'iteini* as "greedily to gulp down."[238] Esau's mindless animalistic eating therefore serves as an example of an inappropriate and unholy way to eat.

Eating food can be a significant part of spiritual living, and rabbinic teachings and practices provide guidance for how to eat in a holy manner. These include being selective and mindful of which foods we eat and how we eat them. In Rabbi Tzadok HaKohen's "A Treatise on Eating," he cites the mystical book of the Zohar, which calls the moment of eating "the time of combat."[239] This is because in eating, a person must engage in the spiritual fight to ensure the act is a holy one. If Esau teaches how *not* to eat, what wisdom does the Torah offer for how we *should* consume in holiness?

Why am I eating? Rebbe Nachman of Breslov identifies the desire for food and drink as the central desire of the human being, and the one from which other desires emanate.[240] Rabbi Shlomo Wolbe teaches that a person needs to distinguish between eating because of a healthy desire of the body (eating in order to be healthy) versus eating out of base physical desire.[241] Of course we also know that many people today also eat out of emotional desire. It is therefore important to clarify, before eating, that it is for the right reason. To eat in a spiritual way, we should eat when we are hungry, to fulfill our body's needs, rather than out of physical or emotional cravings.

---

236 Neril, Yonatan / Sinclair, Yedidya, "We Are How We Eat: A Jewish Approach to Eating and Food," produced by Canfei Nesharim (now a branch of Grow Torah), February 24, 2014, http://canfeinesharim.org/we-are-how-we-eat-a-jewish-approach-to-food-and-sustainability-long-article/
237 Genesis Rabbah 21, Midrash Tanchuma, Pinchas 13; Midrash Genesis Rabbah (Vilna edition), 63:12, citing Mishnah, Shabbat 24:3.
238 Hirsch, Samson Raphael, commentary to Genesis 25:30.
239 Cited in Rabbi Tzadok HaKohen, Kitzur Kuntras Eit HaOchel, §9.
240 Likutei Moharan I, 62:5.
241 Wolbe, Shlomo, *Alei Shor*, Jerusalem, 1998.

How fast do I eat my food? While it is possible to eat a meal quickly in a few minutes, the rabbis caution against doing so. Rabbi Nathan of Breslov states: "Be careful not to swallow your food in a hurry. Eat at a moderate pace, calmly and with the same table manners that you would show if an important guest were present. You should always eat in this manner, even when you are alone."[242] Along with the physicality of his cravings, Esau's fast eating is also considered unholy. A spiritual way of eating includes eating food slowly and consciously.

Where do I eat? In the Talmud, Rabbi Yochanan and Reish Lakish teach that a person's table atones for a person like the Temple did in ancient times. One understanding of their statement is that when a person eats in holiness at their own table, they have made proper use of their table in a way parallel to the altar of the Temple.[243] This underscores the significance in Jewish thought of eating at a table, rather than while standing or walking. Today some of our eating takes place at a desk or even in a car! We will eat more healthfully if we take wholesome meals at a table.

With whom do I eat? Rabbi Shimon teaches: "Three who eat at one table and do not speak words of Torah, it is as if they have eaten sacrifices of the dead... But three who eat at one table and speak words of Torah, it is as if they have eaten at God's table..."[244] The act of eating with others and sharing not only food, but also Torah wisdom, bestows upon the meal an aura of sanctity, and elevates eating to a holy act. A shared opportunity for blessing before and after one eats also serves to connect the act of eating to a higher purpose.[245]

Bringing greater spiritual awareness to our eating will likely have an effect on how much food we eat. The link between *how much* we eat and the environmental "footprint" has been made clear by several studies. Adults in the United States today eat on average 500 calories more per day (about one large hamburger) than they did in the 1970s.[246] Between 1983 and 2000, US food availability (food consumption including waste) increased by 18 percent, requiring an additional 3.1 percent of total US energy consumption as well as more land and water

---

[242] Rabbi Nathan (Sternhartz) of Breslov, *Chayey Moharan*, #515, trans. Rabbi Avraham Greenbaum.
[243] Babylonian Talmud, Chagigah 27a.
[244] Chapter 3, Mishnah 4.
[245] Rabbi Tzadok HaKohen, *Pri Tzadik*, Treatise on the Time of Eating, §6.
[246] Swinburn, Boyd et al., "Increased Food Intake Alone Explains the Increase in Body Weight in the United States," oral presentation, 17th European Congress on Obesity, May 2009, news abstract online at http://www.medicalnewstoday.com/articles/149553.php. The researchers consider this increased food consumption to be the leading cause of the obesity epidemic.

to produce the food.²⁴⁷ Agriculture, forestry, and other land use contribute about 24 percent of global greenhouse gas emissions globally, making them major factors in addressing climate change.²⁴⁸ Modern food production and consumption also contribute to rainforest deforestation (to clear land for cattle and crops) and water pollution (from pesticide and fertilizer use).

Expanding agriculture to meet growing demand based on overeating only exacerbates these impacts. Practices that elevate our eating to become an act of holiness and devotion can also make our food consumption more ecologically sustainable.

3.25 Fast and Slow Food

Appreciating food appropriately is pointed at in the verse Genesis 25:34 – "Jacob then gave Esau bread and lentil stew; he ate and drank, and he rose and went away. Thus did Esau spurn the birthright." In explaining that Esau "ate and drank and rose," the HaKetav VeHaKabbalah commentary²⁴⁹ suggests that he did not sit to eat like his father, Isaac (to whom Jacob beckons, "Please sit up and eat of my game"), and his grandfather Abraham (when he served the angels, "he waited on them under the tree as they ate").²⁵⁰ Esau is uncouth, eating on the run, which shows his lack of self-control and ultimately his lack of qualification to hold the birthright. Esau is the root of wasteful consumption. The first use in the Torah of the word for wasting in relation to a person occurs with regard to Esau. He just thinks about the present without regard for the future, which causes him to waste the future. This is one of the spiritual roots of today's ecological crisis.

With a healthy-looking snail as its logo, the Slow Food Movement (SFM), conceived in 1986 in Bra, Italy by Carlo Petrini,²⁵¹ has grown and inspired the broader "Slow Movement."²⁵² Slow cities, slow tourism, slow money, slow jour-

---

247 Blair, Dorothy / Sobal, Jeffery, "Luxus Consumption: Wasting Food Resources through Overeating," *Agriculture and Human Values*, 23, 1 (2006), 63–74, https://doi.org/10.1007/s10460-004-5869-4
248 "Global Greenhouse Gas Emissions Data," US EPA, accessed June 21, 2020, https://www.epa.gov/ghgemissions/global-greenhouse-gas-emissions-data
249 HaKetav VeHaKabbalah on Genesis 25:34.
250 Genesis 18:8.
251 Petrini, Carlo, *Slow Food Nation: Why Our Food Should Be Good, Clean, and Fair*, New York: Rizzoli Publications, 2013.
252 Honoré, Carl, *In Praise of Slow: How a Worldwide Movement Is Challenging the Cult of Speed*, Toronto: Vintage Canada, 2004.

nalism, slow travel, and slow fashion are a few examples. From its humble origins in a protest against the first McDonald's in Italy (at the Piazza di Spagna in Rome), SFM now has more than 1,500 "convivia" or local chapters, with more than 100,000 members in 160 countries.[253] Its members advocate a return to simple local food and leisure, benefiting local communities and reducing our carbon footprint. Esau is the antithesis of this ideology, and Jacob is its advocate – described by the Torah as "a mild man who stayed in camp."[254]

3.26 Isaac and Water Mapping

The Midrash explains that Isaac's bountiful harvest came during a year of famine in the region.[255] Genesis 26:12,15 – "Isaac sowed in that land and reaped a hundredfold the same year. The Lord blessed him [...] The Philistines stopped up all the wells which his father's servants had dug in the days of his father Abraham, filling them with earth."

God blessed him with a successful crop when the rest of the country was suffering a famine. The Philistines apparently stopped up the wells of Abraham only after Isaac's bountiful harvest. Isaac therefore likely knew the locations of these wells, perhaps with maps, and drew water from them before they were stopped up.

Today, computerized maps known as Geographic Information Systems (GIS) are critical in the identification and management of underground water sources and inland fisheries.[256] Yet underground water sources are threatened by a relatively new form of fossil fuel extraction – hydraulic fracturing.[257] Fracking uses water to break up rock in order to force out natural gas. Most of the water used remains in the rock.

As Rabbi David Seidenberg writes:

> Fracking is unique, because the many billions of gallons of water involved are being used up, taken out of the cycle that would have seen them flow through the earth's streams and seas and atmosphere as part of the life-blood of this planet, for potentially millions of

---

253 Wexler, Mark N. / Oberlander, Judy / Shankar, Arjun, "The Slow Food Movement: A 'Big Tent' Ideology," *Journal of Ideology* 37, 1 (2017).
254 Genesis 25:27.
255 Rashi on Genesis 26:12, citing Midrash Genesis Rabbah ad loc.
256 Jenness, Jeff / Dooley, Joe / Aguilar-Manjarrez, Jose/ Riva, Claudia, *African Water Database*, Rome: FAO, 2007, www.fao.org/3/a1170e/a1170e.pdf
257 Kondash, Andrew J. / Lauer, Nancy E. / Vengosh, Avner, "The Intensification of the Water Footprint of Hydraulic Fracturing," Science Advances 4, 8 (2018), DOI: 10.1126/sciadv.aar5982

years. What does it mean to lose that water, essentially forever? According to Kabbalah, it could be considered a sin against the water itself.

The way the natural world is imagined in Kabbalah, its elements are yearning, longing to be raised higher and higher into consciousness, into the process of life and love. This can happen whenever a more sentient life form like a human being takes in a more basic substance (like when we drink water or eat plants), and it happens through the process of evolution itself, where life comes from the elements and develops greater and greater capacities for connection and awareness. In Kabbalah, the very symbol of blessing and life – of *chesed* (or "loving-kindness") – is water. If we take these ideas seriously, then the water that stays in that fracked rock is deprived of fulfilling its deepest purpose.[258]

3.27 Water Wars (*by* Rabbi Yuval Cherlow)[259]

Isaac's conflict with the Philistines and the people of Gerar is rooted in the age-old struggle for scarce water. Genesis 26:20 – "The herdsmen of Gerar quarreled with Isaac's herdsmen, saying, 'The water is ours.' He named that well Esek [contention], because they contended with him." The shepherds of Gerar claim, "The water is ours," and effectively expel Isaac from the area of the well in contention, forcing him to find a new source of water. The Philistines go further, filling the wells Isaac used with dirt rather than sharing them with him. So fierce is their enmity that they destroyed some of their own vital water sources to expel him and attain their political end.

Access to fresh water is arguably the primary environmental issue in the history of humankind. Our need for clean water is the concern that requires us to directly face the undeniable and harsh consequences of depleting a critically limited natural resource.

The narrative of Isaac and the wells offers us insight into how to deal with the contemporary water crisis. The first teaching is the necessity to protect natural resources from destruction in times of conflict and war. The deliberate destruction of the wells by the Philistines, to expel Isaac from their midst, illustrates the danger of war fought without regard for the environment. The Torah places limits on how harshly we respond during war. It forbids us from wantonly destroying fruit-bearing trees as a military tactic.[260] Even in the midst of struggle,

---

258 Seidenberg, Rabbi David, "How Fracking Conflicts with Kabbalah," *Forward*, July 16, 2013, https://forward.com/opinion/180507/how-fracking-conflicts-with-kabbalah/
259 This content was produced by Canfei Nesharim, a branch of Grow Torah. It is available at http://canfeinesharim.org/parshat-toldot-digging-the-wells-the-importance-of-protecting-our-natural-resources/
260 Deuteronomy 20:19.

we must consider the "day after" and understand the profound need for sustainability for both sides of the conflict.

The narrative continues with Isaac developing additional water sources after being forced to abandon the wells of his father, as well as some of his own. He continuously searches for new sources of water.[261] We too are bound by the unremitting task of expanding and protecting our water resources, rather than relying solely on our current "wells." There are many ways to increase access to potable water. One is to capture rainwater, instead of letting it run off into the sea. Another highly successful method is recycling and purifying wastewater, as is commonly done in Israel's agricultural sector and increasingly in other countries. In addition, the Israeli invention of drip irrigation in 1965 revolutionized agriculture. Implemented in over 110 countries, over 150 billion dripper mechanisms have been sold.[262]

The ethics for wise and appropriate water consumption practices are included in the general prohibition of wanton destruction (*ba'al tashḥit*). Due to the direct connection between water and life, the conservation of water also becomes a Jewish legal obligation.

In the semi-arid and arid Middle East, the lack of fresh water often adds fuel to the existing political conflagrations. Climate change is making the Middle East drier and water scarcer. Some scientists understand the 2006–7 drought – the worst in 900 years – to be a key driver of the Syrian civil and regional war.[263] May we look to a future where peace between nations is fostered by our shared water resources.

3.28 Hunters and Farmers

Esau was a hunter and Jacob a farmer. In investigating why ancient communities transitioned from hunting to more sustainable farming, researchers found three drivers: populations structured into small groups, farming-friendly property

---

[261] Genesis 26:18–22.
[262] Gass, Morgan / Freire Haddad, Helena, "Revolutionizing Sustainable Agriculture," Northwestern University Center for Water Research, September 19, 2019, https://water.northwestern.edu/2019/09/19/get-water-blog-2-revolutionizing-sustainable-agriculture/
[263] Kelley, Colin et al., "Climate Change in the Fertile Crescent and Implications of the Recent Syrian Drought," *Proceedings of the National Academy of Sciences of the United States of America* 112, 11 (2015) 3241–3246. www.jstor.org/stable/26462026

rights, and a conservative mindset.²⁶⁴ We learn that Isaac set up a small settlement in Beersheba, away from the Philistines.²⁶⁵ Additionally, property rights had just been established through a pact with the king of the Philistines, Abimelech.²⁶⁶ The final ingredient, a conservative mindset, was more an aspect of Jacob's personality ("a mild man who stayed in camp") in contrast to Esau's ("a man of the field").²⁶⁷

This may be why Jacob became the farmer: Genesis 27:6–9 – "Rebecca said to her son Jacob, 'I overheard your father speaking to your brother Esau, saying, 'Bring me some game and prepare a dish for me to eat, that I may bless you, with the Lord's approval, before I die.' Now, my son, listen carefully as I instruct you. Go to the flock and fetch me two choice kids, and I will make of them a dish for your father, such as he likes.'"

Today, society is structured into large groups, property rights are well established in most countries, and the greatest challenge to greater sustainability is creating a conservationist mindset that thinks long term about preventing future environmental risks. How does humankind become more long-term oriented? This is an important role for religious educators who are accustomed to seeing life patterns over thousands of years, more so than for politicians who typically are focused on the next two or four years.

3.29 Doing All We Can

Isaac's blessing contains a powerful lesson, in Genesis 27:28 – "And may God give you of the dew of heaven and the fat of the earth, abundance of new grain and wine." Kli Yakar explains that the blessing is introduced with the word "and" because God's blessing is given only after a person has done all they can do. Then, and only then, "nature will complete the miracle."²⁶⁸

How can one do all that is possible? The work of achieving sustainability in our lives and on our planet seems infinite, and potentially discouraging to any one person. Group, community, and even interfaith collaboration greatly ex-

---

264 Gallagher, Elizabeth M. / Shennan, Stephen J. / Thomas, Mark G., "Transition to Farming More Likely for Small, Conservative Groups with Property Rights, but Increased Productivity Is Not Essential," *Proceedings of the National Academy of Sciences* 112, 46 (2015), 14218–14223, https://doi.org/10.1073/pnas.1511870112
265 Genesis 26:33.
266 Ibid., 26:28.
267 Ibid., 25:27.
268 Kli Yakar on Genesis 28:27.

pands our capacity. Since 2010, The Interfaith Center for Sustainable Development has been revealing the connection between religion and ecology and has been mobilizing people to act. It has co-organized twelve conferences in Israel and the United States, bringing together current and emerging clergy from many faiths for engagement on religion and ecology.[269]

Permissions

Content from Canfei Nesharim articles have been reprinted by permission of Canfei Nesharim, a branch of Grow Torah.
Content from Eco Bible volume 1 has been reprinted with permission of The Interfaith Center for Sustainable Development
Scripture quotations are from the New JPS translation of the Tanakh: The Holy Scriptures and are used by permission of the University of Nebraska Press. Copyright 1985 by The Jewish Publication Society, Philadelphia.

Sources

Kohn, Daniel, oral teaching, Yeshivat Sulam Yaakov, Jerusalem, May 2011.
Riskin, Shlomo, oral teaching, Yeshivat Hamivtar, Migdal Oz, November 2009.
Tzadok HaKohen Rabinowitz of Lublin, "Section 8: Genesis," in: *Pri Tzadik*.
Waskow, Arthur, "Torah and the Climate Crisis", webinar, May 2019.
http://canfeinesharim.org/the-conflict-of-yaakov-and-esav
http://canfeinesharim.org/noach-a-paradigm-for-environmental-consciousness/
http://canfeinesharim.org/lech-lecha-joining-together-for-justice-in-the-land/
http://canfeinesharim.org/parshat-toldot-digging-the-wells-the-importance-of-protecting-our-natural-resources/
CO2 Earth, accessed June 21, 2020, https://www.co2.earth/
"Impacts of Acid Rain on Soils," *Air Pollution UK*, accessed May 16, 2019, http://www.air-quality.org.uk/16.php
https://en.wikipedia.org/wiki/List_of_ammonium_nitrate_disasters
"Top Chain Restaurants Worldwide," Restaurant Engine, accessed June 17, 2020, https://restaurantengine.com/top-chain-restaurants-worldwide/
"UN Agency Sounds Alarm: Dwindling Agrobiodiversity 'Severe Threat' to Food Security," *UN News*, November 14, 2019, https://news.un.org/en/story/2019/11/1051411
US Census Bureau, World Population 1950–2050. https://www.census.gov/library/visualizations/2011/demo/world-population-1950-2050.html

---

[269] The Interfaith Center for Sustainable Development, www.interfaithsustain.com

Bibliography

Acevedo-Whitehouse, Karina / Duffus, Amanda L. J., "Effects of Environmental Change on Wildlife Health," *Philosophical Transactions of the Royal Society B*, Biological Sciences 364, no. 1534, November 2009, 3429–3438, https://doi.org/10.1098/rstb.2009.0128

Altman, Yair, "Shortage of 1.5 Million Graves in the Center of Israel" (Hebrew), *Israel Hayom*, March 23, 2020, https://www.israelhayom.co.il/article/744597

American Chemical Society (eds.), "Missing Link in Coronavirus Jump from Bats to Humans Could Be Pangolins, Not Snakes," March 26, 2020, https://www.acs.org/content/acs/en/pressroom/newsreleases/2020/march/missing-link-in-coronavirus-jump-from-bats-to-humans-could-be-pangolins-not-snakes.html

Anderegg, William R. L. et al., "Hydraulic Diversity of Forests Regulates Ecosystem Resilience during Drought," *Nature 561*, no. 7724, September 2018, https://doi.org/10.1038/s41586-018-0539-7

Benstein, Jeremy, *The Way Into Judaism and the Environment*, Vermont: Jewish Lights Publishing, 2008.

Berezovsky, Shalom, *Netivot Shalom*, Jerusalem: Yeshivat Beit Avraham Slonim, 2000.

Blair, Dorothy / Sobal, Jeffery, "Luxus Consumption: Wasting Food Resources through Overeating," *Agriculture and Human Values*, vol. 23, Number 1, 2006, 63–74, https://doi.org/10.1007/s10460-004-5869-4

Borenstein, Seth / Keaten, Jamey, "UN Climate Report: Change Land Use to Avoid a Hungry Future," Phys.org, August 8, 2019, https://phys.org/news/2019-08-climate-hungry-future.html

Buber, Martin, *I and Thou*, London: A&C Black, 1937.

Canadian Association of Petroleum Producers (eds.), "What Are the Oil Sands?, accessed March 1, 2020, https://www.capp.ca/oil/what-are-the-oil-sands/

Ceballos, Gerardo / Ehrlich, Paul R. / Raven, Peter H., "Vertebrates on the Brink as Indicators of Biological Annihilation and the Sixth Mass Extinction," *Proceedings of the National Academy of Sciences*, June 16, 2020, 117 (24) 13596–13602, https://doi.org/10.1073/pnas.1922686117

Ceccanti, Costanza et al., "Mediterranean Wild Edible Plants: Weeds or 'New Functional Crops'?" *Molecules 23*, no. 9, September 2018, 2299, https://dx.doi.org/10.3390%2Fmolecules23092299

Chiba, Sanae et al., "Human Footprint in the Abyss: 30 Year Records of Deep-Sea Plastic Debris," *Marine Policy 96*, October 2018, 204–212, https://doi.org/10.1016/j.marpol.2018.03.022

Crouch, David, "The Swedish 15-Year-Old Who's Cutting Class to Fight the Climate Crisis," *The Guardian*, September 1, 2018, https://www.theguardian.com/science/2018/sep/01/swedish-15-year-old-cutting-class-to-fight-the-climate-crisis

Denworth, Lydia, "Children Change Their Parents' Minds about Climate Change," *Scientific American*, May 6, 2019, https://www.scientificamerican.com/article/children-change-their-parents-minds-about-climate-change/?redirect=1

Devereux, Stephen, "Famine in the Twentieth Century," *IDS Working Papers*, 105, January 2000.

Diamond, Jared, *Collapse*, London: Penguin, 2005.

Eisenberg, Evan, "The Mountain & the Tower," in: Arthur Waskow (ed.), *Torah of the Earth, vol. 1,* Vermont: Jewish Lights Publishing, 2000.

Energy Education, University of Calgary (eds.), "Bitumen," last modified June 25, 2018, https://energyeducation.ca/encyclopedia/Bitumen

Everington, Keoni, "Taoyuan's Zhongli District Has Worst Acid Rain in Taiwan," *Taiwan News,* August 19, 2019, https://www.taiwannews.com.tw/en/news/3764930

Gallagher, Elizabeth M. / Shennan, Stephen J. / Thomas, Mark G., "Transition to Farming More Likely for Small, Conservative Groups with Property Rights, but Increased Productivity Is Not Essential," *Proceedings of the National Academy of Sciences* 112, no. 46 (November 2015): 14218–14223, https://doi.org/10.1073/pnas.1511870112

Gass, Morgan / Haddad, Helena Freire, "Revolutionizing Sustainable Agriculture," Northwestern University Center for Water Research, September 19, 2019, https://water.northwestern.edu/2019/09/19/get-water-blog-2-revolutionizing-sustainable-agriculture/

Gerstenfeld, Manfred, *The Quality of the Environment,* Israel: The Jerusalem Institute for Research, 2002.

Giaimo, Cara, "Crocodiles Went Through a Vegetarian Phase, Too," *The New York Times,* June 27, 2019, https://www.nytimes.com/2019/06/27/science/crocodiles-vegetarian-teeth.html

Greshko, Michael, "What Are Mass Extinctions, and What Causes Them?", *National Geographic,* https://www.nationalgeographic.com/science/prehistoric-world/mass-extinction/

Grooten, M. / Almond, R.E.A. (eds.), "Living Planet Report–2018: Aiming Higher," WWF, Gland, Switzerland, https://www.wwf.org.uk/sites/default/files/2018-10/wwfintl_living planet_full.pdf

Hausfather, Zeke, "Analysis: Why Scientists Think 100% of Global Warming Is Due to Humans," *Carbon Brief,* December 13, 2017, https://www.carbonbrief.org/analysis-why-scientists-think-100-of-global-warming-is-due-to-humans

He, Jinxing et al., "Quantifying the Effects of Climate and Anthropogenic Change on Regional Species Loss in China," *PLOS One 13,* no. 7, July 25, 2018, https://doi.org/10.1371/journal.pone.0199735

Hirsch, Samson Raphael, *The Nineteen Letters of Ben Uziel,* New York: BN Publishing, 2011.

Hirsch, Samson Raphael, *The Pentateuch,* vol. 1: Genesis, Gateshead, England: Judaica Press, 1989.

Hirsch, Samson Raphael, *The Pentateuch,* vol. 4: Numbers, Gateshead, England: Judaica Press, 1989.

Hochman, Mordechai, "Footnote 1 based on the Midrash," in: *The Bird That Brings Life to the Carcasses,* Yeshiva Beit El, published Kislev 5, 5770, https://www.yeshiva.org.il/midrash/12714

Honoré, Carl, *In Praise of Slow: How a Worldwide Movement Is Challenging the Cult of Speed,* Toronto: Vintage Canada, 2004.

Hughes, J. Donald / Thirgood, J.V., "Deforestation, Erosion, and Forest Management in Ancient Greece and Rome," *Journal of Forest History* 26, no. 2, April 1982, 60–75, https://doi.org/10.2307/4004530

Ippolito, Jim / Al-Kaisi, Mahdi, "The Dirt on Soil Loss from the Midwest Floods," Colorado State University, April 16, 2019, https://source.colostate.edu/the-dirt-on-soil-loss-from-the-midwest-floods/

Intergovernmental Panel on Climate Change (eds.), "Climate Change and Land, An IPCC Special Report on Climate Change, Desertification, Land Degradation, Sustainable Land Management, Food Security, and Greenhouse Gas Fluxes in Terrestrial Ecosystems," *Summary for Policymakers*, IPCC, 2019, https://www.ipcc.ch/site/assets/uploads/2019/08/4.-SPM_Approved_Microsite_FINAL.pdf

Intergovernmental Panel on Climate Change (eds.), "History of the IPCC," accessed March 1, 2020, https://www.ipcc.ch/about/history/

Israel Central Bureau of Statistics (ed.), "Agricultural Statistics Quarterly July–September 2019," https://www.cbs.gov.il/en/publications/Pages/2020/Agricultural-Statistics-Quarterly-July-September-2019.aspx

Israel Ministry of Foreign Affairs (eds.), "Article 6" in: "Treaty of Peace between the State of Israel and the Hashemite Kingdom of Jordan," October 26, 1994, https://mfa.gov.il/mfa/foreignpolicy/peace/guide/pages/israel-jordan%20peace%20treaty.aspx

Israel Water Authority (eds.), "Saving the Dead Sea," accessed June 18, 2020, http://www.water.gov.il/Hebrew/Water-Environment/Dead-Sea/DocLib1/saving-dead-sea-eng.pdf

Jacobson, Yosef Y., "The Burning Palace," Chabad, September 11, 2002, https://www.chabad.org/library/article_cdo/aid/59473/jewish/The-Burning%20-Palace.htm

Jacobson, Marc Z. et al., "100% Clean and Renewable Wind, Water, and Sunlight All-Sector Energy Roadmaps for 139 Countries of the World," *Joule 1*, 108–121 September 6, 2017, Elsevier Inc. http://dx.doi.org/10.1016/j.joule.2017.07.005

Jones, Steven A. (ed.), *World Green Building Trends 2018: Smart Market Report*, Bedford: Dodge Data Analytics, 2018, https://www.worldgbc.org/sites/default/files/World%20Green%20Building%20Trends%202018%20SMR%20FINAL%2010-11.pdf

Kelley, Colin et al., "Climate Change in the Fertile Crescent and Implications of the Recent Syrian Drought," *Proceedings of the National Academy of Sciences of the United States of America* 112, no. 11, 2015, 3241–3246. www.jstor.org/stable/26462026.

Keynan, Eldad, "Private vs. Public Burials: Differences and Time Span," *The Bible and Interpretation*, The University of Arizona, October 2010, http://www.bibleinterp.com/articles/burial357907.shtml#sdfootnote9sym

Kingdon, Jonathan, *East African Mammals: An Atlas of Evolution in Africa, Volume 1*, Chicago: University Of Chicago Press, 1984.

Kondash, Andrew J. / Lauer, Nancy E. / Vengosh, Avner, "The Intensification of the Water Footprint of Hydraulic Fracturing," *Science Advances* 4, no. 8, August 2018, DOI: 10.1126/sciadv.aar5982

Kook, Abraham Isaac, *Gold from the Land of Israel*, Chanan Morrison ed., California: CreateSpace Independent Publishing Platform, 2017.

Kook, Abraham Isaac, "Selections From 'A Vision of Vegetarianism And Peace'," in: Rabbi David Cohen and Jonathan Rubenstein (eds.), *The Vision of Eden: Animal Welfare and Vegetarianism in Jewish Law and Mysticism*, California: CreateSpace Independent Publishing Platform, 2nd edition, 2014.

Kook, Abraham Isaac, "On Torah for its Own Sake," *Orot HaTorah II*, Jerusalem: Sifriat Hava, 2005.

Kurian, Bijumon, "Farmers Plant 200,000 Seedlings to Replace Lost Crops after Kerala Floods," Fairtrade Foundation, November 27, 2018, https://www.fairtrade.org.uk/Media-Centre/Blog/2018/November/Farmers-become-earth-builders-after-Kerala-floods

Lamm, Norman, *Derashot Ledorot: A Commentary for the Ages – Genesis*, Jerusalem: OU Press and Maggid Books, 2012.

Lamm, Norman, *Faith and Doubt,* Brooklyn: KTAV Publishing House, 1986.

Leahy, Stephen, "This Is the World's Most Destructive Oil Operation – and It's Growing," *National Geographic,* April 11, 2019, https://www.nationalgeographic.com/environment/2019/04/alberta-canadas-tar-sands-is-growing-but-indigenous-people-fight-back/

Linden, Eugene, "How Scientists Got Climate Change So Wrong," *The New York Times,* November 8, 2019, https://www.nytimes.com/2019/11/08/opinion/sunday/science-climate-change.html

Maslin, Mark, *Global Warming, A Very Short Introduction,* Oxford: Oxford University Press, 2004.

Mcgowan, Elizabeth / Song, Lisa, "The Dilbit Disaster: Inside the Biggest Oil Spill You've Never Heard Of," *InsideClimate News,* Jun 26, 2012, https://insideclimatenews.org/news/26062012/dilbit-diluted-bitumen-enbridge-kalamazoo-river-marshall-michigan-oil-spill-6b-pipeline-epa/

Midrash Rabbah: Genesis, trans. Harry Freedman and Maurice Simon, London: Soncino Press, 1983.

Mikati, Ihab et al., "Disparities in Distribution of Particulate Matter Emission Sources by Race and Poverty Status," *American Journal of Public Health 108*, no. 4, April 1, 2018, 480–485, https://doi.org/10.2105/AJPH.2017.304297

Neril, Yonatan, "Countering Destruction: Lessons from Noach," Canfei Nesharim, a branch of Grow Torah, February 19, 2004, http://canfeinesharim.org/countering-destruction-lessons-from-noach-longer-article/

Neril, Yonatan, "Genesis and Human Stewardship of the Earth," February 24, 2014, content produced by Canfei Nesharim, a branch of Grow Torah. It is available at http://canfeinesharim.org/genesis-and-human-stewardship-of-the-earth/

Neril, Yonatan / Sinclair, Yedidya, "We Are How We Eat: A Jewish Approach to Eating and Food," produced by Canfei Nesharim (now a branch of Grow Torah), February 24, 2014, http://canfeinesharim.org/we-are-how-we-eat-a-jewish-approach-to-food-and-sustainability-long-article/

Nielsen, Knut Schmidt, *Animal Physiology: Adaptation and Environment,* Cambridge: Cambridge University Press, 5th ed., 1997.

Oratz, Efraim (ed.), *The Pentateuch,* trans. Gertrude Hirschler, New York: Judaica Press, 1986.

Oron, Asaf et al., "Early Maritime Activity on the Dead Sea: Bitumen Harvesting and the Possible Use of Reed Watercraft," *Journal of Maritime Archaeology 10*, no. 1, April 2015, 65–88, https://doi.org/10.1007/s11457-015-9135-2

Pachauri, Rajendra K. / Meyer, Leo (eds.), *Climate Change 2014: Synthesis Report. Contribution of Working Groups I, II and III to the Fifth Assessment, A Report of the Intergovernmental Panel on Climate Change,* IPPC, 2014, https://www.ipcc.ch/site/assets/uploads/2018/05/SYR_AR5_FINAL_full_wcover.pdf

Pachauri, Rajendra K. / Meyer, Leo (eds.), *Climate Change 2014: Synthesis Report Summary for Policymakers,* Geneva, IPCC, 2014, https://www.ipcc.ch/site/assets/uploads/2018/02/AR5_SYR_FINAL_SPM.pdf

Pe'er, Guy / Safriel, Uriel N., *Climate Change Israel National Report: Impact, Vulnerability and Adaptation,* Israel: Blaustein Institute for Desert Research, Ben-Gurion University of the Negev, October 2000.

Petrini, Carlo, *Slow Food Nation: Why Our Food Should Be Good, Clean, and Fair,* New York: Rizzoli Publications, 2013.
Podesta, John, "The Climate Crisis, Migration, and Refugees," The Brookings Institution, July 25, 2019, https://www.brookings.edu/research/the-climate-crisis-migration-and-refugees/
Rigaud, Kanta Kumari et al., "Groundswell: Preparing for Internal Climate Migration," World Bank Group, 2018, https://openknowledge.worldbank.org/handle/10986/29461
Rignot, Eric et al., "Four Decades of Antarctic Ice Sheet Mass Balance from 1979–2017," *Proceedings of the National Academy of Sciences 116,* no. 4, January 2019, 1095–1103, https://doi.org/10.1073/pnas.1812883116
Riskin, Shlomo, "The 'Noah Covenant' with Mankind," Arutz Sheva, October 31, 2018, http://www.israelnationalnews.com/Articles/Article.aspx/8340
Ritchie, Hannah / Roser, Max, "CO2 and Greenhouse Gas Emissions," Our World in Data, revised December 2019, https://ourworldindata.org/co2-and-other-greenhouse-gas-emissions#co2-in-the-atmosphere
Rosen, David, "Jewish Ethics, Animal Welfare, and Veganism: A Panel of Rabbis and Experts," interview, Jewish Eco Seminars Productions, January 2018, https://www.youtube.com/watch?v=UHIyXrN1JAI
Rosenberg, Kenneth et al., "Decline of the North American Avifauna," *Science,* 2019, https://www.birds.cornell.edu/home/wp-content/uploads/2019/09/DECLINE-OF-NORTH-AMERICAN-AVIFAUNA-SCIENCE-2019.pdf
Samet, Elchanan, "The Story of Creation and Our Ecological Crisis," *Yeshivat Har Etzion VBM,* 2002, https://www.etzion.org.il/en/story-creation-and-our-ecological-crisis
Sacks, Jonathan, *The Dignity of Difference: How to Avoid the Clash of Civilizations,* London: Continuum, 2003.
Sacks, Jonathan, "The Stewardship Paradigm," January 14, 2014, http://rabbisacks.org/tu-bshvat/
Sacks, Jonathan, *Radical Then, Radical Now,* London: Continuum, 2000.
Savoca, Matthew, "The Bad News Is That Fish Are Eating Lots of Plastic. Even Worse, They May Like It," *The Washington Post,* April 9, 2017, https://www.washingtonpost.com/national/health-science/the-bad-news-is-that-fish-are-eating-lots-of-plastic-even-worse-they-may-like-it/2017/09/01/54159ee8-8cc6-11e7-91d5-ab4e4b76a3a_story.html
Sears, David, "Selections From 'A Vision of Vegetarianism and Peace'," in: David Cohen / Jonathan Rubenstein (ed.), *The Vision of Eden: Animal Welfare and Vegetarianism in Jewish Law and Mysticism,* trans. David Sears, California: CreateSpace Independent Publishing Platform, 2nd edition, 2014. https://www.jewishveg.org/DSvision.html
Schneider, Susan (Sarah Yehudit), *Eating as Tikun,* Jerusalem: A Still Small Voice, 1996.
Seidenberg, David, "Crossing the Threshold: God's Image in the More-Than-Human World," PhD thesis, Jewish Theological Seminary, 2004.
Seidenberg, David, "How Fracking Conflicts with Kabbalah," *Forward,* July 16, 2013, https://forward.com/opinion/180507/how-fracking-conflicts-with-kabbalah/
Siegelbaum, Chana Bracha, "Discovering the Camel Connection: Nature in the Parasha: Parashat Chayei Sarah," *Women on the Land,* November 11, 2014, http://rebbetzinchanabracha.blogspot.com/2014/11/discovering-camel-connection.html

Sokol, Sam, "Squeezed for Burial Space, Jerusalem Prepares an Underground City of the Dead," *The Times of Israel*, October 26, 2019, https://www.timesofisrael.com/squeezed-for-burial-space-jerusalem-prepares-an-underground-city-of-the-dead/

Song, Lisa, "Why Tar Sands Oil Is More Polluting and Why It Matters," *Reuters*, May 22, 2012, https://www.reuters.com/article/idUS201043482520120522

Stevens, William K., "To Treat the Attack of Acid Rain, Add Limestone to Water and Wait," *The New York Times*, January 31, 1989, https://www.nytimes.com/1989/01/31/science/to-treat-the-attack-of-acid-rain-add-limestone-to-water-and-wait.html

Stokar, Saul, "The Environment in Jewish Thought and Law," *Sviva Israel* (2018).

Swinburn, Boyd et al., "Increased Food Intake Alone Explains the Increase in Body Weight in the United States," oral presentation, 17th European Congress on Obesity, May 2009, news abstract online at http://www.medicalnewstoday.com/articles/149553.php

Symonds, Alexandria, "Amazon Rainforest Fires: Here's What's Really Happening," *The New York Times*, August 28, 2019, https://www.nytimes.com/2019/08/23/world/americas/amazon-fire-brazil-bolsonaro.html

Tirole, Jean, "Some Economics of Global Warming," *Rivista di Politica Economica* 98, no. 6, November 2008, 9–42.

Turkewitz, Julie / Fernandez, Manny / Blinder, Alan, "In Houston, Anxiety and Frantic Rescues as Floodwaters Rise," *The New York Times*, August 27, 2017, https://www.nytimes.com/2017/08/27/us/hurricane-harvey-texas.html?_r=0

United Nations (eds.), "UN Report: Nature's Dangerous Decline 'Unprecedented'", May 6, 2019, https://www.un.org/sustainabledevelopment/blog/2019/05/nature-decline-unprecedented-report/

University of California – San Diego (eds.), "Climate Change and Deforestation Will Lead to Declines in Global Bird Diversity, Study Warns," *ScienceDaily*, June 5, 2007, www.sciencedaily.com/releases/2007/06/070604205627.htm

University of Michigan, Center for Sustainable Systems (eds.), "U.S. Environmental Footprint Factsheet," accessed December 12, 2019, http://css.umich.edu/factsheets/us-environmental-footprint-factsheet

UN Environment Programme (eds.), "Dreams to Action: Beginning a Meaningful Conversation with Young Leaders," published April 23, 2019, https://www.unenvironment.org/news-and-stories/story/dreams-action-beginning-meaningful-conversation-young-leaders

US Environmental Protection Agency (eds.), "Mercury and Air Toxics Standards," accessed June 7, 2020, https://www.epa.gov/mats.

US EPA (eds.), "Acid Rain Program," accessed June 22, 2020, https://www.epa.gov/acidrain/acid-rain-program

US EPA (eds.), "Global Greenhouse Gas Emissions Data," accessed June 21, 2020, https://www.epa.gov/ghgemissions/global-greenhouse-gas-emissions-data

US Geological Survey (eds.), "Ice, Snow, and Glaciers and the Water Cycle," Water Science School, accessed February 18, 2020, www.usgs.gov/special-topic/water-science-school/science/ice-snow-and-glaciers-and-water-cycle?qt-science_center_objects=0#qt-science_center_objects.

Uslu, Aysel / Barış, Emin / Erdoğan, Elmas, "Ecological Concerns over Cemeteries," *African Journal of Agricultural Research* 4, 13, December 2009, 1505–1511.

Weinberg, Matis, *Frameworks: Genesis*, Boston: Foundation for Jewish Publications, 1st edition, 1998, 100–101.

Velasquez-Manoff, Moises, "Can Humans Help Trees Outrun Climate Change?", *The New York Times*, April 25, 2019, https://www.nytimes.com/2019/04/25/climate/trees-climate-change.html?searchResultPosition=7

Wexler, Mark N. / Oberlander, Judy / Shankar, Arjun, "The Slow Food Movement: A 'Big Tent' Ideology," *Journal of Ideology* 37, no. 1 (January 2017).

Wilson, Edward O., *The Creation: An Appeal to Save Life on Earth*, New York: W.W. Norton & Company, 2006.

Wolbe, Shlomo, *Alei Shor*, Jerusalem, 1998.

World Economic Forum (eds.), "The New Plastics Economy: Rethinking the Future of Plastics," 2016, http://www3.weforum.org/docs/WEF_The_New_Plastics_Economy.pdf

Xu, Haigen et al., "The Distribution and Economic Losses of Alien Species Invasion to China," *Biological Invasions 8*, October 2006, 1495–1500, https://doi.org/10.1007/s10530-005-5841-2

Suggestions for further reading

Eisenberg, Evan, *The Ecology of Eden*, New York: Alfred A. Knopf, 1998.

Issacs, Ronald H., *The Jewish Sourcebook on the Environment and Ecology*, Northvale, N.J.: Jason Aronson Inc., 1998.

Neril, Yonatan / Dee, Leo, *Eco Bible: Volume One: An Ecological Commentary on Genesis and Exodus*, Verona, New Jersey: The Interfaith Center for Sustainable Development, 2020.

Neril, Yonatan / Dee, Leo, *Eco Bible: Volume Two: An Ecological Commentary on Leviticus, Numbers, and Deuteronomy*, Verona, New Jersey: The Interfaith Center for Sustainable Development, 2021.

Rose, Aubrey (ed.), *Judaism and Ecology*, New York: Cassell Publishers, Ltd., 1992.

Toperoff, Shlomo Pesach, *The Animal Kingdom in Jewish Thought*, Northvale, N.J.: Jason Aronson Inc, 1995.

Yoreh, Tanhum, *Waste Not: A Jewish Environmental Ethic*, Albany, NY: State University of New York Press, 2019.

Waskow, Arthur (ed.), *Torah of the Earth: Exploring 4,000 Years of Ecology in Jewish Thought*, volumes one and two: Woodstock, Vermont: Jewish Lights Publishing, 2000.

Kerstin Schlögl-Flierl
The Concept of Environment in Christianity

Environment as a Significant Issue in Christianity –
as a Challenge and Option for the Future

The Corona crisis can be considered a stimulant for a new perception of the environment. This results from a lack of attention to the One Health approach, due to which the environmental side of health has been given little consideration in the past. Thus, the risk of zoonotic diseases has been underestimated. This applies also to a religious, more specifically, the Christian tradition in thinking about environmental issues.

In order to get an initial idea of a Christian understanding of environment, a general approach to the issue of environment in Christianity is to start from an interreligious comparison of the topic of nature. Principally, four elementary religious forms of understanding nature can be found. Firstly, nature is understood "as the work of the Creator, who sustains it and to whom people owe an account (Judaism, Christianity, Islam)"[1]. Secondly, the essential equality of human beings, animals, and plants can be postulated. This results in the need for respectful interaction (Buddhism, Hinduism, and other Asian religions). A third approach takes into account the cosmic harmony of the God-given natural order, which must be recognized and taken as the basis for a successful life (for example in Taoism). The fourth approach is the idea of earth-connected gods that human beings encounter in nature and that need to be amended positively through rites (for example tribal religions in Africa, America, and Australia)[2].

The question will be what characterizes the concept of Christianity in a further manner. On a purely conceptual level, the idea of ecumenism is guiding. It expresses living together in *one house*, that is, it does not refer to the Christian denominations, but to all fellow creatures. It "takes shape [thus] as an interdenominational, intercultural, interreligious and ecological learning process that cannot be concluded"[3].

Ecology, thus, also forms the framework for religious discourse. Here in the present contribution, the genuinely Christian is formulated, whereby the term Christian also offers a wide field. Pope Benedict XVI – as a risk and a crisis –

---
[1] Vogt, Markus, *Christliche Umweltethik. Grundlagen und zentrale Herausforderungen*, Freiburg et al.: Herder, 2021, 268 [translation K.S.F. with the help of Pia Heutling].
[2] Cf. Vogt, *Christliche Umweltethik*, 268.
[3] Vogt, *Christliche Umweltethik*, 283f. [translation K.S.F.].

pointed to a new covenant between human beings and the environment.⁴ This culminated in Pope Francis' encyclical, *Laudato Si'*, which will be presented in this article.

In particular, it is a Catholic point of view on Environment in Christianity, which seeks to incorporate Protestant and Orthodox views. This also reveals itself to be a challenge and will be addressed in this contribution.

For the purpose of contextualizing, the discussions about the concept of "environment" and its meaning are taking place in times of the Anthropocene. Are humans considered engineers of the biosphere in this context? The term of human beings as engineers, which already existed before, was mentioned by Paul Crutzen⁵. He also explains the term "Anthropocene" and correlates it with analyses that found air trapped in polar ice. This could be dated back to the late 18th century, where the beginning of growing global concentrations of carbon dioxide and methane began taking place.⁶ Crutzen emphasizes the impact of mankind and its behavior towards the environment. Finding environmentally sustainable management tools is crucial for the Anthropocene. Apart from various international programs and large-scale geo-engineering projects, scientists are still largely treading on terra incognita.⁷

The social ethicist, Markus Vogt, points out, that this understanding as human engineers of the environment suggests the human invention (from Latin *ingenium*, invention) of the environment. Dissolving the dualism of man and environment in favor of man and culture, encompasses supposedly everything.⁸ This is opposed by a biblical image of the environment.

1 The Bible and the Environment

A glimpse into the biblical text also helps to understand environment in Christianity.

---

4 Cf. Caritas in Veritate, no. 48–52.
5 Cf. Crutzen, Paul, "The Geology of mankind", *Nature* 415 (2002), 23.
6 Cf. Crutzen, *Geology*, 23.
7 Cf. Crutzen, *Geology*, 23.
8 Cf. Vogt, *Christliche Umweltethik*, 132.

1.1 Paradise Narrative/Creation Account

A central biblical text that gives voice to ideas of the environment is the paradise narrative. Da Silva[9] points out that this is a yearning harmonious image that actively places the task of preservation on mankind. Human beings are, therefore, responsible for the preservation of the divine creation.

Mankind is expelled from paradise and must till the soil there (Gen 3:23–24) as God's punishment. This can be linked to the liberation of the world from chaos outside of paradise, which is, thereby, brought about. Human beings know themselves to be co-creators with God.

The expulsion from paradise is a result of the tensions and conflicts between God and mankind. For Gen 2–3 makes it clear that next to God's divine life-giving power of creation, which has its climax in the fertility of the land and the women as the bearers of life, there is mankind's striving towards being able to distinguish between good and evil. Mankind wants to be like God – Godkind, so to say – hence mankind's task is to protect and to preserve what is given to it. The space to be preserved and protected is provided by the surroundings in the form of soil, water, plants, animals, and people, who all function as bearers of life.

After having focused on Gen 2–3, the attention is now turned to Gen 1. The following verbs are crucial here: The verbs *radah* and *kabash* used in Hebrew can be translated as *to tread down, to kick (the winepress), to stomp, to subjugate, to rape sexually*. They, thus, imply a violent dimension of meaning. In Gen 1:26, however, *radah* clearly means "to subdue", which is to be interpreted as a correspondence to God's rule, which is founded in the likeness of man and, from there, as a mandate of responsibility.

Gen 1:28 has been newly considered and analyzed because of an established aggressive interpretation.[10] Bernd Janowski structures previous interpretations into two interpretive models for the Hebrew root *radah:* "to rule" as "to trample (down)" and "to rule" as "to accompany, to lead along". The first interpretive model, with reference to Joel 4:13, where the treading of grapes in the winepress is described, depicts an action that is clearly directed from above downward and is associated with violence. Consequently, man could be understood as the

---

9 Cf. da Silva, Jorgiano dos Santos, *Füllet die Erde und macht sie euch untertan! (Gen 1,28). Strukturen einer alttestamentlich begründeten Schöpfungstheologie und deren Konsequenzen für eine biblisch orientierte Umweltethik*, Münster: LIT, 2018, 81ff.
10 Cf. Janowski, Bernd, "Herrschaft über die Tiere. Gen 1,26–28 und die Semantik von רדה", in: id., *Die rettende Gerechtigkeit. Beiträge zur Theologie des Alten Testaments 2*, Neukirchen–Vluyn: Neukirchner, 1999, 33–48, here: 33.

"down tramper" and spreader of terror among all creatures. The second model of interpretation describes an interpretation based on the context of Gen 1:28 with verses 29f., which speak of blessing: Gen 1:22 and Gen 2:3 coupled with God's resting on the seventh day (Gen 2:2f.). In 1972, James Barr[11], therefore, proposed the interpretation of man as the royal shepherd rather than the conqueror of all creatures.[12]

According to Norbert Lohfink, the *radah* used here corresponds to the Akkadian *redû(m)*, which means "to accompany, to lead (with oneself), to go". This corresponds to the idea and word usage for droving and leading animals.[13] Erich Zenger[14] understands man as a royal agent of the Creator God and, thus, does not empower him to unrestrained rule. Zenger's justification lies in the semantics of the verb as well as in the ancient oriental conception of the divine shepherd. The shepherd cares for his flock, which in this case are the people, and is represented by the king as a living image. This is opposed by Klaus Koch with his royal ideological interpretation based on Ez 34:4, Ps 49:15 and the Akkadian *redû(m)*.[15] Janowski calls his interpretation restrictive, when Koch only speaks of "leading animals", more precisely, for example, in a caravan. Koch's general interpretation of a grazing, guiding, and tending behavior of man originates form this interpretation.[16]

Janowski dared a new interpretation, which became necessary because of the previous interpretation models and critical objections to them. The overall context of Gen 1:28 – together with 1:29f. and 1:31 – contradicts the first model of interpretation by pointing to an overall peaceful mood, which has its opposite in the state of war as seen in Gen 9:1–3 and Gen 6:11f.13.[17] The second model of

---

[11] Cf. Barr, James, "Man and Nature. The Ecological Controversy and the Old Testament", *Bulletin of the John Rylands Library* 55 (1972/73), 1–28.
[12] Cf. Janowski, *Herrschaft*, 33f.
[13] Cf. Lohfink, Norbert, "'Macht euch die Erde untertan'?" (1974), in: id., *Studien zum Pentateuch*, SBAB 4, Stuttgart: Verlag katholisches Bibelwerk, 1988, 11–28, 22.
[14] Cf. Zenger, Erich, *Gottes Bogen in den Wolken. Untersuchungen zu Komposition und Theologie der priesterschriftlichen Urgeschichte*, SBS 112, Stuttgart: Verlag katholisches Bibelwerk, ²1987, 90.
[15] Cf. Koch, Klaus, "Gestaltet die Erde, doch hegt das Leben! Einige Klarstellungen zum *dominium terrae* in Genesis 1" (1983), in: id., *Spuren des hebräischen Denkens. Beiträge zur alttestamentlichen Theologie. Gesammelte Aufsätze 1*, Bernd Janowski / Martin Krause (eds.), Neukirchen-Vluyn: Neukirchener, 1991, 223–237, here: 225, 231ff.
[16] Cf. Janowski, *Herrschaft*, 36f.
[17] Cf. Lohfink, Norbert, "Die Priesterschrift und die Grenzen des Wachstums", in: id., *Unsere großen Wörter. Das Alte Testament zu Themen dieser Jahre*, Freiburg et al.: Herder, 1977, 156–171, here: 168f. See also: Uehlinger, Christoph, "Vom dominium terrae zu einem Ethos der Selbstbeschränkung? Alttestamentliche Einsprüche gegen einen tyrannischen Umgang mit der Schöpfung", *Bibel und Liturgie* 64 (1991), 59–74, here: 61. And: Link, Christian, *Schöpfung. Schöp-*

interpretation is countered by the accusation of pacification and the subliminal introduction of a modern collective responsibility conception for creation. This is not appropriate to the texts.[18] Janowski makes it his task to develop an understanding of *radah* that considers both the propositional disparity of Gen 1:26–28 and its embeddedness in the context. He proposes the metaphor of the royal man for this purpose.[19]

Janowski understands the meaning of *radah* against the backdrop of the Akkadian *redû(m)*, too. This is syntactically constructed with an object denoting a spatial totality ("all lands") or a totality of living beings ("mankind").[20] Thus, dominion must be understood in terms of the boundaries of creation. According to Gen 1:28, man's task is determined in a twofold sense: claiming the earth and ruling over the animals. The image of God as an originally royal motive in Gen 1:26ff. denotes an image of God acting responsibly in relation to his living space and all living beings in it. The allocation of food in Gen 1:29f. regulates the coexistence of living beings. Community (same habitat) and difference (different food) intermingle with each other here.[21]

In addition, the demarcation of Gen 1:26–28 and Gen 9:2f. emphasizes that Gen 1:26–28 calls mankind not to fail in its humanity, as the image of God is adversatively described in Gen 6:11ff. The mandate to rule in Gen 1:26–28 does not reduce the world to the ideal of a perfect world, but in comparison with Gen 9:2f. calls on man not to leave it at the normativity of the factual, but to limit rule.[22]

In the so-called first creation narrative in Gen 1:1–2:3 the human being is particularly singled out in two ways: once by the so-called "dominion order" and by the God-likeness (imago Dei). Man is created at the same time, as are the animals, by the verb *barah*, and he shares the seventh day with the animals as a distinction by divine blessing. However, what is lacking, is that God evaluates man as good and provides him with this form of approval. The position of man according to Gen 1 is, thus, clearly more ambivalent than commonly received and suggested by the speech of the "crown of creation". This speech can-

---

fungstheologie angesichts der Herausforderungen des 20. Jahrhunderts, Handbuch Systematischer Theologie 7/2, Gütersloh: Mohn, 1991, here: 396.
18 Cf. Ebach, Jürgen, "Bild Gottes und Schrecken der Tiere. Zur Anthropologie der priesterlichen Urgeschichte", in: id., *Ursprung und Ziel. Erinnerte Zukunft und erhoffte Vergangenheit. Biblische Exegesen, Reflexionen, Geschichten*, Neukirchen–Vluyn: Neukirchener, 1986, 16–47, here: 32. Also: Uehlinger, *dominium terrae*, 61.
19 Cf. Janowski, *Herrschaft*, 38.
20 Cf. Janowski, *Herrschaft*, 40.
21 Cf. Janowski, *Herrschaft*, 44.
22 Cf. Janowski, *Herrschaft*, 45.

not refer to Gen 1. Gen 1 is understood as a theological concept, not an anthropocentric one, culminating in God's resting on the seventh day. According to Gen 1, the "crown of creation" is the seventh day and mankind a *primus inter pares*.[23]

In summary, the environment is created by God and there is a special relationship between God and humankind concerning the tasks for the environment. But other (biblical) books and authors give an impetus for the conception of environment in Christianity, too.

1.2 Prophets

For example, Hilary Marlow[24] re-reads the Old Testament prophets Amos and Hosea in the context of contemporary environmental ethics. She points out that especially the rhetorical structure of the Book of Amos shows the powerful and all-encompassing nature of God, which finds expression especially in the non-human creation. The Book of Amos invites an environmentally interested reader to understand the cooperation of the non-human world with its creator as opposed to human rebellion against both. This finds expression in a cause and effect pattern: in disasters such as, for example, droughts, earthquakes or floods. YHWH first warns the human beings and then judges.[25]

Hosea – in contrast to Amos, who presents YHWH as a cosmic power and as creator and judge – focusses exclusively on land and its produce when referring to non-human creation. Hosea uses almost no description of cosmic powers or global disorder.[26] More generally, Marlow finds out that the non-human creation in the Book of Hosea is structurally and thematically less important than in the Book of Amos.[27]

---

23 Cf. Schmitz, Barbara, "Der Mensch als 'Krone der Schöpfung'. Anthropologische Konzepte im Spannungsfeld von alttestamentlicher Theologie und moderner Rezeption", *Kirche und Israel* 27.1 (2012), 18–32, here: 22.
24 Cf. Marlow, Hilary, *Biblical Prophets and Contemporary Environmental Ethics. Re-Reading Amos, Hosea, and First Isaiah*, Oxford: Oxford University Press, 2009.
25 Cf. Marlow, *Prophets*, 157.
26 Cf. Marlow, *Prophets*, 158f.
27 Cf. Marlow, *Prophets*, 194.

1.3 Creation in the Book of Psalms

Especially Ps 8 and Ps 104 should be examined in this context. Ps 8 reads as follows:

> 1 To the choirmaster: according to The Gittith. A Psalm of David. O Lord, our Lord, how majestic is your name in all the earth! You have set your glory above the heavens.
> 2 Out of the mouth of babies and infants, you have established strength because of your foes, to still the enemy and the avenger.
> 3 When I look at your heavens, the work of your fingers, the moon and the stars, which you have set in place,
> 4 what is man that you are mindful of him, and the son of man that you care for him?
> 5 Yet you have made him a little lower than the heavenly beings and crowned him with glory and honor.
> 6 You have given him dominion over the works of your hands; you have put all things under his feet,
> 7 all sheep and oxen, and also the beasts of the field,
> 8 the birds of the heavens, and the fish of the sea, whatever passes along the paths of the seas.
> 9 O Lord, our Lord, how majestic is your name in all the earth![28]

Ps 8 suggests itself as a biblical text relevant to environmental ethics because it uses the verb *to crown*, suggesting an association with the formulation of man as the "crown of creation". Ps 8 begins with the invocation of God (YHWH) as Lord, the ruler whose name is mighty all over the earth. Verses 2 and 10 are identical, framing the psalm in an invocation to God.[29] Text-critically, there is even a hymnic explication as majesty in verses 2b and 3. More precisely, God's majesty is not meant in military, economic, or political terms, but it is clearly distinguished from that of worldly rulers. God's extraordinary power, which comes from the "mouth of babies and infants", determines all reality (Ps 8:2). The function of man in this is posited in verses 4–6: there is an anthropological self-determination (not a philosophical discourse) of an individual in prayer before God and in the presence of God. The self-designation of man in verse 5 as *'enosh* is a generic designation and may particularly emphasize his limitedness (in the possible translation as "little man" or the German "Menschlein"). In addition, the designation *ben 'adam* is found, in which references to the individual human being can be made to Gen 2–4 and the son of Adam. The focus here could be on the transience of man and his potential guilt. The continuation in verse 6 crowns

---

28 Ps 8 (ESV).
29 Cf. Schmitz, *Mensch*, 22.

man with "glory" and "honor", qualifications otherwise ascribed to God.[30] In Ps 21 alone, these qualities come to a human being, a king, however. In Ps 8, though, this qualification happens to all men, making man a king with such a function and basic determination. The king function is opened and democratized.[31]

Contrary to the first intuition of verse 4, according to verses 5 and 6, man is not nothing, he is only slightly inferior to God and crowned with splendor and glory. This appreciative singling out of man makes the question of the distance between man and God important in an exacerbated way[32]: for, what is man, singled out by God and endowed with royal functions, in view of his Creator and the world he has made?

Verses 7–9 explain the kingly function as the function of ruling. Man's being king does not shape up as a privileged way of life, but as the hard and stony task of being a good king. According to Ps 8:7–9, this task does not refer to the world and not to nature and not to other people, but to the animal world. In short, it can be stated that Ps 8 formulates an anthropological concept that humans are to be good shepherds over the animal world. Together with the essential framework of the psalm, Ps 8 is not about the rule of man and his supposed privileged position, but about the hymnically praised rule of God in which man has a function.[33]

Like Gen 1, Ps 8 is not an anthropocentric but a theocentric text. The designation as a creation hymn is, therefore, appropriate.[34]

The 104th Psalm can be classified as a creation psalm. While at the beginning (verse 1) and at the end of the psalm (verses 33–35) the poet or the poetess stands out, in the main part (verses 2–32), YHWH, the God of Israel, is praised as creator and sustainer of the world. The direction of the praise goes from heaven (verses 1–4) to the separation of water and land (verses 5–9) to life on earth (verses 10–24) and the sea (verses 25–26). All life thereby depends on YHWH (verses 27–32). Various conceptions of God become clear: YHWH appears as a weather god who brings rain or symbolizes the sun; that is, as a fighter against primeval chaos. Linguistic signals also point to this, for example the change in address

---

[30] See: Ps 29:3; 145:5, 12; Isa 35:2.
[31] Cf. Schmitz, *Mensch*, 23.
[32] Cf. Schmitz, *Mensch*, 23.
[33] Cf. Schmitz, *Mensch*, 24.
[34] Cf. Schmitz, *Mensch*, 24.

between the 2nd person compared to statements about YHWH in the 3rd person. The exact textual genesis and precursors of the text are disputed.[35]

In the 21st century, Ps 104 is particularly relevant because of its framing of man's position in creation. The notion of not understanding animals as fellow human beings and, therefore, understanding them merely as a means to achieve any purpose cannot be based on Ps 104 and the Bible. Human beings do experience a special place in the world – as they do in Ps 104 – but this does not mean that the rest of creation is available for processing and preparation of food. Animals eat what they find (verses 11.14.21). Human beings must prepare, process, and manufacture it (verses 23.14–15). Human beings may at best marvel at the world of animals from a distance according to Ps 104: wild asses, ibexes, klipsheep (verses 11–18), birds (verses 12–17) or the leviathan in the sea (verse 26). God turns to this world while man has no place in the animal world. Rainer Kessler reads Ps 104 as an invitation to mankind to learn again not to be masters and owners of nature, but a part of it. Only in this way, upcoming catastrophes can be averted.[36]

Verse 35, which urges that sinners may disappear from earth, so that there are no more workers of iniquity on earth, is preceded by a final repetition of the beginning ("Bless, my inmost being, YHWH!") and the Hallelujah shout that ties Ps 104–106 together into a triad.[37] The sinners and transgressors here can be identified with those who threaten to destroy the divine creation itself. Therefore, they should no longer exist. Rainer Kessler suggests reading Ps 104 as a self-question whether each and every one himself belongs to the sinners and workers of iniquity as described in the psalm. This question is central and should be answered independently of how politicians like Donald Trump or Jair Bolsonaro act in relation to our planet or that, according to Oxfam's 2020 report, the richest 10% of the earth's population are responsible for over half of the greenhouse gas emissions of the last quarter century.[38]

Peter Riede asks what we can learn from Ps 104 for our understanding of the world today. In doing so, he draws attention to the interdependence of the whole of creation and the guiding principle of "life" in contrast to the guiding principle of progress in the 20th century, where man is the central focus. He understands this concept not as a romanticism of nature or as a naïve "back to nature", but as an understanding of the world as an organism of life with manifold life-perform-

---

35 Cf. Kessler, Rainer, "'Eine Grenze hast du gesetzt' (Ps 104,9). Psalm 104 im Horizont globaler Krisen", *Bibel und Kirche* 76.1 (2021), 22–27, here: 22f.
36 Cf. Kessler, *Grenze*, 25.
37 Cf. Kessler, *Grenze*, 25.
38 Cf. Kessler, *Grenze*, 26.

ances, which makes God's reign over the world clear. Creation is, thus, the place where the healing and saving God wants to be revealed. Within a new ethics of creation, this means turning away from the dominance of the human measure. The non-human creation thereby experiences intrinsic values[39] and rights in the form of protection of ecosystems and species, the preservation and development of the genetic heritage and a species-appropriate life.[40] In this context, Ps 104 helps to put modern anthropocentrism in its place and to emphasize the intrinsic value of nature.[41]

1.4 New Testament

At first glance, creation is not a central theme of the New Testament – especially in comparison to the magnificent Old Testament descriptions. When continuing on from this, however, one can read in the New Testament about the experience of God's new work of creation.[42] Ritual enactment is the baptism that makes Christians Christians. In the Pauline sense, the focus is on overcoming differences that constitute the present world age: "For neither circumcision counts for anything, nor uncircumcision, but a new creation."[43] "New creation" refers to late descriptions in the Book of Isaiah (Isa 65:17 and 66:20) in order to denote the expectation of a comprehensive reorganization of the entire world. This refers to a change in the identity of individuals, as is expressed programmatically, for example, in the Epistle to the Galatians in the polemic against circumcision to distinguish Judaism from paganism. According to Paul, it is genuinely Christian to overcome ethnic and social backgrounds, as well as the sex of human beings: "There is neither Jew nor Greek, there is neither slave nor free, there is no male and female, for you are all one in Christ Jesus."[44] A new way of perception is also part of Paul's new creation thought: "From now on, therefore, we regard no one

---

[39] "Intrinsic value" vs. "inherent value" for German "Eigenwert": according to a short research, intrinsic is more often used for nature in general and inherent is explicitly used in the context of animal rights.
[40] Cf. Riede, Peter, "Mensch und Welt in der Sicht des Alten Testaments. Am Beispiel von Psalm 104", in: id., *Schöpfung und Lebenswelt. Studien zur Theologie und Anthropologie des Alten Testaments*, Leipzig: Evangelische Verlagsanstalt 2009, 101–117, here: 116.
[41] Cf. Riede, *Mensch*, 117.
[42] Cf. Vollenweider, Samuel, "Wahrnehmungen der Schöpfung im Neuen Testament", *Zeitschrift für Pädagogik und Theologie*, 55 (2003), 246–253, here: 246.
[43] Gal 6:15 (ESV).
[44] Gal 3:28 (ESV), paragraph: cf. Vollenweider, *Wahrnehmungen*, 247.

according to the flesh. Even though we once regarded Christ according to the flesh, we regard him thus no longer."[45]

Because of the uncontroversial assumption by early Christians that God the Creator created the world and continues to sustain it, both processes are addressed only in passing. An exception is the Lucan version of Paul's speech on the Areopagus (Acts 17:16–34, compare 14:15–17). Biblical and Hellenistic convictions are brought into conversation with each other, for example temple and cult criticism, the animation of creation with life and spirit, the origin of mankind, the order of spaces and times, the nearness and sonship of God.[46]

Moreover, Christ is identified as the basic figure of creation (1 Cor. 8:6; Col. 1:15–20; Heb. 1:2f.; Jn. 1:1ff.). The prologue of John is a central text, in which the beginning of Genesis is used to give weight to the Jesus story in connection with it. Through creation theology, Jesus is given and presented to the world by John. The praise of Christ in the Letter to the Colossians also joins this sequence of texts. The focus here is on the interplay of creation and redemption with recourse to Greek Hellenistic cosmologies. The Church as the Body of Christ growing into the cosmos is the place where the cosmic presence of Christ can be perceived (Col 1:12–14, 21–23). This is a critical interpretation of wisdom theology as well as philosophical cosmologies in Colossians.[47]

1.5 A Summary of the Reflections on the Bible

It can be stated that the entire biblical canon is framed by the notion of creation. Mankind's task on earth can be summarized as striving to create paradise on earth. The attempt to be like God can only harm and destroy what has been created. A paradise on earth appears wherever people succeed in protecting and preserving creation. Gen 2–3, thus, conceives of a holistic ecology including the human being. A human ecology that thinks God and human beings in accordance with each other and assigns a new place to human beings in cooperation with other human beings as well as with God is a challenge.[48]

Considering various discussions on and misinterpretations of the biblical texts, Jürgen Manemann speaks of man's gardening in the world. He takes a close look at the mission of dominion as a basis. The new world gardeners are engineers and geologists: they appear as *anthropocentrists*, who see themselves

---

[45] 2 Cor 5:16 (ESV), paragraph: cf. Vollenweider, *Wahrnehmungen*, 248.
[46] Cf. Vollenweider, *Wahrnehmungen*, 249f.
[47] Cf. Vollenweider, *Wahrnehmungen*, 250f.
[48] Cf. da Silva, *Füllet die Erde*, 81ff.

as world gardeners. There is planetary gardening and there are plant gardens that are created by order. Humankind is responsible, also, for the environment remaining wild and 'natural'.

However, the question remains: who determines this? Who makes the decisions? Perhaps the Christian tradition helps to see clearer.

2 The Tradition

Jame Schaefer suggests reading the (Catholic) theological tradition through an ecological lens. In order to do so, she starts by indicating the pivotal role of religious communities to remind their members of traditions that may guide them during the current widespread ecological degradation.[49] For this reason, the National Religious Partnership for the Environment was initiated by Jewish and Christian representatives. Its aim is to care for God's creation throughout religious life through theological reflection, teaching, worship, and public policy initiative.[50]

Jame Schaefer proposes a five-step model, which she calls a modest method for retrieval, reconstruction, and application. The first step explores a certain concept from patristic and medieval texts and estimates its adequateness for ecological concerns. The second step looks at the theologians and their prescientific understanding of the world. Thus, the aim of step two is to reconstruct philosophical and theological backgrounds and a context of the time from which the concepts result. Step three focusses on coherence followed by step four, which ensures the relevance for ecological concerns. Step five finally assesses the helpfulness of the concept in addressing ecological concerns. This method excludes all "is-ought" problems from empirical facts because every process starts in the religious faith in God as creator-initiator and continuous sustainer of the cosmological-biological process.[51] These five steps offer a critical-creative approach for the Catholic, Christian tradition, on how to think and act towards other species, ecosystems and biosphere, beginning with the patristic and medieval texts.[52]

---

[49] Cf. Schaefer, Jame, *Theological Foundations for Environmental Ethics. Reconstruction Patristic and Medieval Concepts*, Washington: Georgetown University Press, 2009, 1.
[50] Cf. Schaefer, *Foundations*, 2.
[51] Cf. Schaefer, *Foundations*, 5f.
[52] Cf. Schaefer, *Foundations*, 7.

2.1 Valuing the Goodness of Creation

Valuing the Goodness of Creation – as the first of all nine concepts Schaefer deals with – is part of various teachings of Augustine, Chrysostom, and Aquinas. Augustine (354–430) derives every existence from God, that he calls the "supremely good Creator"[53]. He created the universe ex nihilo. In his controversy with the Manicheans, he states directly that every being is good according to its characteristics and body. In his great work *De Trinitate* he declares:

> The earth is good by the height of its mountains, the moderate elevation of its hills, and the evenness of its fields; and good is the farm that is pleasant and fertile; and good is the house that is arranged throughout in symmetrical proportions and is spacious and bright; and good are the animals, animate bodies; and good is the mild and salubrious air; and good is the food that is pleasant and conducive to health; and good is health without pains and weariness; and good is the countenance of man with regular features, a cheerful expression, and a glowing color; and good is the soul of a friend with the sweetness of concord and the fidelity of love; and good is the just man; and good are riches because they readily assist us; and good is the heaven with its own sun, moon and stars.[54]

The goodness of the existing continues even in a diminished body as long as it exists.

Aquinas (1224/25–1274), thereafter, draws on Augustine in the affirmation of the goodness of every creature according to the Book of Genesis. The existence of every creature is reasoned in the creation of God, which attributes to every creature its goodness. Moreover, according to Aquinas, every entity is implanted with some kind of innate way of existing that makes it perfect. Criticizing a creature's nature is at the same time criticism on God, who is the creator of nature. However, the ability to comprehend makes human beings distinct, according to Aquinas. Through God's innate way of existing as God intends, goodness receives another dimension: the likeness to God's goodness. "Only intellectual aspects of the human bear God's image, whereas the nonintellectual aspects, those making up the physical body, retain only a likeness of God's goodness through their existence."[55] Schaefer highlights that the goodness, which Augustine and Aquinas attribute to God's creation, is also fixed to God's specificity and his overall plan.

---

53 Cf. Augustine, *The Enchiridion: on Faith, Hope, and Love*, trans. J.F. Shaw, Henry Paolucci (ed.), Chicago: Regnery Gateway, 1961, 10:10.
54 Augustine, *The Trinity*, trans. Stephen McKenna, Washington, DC: Catholic University of America Press, 1963, 8.3.4, 247.
55 Schaefer, *Foundations*, 19 f.

Thus, only rational beings are free to decide, despite it being against the Will of God.[56]

Summing up the first concept Schaefer takes from patristic and medieval tradition, the ethics of intrinsic-instrumental valuing appears as a potentially effective system for the environmental ethics of today. The origin in God attributes to every constituent of the earth an intrinsic-instrumental value, which persists in the ongoing process of existing. In this concept, the idea of a common good, as the sustainability of all constituents in the shared ecosystem and the greater biosphere, solves conflicts between any of those valued beings.[57]

2.2 Appreciating the Beauty of Creation

The second concept Schaefer takes, in particular from eminent theologians of patristic and medieval thought, is an aesthetic concept including affective, cognitive, affective-cognitive, and mysterious dimensions: the concept of "Appreciating the Beauty of Creation".[58] The central theological position was established by Basil of Caesarea (329–379). In his second homily, where he expounds Gen 1, adjectives such as "august, magnificent, wondrous, marvelous, dazzling, pleasant, attractive, enjoyable, and excellent"[59] serve as a means for him to describe the world. In a letter to his friend Gregory of Nazianzus, Basil even proclaims that he found the site to God's providence for example in colorful trees on high mountains, and the evenly sloping plain at the mountain's base where he stays. He compares the site he found to Homer's Calypso Island, which are actually not comparable to one another. His depiction is plausibly given.[60] Aside from Basil's impressions, patristic and medieval theologians find four ways in which they express their aesthetic appreciation for the beauty of God's creation:

> Firstly, "[a]n affective appreciation precipitated by their initial encounter with natural beauty; [secondly,] a combined affective-cognitive appreciation from studying the details of natural beings; [thirdly,] a cognitive appreciation for the harmonious functioning of the world; and [fourthly,] an appreciation that comes with a humble sense of inability to fully comprehend the complex universe."[61] [Annotations K.S.F.]

---

56 Cf. Schaefer, *Foundations*, 27.
57 Cf. Schaefer, *Foundations*, 32.
58 Cf. Schaefer, *Foundations*, 43.
59 Schaefer, *Foundations*, 44.
60 Cf. Schaefer, *Foundations*, 44 f.
61 Schaefer, *Foundations*, 56.

Reconstructing patterns of human behavior by starting not from today's broad scientific findings, but from the context of the patristic and medieval theologians, helps to understand phenomenologically the beauty of natural phenomena, the harmonious function of biota and abiota, and finally the necessity of humble human acting before God's incomprehensible universe in scientific and theological endeavors. The patristic and medieval reflection on the beauty of nature needs to be acquired for today's ecotheological thinking.[62]

2.3 Reverencing the Sacramental Universe

The third concept Schaefer suggests is called "Reverencing the Sacramental Universe". The idea of a sacramental quality of nature means that the visible world, which is nature itself, mediates God's invisible presence and his attributes. Patristic and medieval theologians spoke about a "book of nature" in which he reveals himself.[63] Clement of Alexandria (ca. 150–216) addresses God's discernible power, Athanasius (295–373) reflects on God's Activity, and the Syrian theologian, Ephrem (303–373), examines the symbolic creation.

Basil of Caesarea again focusses on the world's sacramental beauty. God's creative act evokes our admiration for God's work at the same time as the world manifests God's "artistic processes of thought"[64]. Basil's understanding of the beauty of God's creation is also expressed in his prayers, with which he usually closes his homilies. This prayer closes his first homily on the six days of creation:

> Let us glorify the Master Craftsmen for all that has been done wisely and skillfully; and from the beauty of the visible things let us form an idea of Him who is more than beautiful; and from the greatness of these perceptible and circumscribed bodies let us conceive of Him who is infinite and immense and who surpasses all understanding in the plentitude of His power. For, even if we are ignorant of things made, yet, at least, that which in general comes under our observation is so wonderful that even the most acute mind is shown to be at a loss as regards the least of the things in the world, either in the ability to explain it worthily or to render due praise to the Creator; to whom be all glory, honor, and power forever. Amen.[65]

---

62 Cf. Schaefer, *Foundations*, 57.
63 Cf. Schaefer, *Foundations*, 65.
64 Basil of Caesarea, On the Hexaemeron, in *Exegetic Homilies*, trans. Sister Agnes Clare Way, Fathers of the Church 46, Washington, DC: Catholic University of America Press, 1963, 3–150, esp. homily 1.7, 112.
65 Basil of Caesarea, *Hexaemeron*, 1.11, 19; quoted from Schaefer, *Foundations*, 68f.

Also, at the end of his sixth homily, he stressed God's gift of intelligence to humans:

> May he who has granted us intelligence to learn of the great wisdom of the artificer from the most insignificant objects of creation permit us to receive loftier concepts of the Creator from the mighty objects of creation ...Truly, it is not possible to attain a worthy view of God of the universe from these things, but to be led on by them, as also by each of the tiniest of plants and animals to some slight and faint impression of Him.[66]

The sacramental character of microcosmic and macrocosmic phenomena was crucial for Basil and he would not regress to any other understanding of God's creation. At the same time, Basil stressed the human acceptance and openness towards natural phenomena and their sacramental quality that is the precondition for their manifestation of God. This is shown theologically and morally in the shape of "God's governance [...] imbedded in the laws of nature telling us how we ought to act"[67]. Observing animals, such as crawling creatures, fish, sea urchins, oysters, sea monsters, and other marine animals is the moral lesson to be learned by human beings, according to Basil.[68]

Augustine presents his trinitarian perspective also related to the invisible God's creation and its presence in the sacramentally qualified nature. According to Augustine, nature and the physical world represent God's wisdom, which is why any approach to the ultimate truth of the universe is only possible through faith in God. For Augustine, knowing God results also in the ability to understand God's self-communication through the world's constituents. The image of God in a human's soul assures the ability to see and understand God. God's self-revelation to the world happens in his trinity, which Augustine concludes from the refrain of Gen 1 "and God saw that it was good". Additionally, every creation manifests a unity, form, and order in itself. All this is God's active, but hidden, governance. God, therefore, works providentially through his created world by a double function of providence: a natural one (provided in the soul and through birth) and a voluntary one (human beings learn and exercise free will and decide on food and clothing). Human beings resemble the Divine Trinity through existing, according to Augustine's reflection[69]. Rejoicing, he prayed and gave thanks to God[70]:

---

[66] Basil of Caesarea, *Hexaemeron*, 6.11, 102–3; quoted from Schaefer, *Foundations*, 69.
[67] Schaefer, *Foundations*, 69.
[68] Cf. Schaefer, *Foundations*, 69; following: Basil, *Hexaemeron*, 7.4, 112.
[69] Cf. Augustine, *Concerning the City of God against the Pagans*, trans. John O'Meara, London: Penguin Books, 1972, 11.26, 459–60.
[70] Cf. Schaefer, *Foundations*, 69 f.

Let him who sees this, either in part, or through a mirror, or in an obscure manner, [Cor 13:12] rejoice that he knows God, and let him honor Him as God and give thanks. But let him who does not see, strive to see through His piety, and not raise captious objections through his blindness. For God is one, yet a trinity. Nor are the words: 'From whom all things, through whom all things, and unto whom all things', to be taken in a confused sense, nor as meaning many gods, but 'to him be the glory forever. Amen.'[71]

Schaefer reconstructs the patristic and medieval concept of sacramentality, which is extremely different from a modern scientific concept. Opposed to empirical findings by quantum physicists, cosmologists, evolutionary and molecular biologists, and ecologists who reconstruct a historically emergent, evolutionary, dynamic, holistic, and prospectively opened view on the natural world, patristic and medieval theologians view the natural world as a divinely designed, static, and geocentric organism with a God-given purpose for existing and acting. The teleological view of the world was hierarchically with God outside the hierarchy, but nevertheless present to it. Human beings were on top of the ladder concerning material beings. The view on the natural world was qualitative rather than quantitative and, above all, of a sacramental nature.[72]

Schaefer calls for the training of sacramental sensibilities, which she deduces from patristic and medieval texts. Because of the modern scientific view since the Enlightenment, this task might seem formidable; however, it is crucial in order to understand the significance of ecological concerns.[73]

God's power, wisdom, and goodness become obvious through a theological reflection on and faith-based approach to the sacramentality of creation in patristic and medieval texts. People who believe in God should be prompted by this concept "to revere the diverse species, ecosystems, and biosphere that constitute Earth. They are means through which God can be experienced and known when they are existing and functioning according to their natures."[74]

2.4 Other Approaches

Another concept that Schaefer cites, and which is relevant to the current contribution, is the concept of "acknowledging kinship and practicing companionship". It serves to explore a Christian ethic on the bases of a metaphysical hy-

---

71 Augustine, *Trinity*, 6.10.12, 241–15, citing Rom 11:36; quoted from Schaefer, *Foundations*, 71.
72 Cf. Schaefer, *Foundations*, 80 f.
73 Cf. Schaefer, *Foundations*, 86.
74 Schaefer, *Foundations*, 92 f.

pothesis of presumed biophilia in order to rethink the human relationship with other species and the natural environment.[75] The terms kinship and companionship are central and part of a process that targets a range of various roles, from kinship to companionship. The idea was presented by the Lutheran theologian Joseph Sittler (1904–1987) and the Catholic theologians Michael J. Himes (1947–2022) and Kenneth R. Himes (*1950). Other species and nature are thought of together, as companions (including an intrinsic value), rather than as strictly instrumental for human beings (only instrumental value for human beings). This is expressed also in the language they use: terms of intimacy, dignity, and equality.[76] An example of such an approach is the demonstrating of piety towards creatures which can be found in Francis's of Assisi and Bonaventure's writings. This piety substantiates in loving the creatures for themselves, devoting themselves to their interests, showering them with affection, being kind to them, standing up for and with them before others, showing compassion for their suffering and acting generously toward them without interfering with their self-expressions.[77]

The seventh concept Schaefer offers is the use of creation with gratitude and restraint.[78] The US Catholic bishops and Pope Benedict XVI have called attention to climate change and the challenge of preserving the earth as a livable place. Several and various consequences of the global warming have been predicted by many scientists: physically, ecologically, economically, socially, and in terms of health. The earth and its inhabitants will be threatened by high risks of extreme weather, the destruction of most of the Amazon rainforest, a decrease in freshwater availability, the need to grow new crops, because old crops will not grow anymore, hunger and malnutrition, an increase in infectious diseases, and an increase in poverty.[79] At this point, only a short summary of the effects have been mentioned, previously undiscovered effects might also occur. They demand gratitude to God for the use of his creation. In an analysis, Patristic-medieval teaching suggests at least seven ways of using God's creation: acknowledging and thanking God for the blessing of the earth, recognizing human accountability to God, reasoning carefully about the appropriate use, limiting use to the necessities of life, ensuring availability for future human use, use in order to gain knowledge about God's creation, and use in order to know God. "In these [at least seven] uses, the faithful will be thankful to God for the many blessings

---

75 Cf. Schaefer, *Foundations*, 149.
76 Cf. Schaefer, *Foundations*, 173.
77 Cf. Schaefer, *Foundations*, 175 f.
78 Cf. Schaefer, *Foundations*, 193 ff.
79 Cf. Schaefer, *Foundations*, 208 f.

of species, land, water, and air that God empowers forth from the cosmological-biological evolutionary process and calls to completion."[80] [Annotations K.S.F.] The actuality of the instructions, which can be found in patristic and medieval writing, is still high. They transcend time and cultures because they "present serious challenges to the ways in which too many humans are over-using, over-consuming, and wasting the goods of Earth today".[81]

Her ninth and last concept, Schaefer calls "Loving earth".[82] An image for this concept might be the hazelnut in Julian of Norwich's (1342–ca. 1416) hand. The little hazelnut, that exists like every other creature on earth because God loves it, envisions three characteristics: God made it, God loves it, and God preserves it. God, therefore, appears as creator, protector, and lover in Julian's words.[83]

Finally, Schaefer entitles the various models of human behavior that can be concluded from the nine concepts analyzed before in her research. She is modelling the human in an age of ecological degradation.[84]

Now, that the biblical and patristic foundations have been consulted, systematic considerations must be made.

3 Systematic Approach

Describing the environment in Christianity is first done by describing the relationship between human beings and the environment. It is a core issue of environmental ethics[85] to consistently think human beings as part of nature without levelling their responsibility as moral subjects.[86] However, to separate the social or natural environment is only theoretically possible but not practically.

---

80 Schaefer, *Foundations*, 215.
81 Schaefer, *Foundations*, 215.
82 Cf. Schaefer, *Foundations*, 255.
83 Cf. Schaefer, *Foundations*, 258. See also: Norwich, Julian of, *Showings*, trans. Edmund Colledge / James Walsh, New York: Paulist Press, 1978, 184.
84 Cf. Schaefer, *Foundations*, 267 ff.
85 For an overview see: Ott, Konrad / Dierks, Jan / Voegt-Kleschin, Lieske (eds.), *Handbuch Umweltethik*, Stuttgart: J. B. Metzler Verlag, 2016.
86 Cf. Vogt, *Christliche Umweltethik*, 24.

3.1 Models of the Relationship of Humankind and Nature

The central term in this context is *anthropocentrism*. It means, that environmental ethical concerns are always traced back to human concerns. In contrast, there are nature-centered or physio-centered approaches, which focus on environmental protection not only for the sake of human beings but directly for the sake of other natural entities, as well. Additionally, those approaches also ascribe a moral intrinsic value to natural entities.

One specific type of anthropocentrism is *normative anthropocentrism*. It addresses the question, for the benefit of which beings we actually want to bind our actions to normative restrictions. Such beings could certainly have unconstrained moral values or a moral intrinsic value themselves. One might distinguish three variants of the normative anthropocentrism: one position accepts its only normative restrictions for the sake of human beings. It is called the *exclusive anthropocentrism*. The second position identifies the human interest in the environment also as an aesthetic appreciation or the admitting of the *value of experiencing nature*. A third possibility to think normative anthropocentrism includes positions that accept moral restrictions also for the sake of other entities. But they give greater weight to the moral value of human beings than to the moral value of non-human entities. One might call this position *anthropocentric in a weak or inclusive* sense. Moreover, there is a *metaphysical anthropocentrism*, which depicts the teleologically understood ultimate purpose in this world. It is, therefore, a form of teleological thinking that fundamentally assumes that everything in the world has a purpose in contrast to a modern scientific worldview that denies this approach. Anthropocentrism, in general, defines that all our knowledge and values are always of human origin, including human language and human concepts. A non-human perspective of knowledge and evaluation is simply not accessible to us. The approach called *epistemic anthropocentrism* focusses on this fundamental realization.

There are several alternatives to anthropocentrism, which offer other perspectives on environment than the different anthropocentric approaches. The *pathocentrism* (from Greek *pathos*, engl. suffering) or the *sentientism* (from Latin *sentire*, engl. feeling) claim that the interests of all sentient beings are to be taken into account. Sentient beings are not only human beings, but certainly animals and perhaps even plants may count as sentient beings.

The biocentrism (from Greek *bios*, engl. life) attributes moral intrinsic value to every living being and is, therefore, classified as the broader term in comparison to pathocentrism and sentientism. Even broader is the holistic approach (*Holism*), which regards the whole ecosystem, the biosphere, the entirety of earth, nature, or world as morally and intrinsically valuable.

Accordingly, the more things acquire moral intrinsic value, the more difficult the question of prioritizing those moral claims and duties from which they derive necessarily. Each position mentioned so far, contains hierarchical-gradualist as well as egalitarian variants itself.

The holistic thinking of process theology turns out to be its unique feature and shall be discussed hereinafter.

3.2 A Theological Approach: Process Theology

The philosopher Reinhart Maurer[87] demands that in ecological ethics, basic attitudes should be recognized, which are part of the ecological crisis and are mostly accepted without reflection, also in science. He demands that the extra-human nature should also be included in ethics and not exclusively the inter-human part of ethics. Based on this, Degen-Ballmer makes it his task to point out other models of thought that are based on such alternative experiences of nature. A holistic thinking as an ideal of orientation guiding knowledge and action is decisive for him. This begins with a holistically oriented knowledge about nature and creation and functions communicatively. A learning attitude towards nature is suggested, which, in principle, is open to different approaches towards creation and nature. Methodological plurality instead of a mechanistic-analytical-dissecting ideal of knowledge is leading, which, at the same time, dismisses a fragmentation of reality and the analysis of the individual.[88]

The natural sciences hold on to this fragmentation of reality for the time being, but Degen-Ballmer points out the lack of reflection on this approach to nature and creation. Holistic thinking can also include particular, fragmentary thinking, but it is equally valid as sensing, feeling, thinking, and intuitive cognition. Holistic thinking is also a heuristic endeavor that is never fully completed. Possible descriptions of an objective start are, for example, "peace with nature" or "natural togetherness". Theologically, this is the idea of the kingdom of God, as described, for example, in Isa 11:6–9 or Rom 8:18–25. In its precise quality, this can be realized differently, for example, as an individual-ethical spirituality

---

[87] Cf. Maurer, Reinhart, "Ökologische Ethik als Problem", in: Bayertz, Kurt (ed.), *Ökologische Ethik*, München/Zürich: Schnell & Steiner, 1988, 11–30.
[88] Cf. Degen-Ballmer, Stephan, *Gott – Mensch – Welt. Eine Untersuchung über mögliche holistische Denkmodelle in der Prozesstheologie und der ostkirchlich-orthodoxen Theologie als Beitrag für ein ethikrelevantes Natur- und Schöpfungsverständnis*, Frankfurt a.M. et al.: Peter Lang, 2001, 17.

of creation or as a scientific dialogue between the humanities and the natural sciences.[89]

In order to introduce American process theology, Degen-Ballmer discusses the philosopher, Alfred North Whitehead. His organismic philosophy had a strong impact on theology. The main representative of process theology is John B. Cobb. He dealt with a clarification of the relationship between God and man as well as the concept of natural theology. The idea of an event happening in order to describe and grasp nature is methodologically leading in process theology. Not only the understanding of nature, but also the epistemology is determined by this thought. For it leads to the questioning of the common dualisms man vs. nature, God vs. man, or spirit vs. matter. The approach can, thus, be qualified as relational and, thus, as non-substantialist, which directly evokes an ethical relevance. On the Orthodox side, Degen-Ballmer draws on works by Paulos Gregorios concerning the Church Father, Gregory of Nyssa, and statements by various theologians active in ecumenical dialogue. There, nature is to be understood as a system of symbols and, as such, as an expression of God itself.[90]

American process theology, also known as the Chicago School before the end of the 1950s, is a socio-historical theology that sought to provide systematic theological support for church related social commitment under the impact of the movement that became known as the "social gospel". This was done, for example, by reading the biblical scriptures in light of the idea of the "social mind". Henry Nelson Wieman and Charles Hartshorne brought to the Chicago Divinity School the teachings of the philosopher Alfred North Whitehead, which caused a shift towards the question of God. Both theologians elaborated a theology that was characterized by a strong reference to reality in systematic theological questions. They recognized God in the immediate experience of reality and, therefore, called their theology empirical theology. Wieman characterized God as a "creative event", which Hartshorne understood panpsychically as totality.[91] Theologians who followed the two included Bernard Eugene Meland, Daniel Day Williams, Wiliam Temple, and William Norman Pittenger.[92]

Whitehead's organismic philosophy opposes all dualisms on which natural philosophy is built according to the physical worldview of Descartes and the mechanistic one of Newton: subject vs. object, spirit vs. matter, space vs. time,

---

[89] Cf. Degen-Ballmer, *Gott*, 18.
[90] Cf. Degen-Ballmer, *Gott*, 22.
[91] Hartshorne, C., *Beyond Humanism: Essays in the Philosophy of Nature*, Chicago: Willet Clark & Co, 1937.
[92] Cf. Degen-Ballmer, *Gott*, 60.

universality vs. particularity. He presented his outline in 1919 in a lecture in Cambridge, which was published in 1920 under the title "The Concept of Nature". Nature, for Whitehead, is not a substantial collection of static, isolated objects. He refers to the permanence of bodies as a derived quantity due to the organized process of becoming real individual beings in a society. Material nature, as well as our consciousness, are products of this becoming of a process. Nature, therefore, consists of innumerable events, which constitute themselves by processes. Therefore, nature is a process, which can also be called the course or progression of nature.[93]

Whitehead describes nature as an expansive process of development and as a structure of evolutionary processes. Thus, different structural principles interact and are characterized by interactions. For example, gravity, amino acids or an electromagnetic field. Therefore, speaking in terms of natural philosophy, nature is considered as reality. It is a reality that functions as a network of relationships. Nature can be determined as the reality that will come into being. Therefore, nature also refers to the creative and, thus, describes the reality of coming into being (central are principles of order and structures). Creation is the newness of coming into being (dynamics are central). Both poles – nature and creation – equally belong to the process and have an inner relation. By this determination, it succeeds neither to identify the two manifestations nature and creation nor to separate them from each other. Thereby both are scientifically and spiritually connected and secured.[94]

Process theologians often refer to themselves as panentheists, in that they relate creator and creature closely to each other, but do not identify them with each other. A precise definition of the terms "nature", "creation", and "world" is not available in process theology, so that they seem to be used interchangeably. The basic prerequisite is that world and nature are related to God, as a fundamental theological thought. Therefore, nature is creation. As an ethical consequence, it follows from this definition that nature cannot be neutral, as the natural sciences claim. Nature is assigned an intrinsic value that is independent of man. Such a thinking together of nature and creation also contributes to the joint work of natural sciences and humanities. Up to now, there has been, for the most part, a division of scientific research, which is not conducive to scientificity.[95]

---

93 Cf. Degen-Ballmer, *Gott*, 65.
94 Cf. Sander, Hans-Joachim, *Natur und Schöpfung – die Realität im Prozess: A.N. Whiteheads Philosophie als Paradigma einer Fundamentaltheologie kreativer Existenz*, Frankfurt a.M. et al: Peter Lang, 1991, 221f.; paragraph: cf. Degen-Ballmer, *Gott*, 88.
95 Cf. Sander, *Natur*, 223, paragraph: cf. Degen-Ballmer, *Gott*, 89.

L.S. Ford understands God in the context of process theology as a "dynamic source of increasing freedom and intensity of experience"[96]. H. Reitz describes God concretely with a terminology of "constructive", "stringent", "coherent", "relevant", "intelligible".[97] Along with the question of God, process theology also poses the question of evil in the world. It is answered with the ambivalence thesis, according to which suffering, along with enjoyment, is an inevitable consequence of creaturely freedom within creation's process of becoming. This is also reflected in our everyday experience with nature, because becoming and passing away as well as birth and death go into each other here. Because of this, in process theology, when dealing with evil, it is not spoken about in terms of eliminating it, but of overcoming it. What is meant by this is that the creaturely freedom can be used to keep the evil as small as possible. Therefore, according to Degen-Ballmer, a complaint about suffering in the world is also justified. The existence of suffering is unchangeable, but the exact constellation of suffering is not. It is worth pointing out an objection to process theology by W. Pannenberg. He criticizes that in process theology God is ascribed a limited power, which leads to the fact that evil and suffering can be dealt with more easily (in dependence on powers other than God), but at the same time the trust in God's overcoming of evil is devalued.[98]

According to this, there are various consequences for human beings in the context of ecological ethics: human beings are themselves part of the ecological problem and are called upon to act consciously as highly complex beings and in their freedom. Every human being can encounter evil, since evil is not presented as a counterpart to the divine. However, this also makes evil difficult to grasp, especially in relation to natural disasters or the suffering of uninvolved people in wars. Process theology offers a potential for change through human intervention alone and suggests that hope for such change is helpful.[99]

This is a fundamental modern approach for understanding the role of environment in Christianity today. Nevertheless, especially concerning certain fields, the Christian approach is important.

---

[96] Ford, Lewis S., *The Lure of God. A Biblical Background for Process Theism*. Fortress Press: Philadelphia 1978, 63.
[97] Reitz, Helga, "Was ist Prozess-Theologie?", *Kerygma und Dogma* 16.2 (1970), 78–103, here: 78.
[98] Cf. Degen-Ballmer, *Gott*, 130 f.
[99] Cf. Degen-Ballmer, *Gott*, 131.

3.3 Conclusion: Suffering

Another aspect of the systematic-theological question that deals with the significance of the environment in Christianity is reflected in the concept of suffering. With an understanding of creation as sustainable, that is, as existing under constant change, the suffering given by nature also goes along with this existing. The destruction of habitats as well as corrective statements towards previous generations must be avoided. This is especially true against the background of the self-interpretation of the creature. Examples are the intensive agricultural use of former rainforest areas, which are considered destroyed as a result, or the excessive use of groundwater and the resulting salinization of the soil. Also, permanent nuclear wastes are to be mentioned here.[100]

Moreover, and from a different perspective, theological research is not particularly known for quickly taking a position on current issues. But especially in the climate crisis there is a need for such a quick reaction. For this, theology must rethink its basic concepts in order to be able to take into account the signs of the times. One of these basic concepts is expressed in the term "God". Starting from the understanding of God as the alterity that interrupts immanence and supposed normality and, thus, paves the way for the Other, the question is obvious where God remains in the crisis. However, he is not explicitly missed among students who take to the streets in the Fridays for Future protest movement. Surveys among these young people revealed that God is not to be found at the demonstrations. Rather, the young people are afraid of losing their own future and demand fair and just life opportunities from governments and those in power.[101]

4 Contemporary Topics Concerning Environment

Below there are two issues that are addressed in the discussion about the environment in Christianity: biodiversity and sustainability.

---

100 Cf. Anselm, Reiner, "Schöpfung als Deutung der Lebenswirklichkeit", in: Schmid, Konrad (ed.), *Schöpfung*, Themen der Theologie 4, Tübingen: Mohr Siebeck, 2012, 225–294, here: 277.
101 Cf. Bederna, Katrin / Gärtner, Claudia, "Wo bleibt Gott, wenn die Wälder brennen?", *Herder Korrespondenz* 74.3 (2020), 27–29, here: 29.

4.1 Biodiversity

Firstly, a central topic of environmental ethics is biodiversity. The Convention on Biological Diversity (CBD), that was ratified in 1992, now counts 196 states that signed the 42 articles. One of the most central articles of the CBD is article no. 6 that claims:

> Each Contracting Party shall, in accordance with its particular conditions and capabilities:
>
> (a) Develop national strategies, plans or programmes for the conservation and sustainable use of biological diversity or adapt for this purpose existing strategies, plans or programmes which shall reflect, inter alia, the measures set out in this Convention relevant to the Contracting Party concerned; and
> (b) Integrate, as far as possible and as appropriate, the conservation and sustainable use of biological diversity into relevant sectoral or cross-sectoral plans, programs and policies.[102]

Therefore, biodiversity is a global requirement that shall be addressed by any state around the world. Because of its global necessity, it needs to be defined precisely. Biodiversity refers to a biological diversity and variability among living organisms from all sources, including, inter alia, terrestrial, marine, and other aquatic ecosystems and the ecological complexes of which they are part. It includes diversity *within* species and *between* species as well as diversity of ecosystems.

"Conserving biodiversity is a challenge, first because – according to the scientific consensus – biodiversity is declining at a dangerous rate. It should be noted that despite all the research efforts, many of the scientific statements on the development of biodiversity are characterized by a high degree of uncertainty. For example, the total number of existing species is unknown."[103] The most important indicator for the biodiversity loss is species extinction, but also natural, non-human-induced species extinction. In the history of the earth, there repeatedly have been major collapses. "In the long term, species extinction has been more than offset by the emergence of new species, which is why the world today is (still) near a maximum of species diversity in Earth history, despite human-caused species extinction."[104]

---

[102] CBD, "Convention Text", Article 6, https://www.cbd.int/convention/articles/?a=cbd-06, last access: 2021/02/28.
[103] Reder, Michael et al., *Umweltethik. Eine Einführung in globaler Perspektive*, Stuttgart: Verlag W. Kohlhammer, 2019, 123 [translation K.S.F.].
[104] Reder, *Umweltethik*, 124 [translation K.S.F.].

Christians are called to act against this loss of biodiversity with all its consequences.

4.2 Sustainability

Usually, sustainability is divided into ecological, economic, and social dimensions. Those three are fundamental but need to be complemented by the cultural dimension, which also appears in the UN Sustainable Development Goals.[105]

According to Vogt[106], sustainability can be understood as the basis for a new social contract. In this context, it is considered the leading, normative guiding principle of global environmental and development policy and forms a key principle of environmental ethics. The breadth of the concept of sustainability, which occasionally makes it seem diffuse, can be sorted by eight dimensions proposed by Vogt. He speaks of an ecological/silvicultural dimension, a political one, a justice-theoretical one, a socio-ecological one, a democratic one, a cultural one, a time-political one, and a theological one. In order to achieve an ethically appropriate understanding of sustainability, all eight dimensions are equally important and necessary.

Concretizing the ecological and silvicultural understanding of the term, which can be considered the original one, it is necessary to reflect on the concept of ownership. It is central to understand resource ownership as appropriation, which at the same time retains the earning power of what is owned (as *usus fructus*). Thus, man is not the owner of nature, because he did not create it. It remains the task of man not to consume more resources than can be newly formed in the same period of time. The core of sustainability, thus, intends the foresighted and prudent integration of the economy into ecological material cycles and rhythms. Vogt calls for an ethical-cultural anchoring of sustainability and political decisions that set the framework for the permissible use of nature.[107]

The political dimension received a boost from the 1992 UN conference in Rio de Janeiro, where a guiding principle for sustainable development was developed. According to this, three pillars are crucial and must be separated from each other: Ecology, economy, and social factors. It is neither an equation nor an equal coexistence, but the integration and networking, in the sense of retinity (that is overall networking), of these three pillars. Sustainability is, therefore, not

---

105 Cf. https://sdgs.un.org/goals, last access: 2021/10/26.
106 Cf. Vogt, *Christliche Umweltethik*, 482–505.
107 The following explications are based on Vogt, *Christliche Umweltethik*, 509–534.

the sum of social, ecological, and economic goals. This assumption would be a maximalist fallacy that would empty the term by infinite scope. Rather, sustainability refers to an interaction between ecological, social, and economic factors. It is a cross-cutting concept.

In terms of justice theory, reference should also be made to the UN Conference in Rio de Janeiro in 1992. The concept of justice was expanded there to include global and intergenerational aspects. Ethically, the distinction between equity and fairness remains to be discussed in the question of a theory of justice. Here, there is a lack of a differentiated theory of justice that makes an ethical approach to sustainability more challenging. The goal, however, must be to leave behind a world that offers sufficient freedom and means for future generations to make their own decisions. According to Vogt, what is needed is a comprehensive concept of the common good that considers global and ecological public goods such as the climate and water balance, as well as a differentiated theory of justice that understands the common good neither collectivistically nor egalitarianistically.

In socioeconomic terms, sustainability can be concretized as an effort to preserve the natural capital stock. This is done by using the notions of weak (substitution of natural capital is allowed) and strong (substitution not allowed) sustainability. The concept of resource becomes a methodologically problematic concept because it is considered a pre-social fact. However, contrary to this, it depends on technical and social development because of its benefit ratio. Strong sustainability keeps in view an interaction between socio-economic and ecological systems and can be linked to the extension of the concept of utility.

The democratic dimension is concretized in a model of openness in the shaping of sustainability. It is about a demand for co-design and the securing of a participatory democracy. Social innovation processes and the so-called change of values are also part of this. The active co-determination of the population must lead to an awareness of responsibility through recognition and co-design and encourage mature citizens to be resilient towards suggestions of the consumer society. The awareness-building together with a mind-shift is the heart and, at the same time, the engine of sustainability in a democratizing respect. Various problems that arise in this regard are only briefly mentioned: the high complexity of sustainability issues, the self-restriction through the fear for one's job, participation concepts (more precisely: such as those promoting acceptance, hardly offer real space for co-design).

With regard to the cultural dimension, sustainability stands for a new definition of the prerequisites, limits, and goals of progress. It is a matter of securing human habitats, avoiding risk and replacing the goal of the so-called "higher, faster, further". A culture of sustainability recognizes nature conservation as a task for all and integrates environmental quality as a fundamental value in the definition of prosperity. It does not see itself as maximizing growth, but as optimizing quality of life and opportunities for participation for as many as possible in the present and the future. The *Index of Sustainable Economic Welfare* can serve as a measure and control variable in this context. Eco-social development can be measured according to this.

In terms of time politics, humanity is currently so successful that it is destabilizing its own ecological niche through accelerated expansion. The problem of sustainability, therefore, specifically draws attention to the lack of synchronization of social and ecological rhythms. Nature does not have enough time to regenerate its resources and assimilate waste materials. Human progress as a non-stop society consuming energy and transportation is often associated with emancipation from biological rhythms. Vogt sees respect for and rediscovery of natural and social rhythms as a central development principle of sustainability.

Finally, the theological dimension should be mentioned. A change of course towards sustainable development can only succeed if religions share responsibility for it. The decisive corrective here is the awareness of one's own creatureliness, which points to the limits of human ability. Sustainability is not a management rule, but an attitude of mind that is nourished by reverence for creation and holds out the prospect of participation in its creative power. The specific competence of theological ethics lies in conveying a knowledge of critical orientation in the dialectic of progress and risk. Accordingly, the theological dimension suggests neither a promise of harmony and security, nor apocalyptic discourses of fear and guilt.

5 The Roman Catholic Church and Environment Nowadays

One explicitly Christian position on the environmental issue is that of the Roman Catholic Church. The Roman Catholic Church today expresses its interest in God's creation and environmental protection in many ways. Pope Francis can be described as an important player in sustainability issues.[108] With his environmental, social, and spiritual encyclical *Laudato Si'*, he expresses the importance

---

108 Cf. Schlögl-Flierl, Kerstin, "Papst Franziskus als Akteur für Nachhaltigkeit", in: Tögel, Jonas / Zierer, Klaus (eds.), *Nachhaltigkeit ins Zentrum rücken: Ein interdisziplinärer Zugang zu den wichtigsten Fragen unserer Zeit*, Baltmannsweiler: Schneider Verlag Hohengehren, 2020, 156–163.

and urgency of this topic. The encyclical is a milestone in the Christian interpretation of environment. It will be analyzed in the following.

5.1 *Laudato Si'* as a Turning Point for the Catholic Church

The title is taken from the Canticle of the Sun by Francis of Assisi, whose spirituality of joy, simplicity, and fraternal relationship with all fellow creatures is carried over by the encyclical.

5.1.1 St. Francis of Assisi's *Canticle of the Creatures*

The text reads:

> [1]Most High, all-powerful, good Lord,
>   Yours are *the praises*, *the glory*, and *the honor*, and all *blessing*,
> [2]To You alone, Most High, do they belong,
>   and no human is worthy to mention Your name. [...]
> [3]Praised be You, my *Lord*, with all *Your creatures*,
>   especially Sir Brother Sun,
>   Who is the day and through whom You give us light. [...]
> [4]And he is beautiful and radiant with great splendor;
>   and bears a likeness of You, Most High One.
> [5]*Praised* be You, my Lord, through Sister *Moon* and *the stars*,
>   in heaven You formed them clear and precious and beautiful. [...]
> [6]Praised be You, my Lord, through Brother Wind,
>   and through the air, cloudy and serene, and every kind of weather,
>   through whom You give sustenance to Your creatures.
> [7]*Praised* be You, my Lord, through Sister *Water*,
>   who is very useful and humble and precious and chaste.
> [8]*Praised* be You, my Lord, through Brother *Fire*,
>   through whom *You light the night*,
>   and he is beautiful and playful and robust and strong.
> [9]*Praised* be You, my Lord, through our Sister Mother *Earth*,
>   who sustains and governs us,
>   and who produces various *fruit* with colored flowers and *herbs*.
> [10]Praised be You, my Lord, through those who give pardon for Your love,
>   and bear infirmity and tribulation. [...]
> [11]Blessed are those who endure in peace
>   for by You, Most High, shall they be crowned.
> [12]Praised be You, my Lord, through our Sister Bodily Death,
>   from whom no one living can escape. [...]

¹³Woe to those who die in mortal sin.
   Blessed are those whom death will find in Your most holy will,
     for *the second death* shall do them no harm. [...]
¹⁴*Praise* and *bless* my *Lord* and give Him thanks
     and serve Him with great humility.[109]

5.1.2 An Analysis of the Encyclical

Encyclicals are considered letters containing papal teaching of the highest order, but do not have infallibility status. They deal with fundamental theological and social questions that are of (mostly current) interest and articulate a binding position. The encyclical *Laudato Si'* can be described as scientific and theological: scientific in the sense that the Pope draws on the findings of quantum theory, the theory of relativity, ecosystem research, and especially the theory of evolution. Equally, it is a theological positioning that also takes other religions and the pluralistic society into consideration.

It was published in 2015 – with a positive influence on the ratification of the Paris Climate Agreement adopted the following autumn – and is considered particularly vivid due to the Latin American tradition of expressing oneself in a language that is particularly rich in images. Many examples from people's everyday lives are given to help put what is said into practice. Two prayers conclude the encyclical: a Christian one and an interreligious one.

The ecological metaphor, which can be found in the title, "House of the Earth", is a multi-layered play on words: House (Greek *oikos*) is associated with ecology, economy, and ecumenism. Building on this, an ecological concern is programmatically linked with economic questions as well as the claim of worldwide ecumenism across the borders of nations, denominations, religions, and scientific disciplines.

Pope Francis distinguishes within the ecology, as an overall term between different forms of ecology: environmental ecology, economic ecology, social ecology (*Laudato Si'*, no. 138 ff.), cultural ecology (*Laudato Si'*, no. 143 ff.), and the ecology of everyday life (*Laudato Si'*, no. 147 ff.). Part of the ecology of everyday life is also human ecology. This terminology brings to mind the equally named research branches of the various sciences. This means, by way of example, that when the encyclical speaks of cultural ecology, it does not mean the shaping of cultures by their environment, but rather – following liberation theological

---

[109] Canticle of the Creatures, in: *Francis of Assisi: Early Documents*, vol. 1, New York-London-Manila: New City Press, 1999, 113–114, Italics in origin.

debates about inculturation – the process of making cultures conform by human consumerism. This leads to the disappearance of a culture, which can be just as difficult as the disappearance of an animal or plant species.[110]

The encyclical is structured as follows: Part I is an intensive dialogue with various environmental sciences. In this situation analysis, the pollution of the planet Earth is noted. The first chapter deals with the question of what is happening to our House. In the second part follows the theological-ethical judgement. It begins with chapter two, which is entitled the "Gospel of Creation". This is followed by chapter three describing the human root of the ecological crisis and chapter four with the construction of a holistic ecology. Part III is now a practical one, dealing with political-social and pedagogical-spiritual assessments and implications. More specifically, chapter five proposes guidelines for orientation and action, and chapter six addresses ecological education and spirituality.

5.1.3 Certain Eco-Social Issues and Biocentric Perspectives

Vogt classifies the encyclical's specific perspective on eco-social issues through the following four features: he begins with a catastrophe-theoretical approach. It states that ecological capacities are largely overloaded, the stability of ecological systems is endangered, and the habitats of countless people are acutely threatened. Second is a socio-ecological approach, which focuses on the fundamental links between environmental and justice issues and states that global and intergenerational justice cannot be achieved without environmental protection. The third is an eco-theological approach. This follows up on the cry of God's creation and the related plight of the poor, which is a challenge for the church and a call to revise the Christian understanding of nature. Fourthly, and thus finally, Vogt proposes a liberation-theological approach. *Laudato Si'*, thus, not only formulates ethical postulates, but also programmatically addresses questions of power, corruption, and systemic undesirable developments.[111]

Another approach is a biocentric approach. According to this, every living entity contains an intrinsic value. Contrary to modern despotic anthropocentrism, a biocentric approach can be classified in a much more moderate way.

---

[110] Cf. Bederna, Katrin, *Every Day for Future. Theologie und religiöse Bildung für nachhaltige Entwicklung*, Ostfildern: Matthias Grünewald Verlag, 2019, 68.
[111] Cf. Vogt, Markus, "Ein neues Kapitel der katholischen Soziallehre. Ganzheitliche Ökologie – Eine Frage radikal veränderter Lebensstile und Wirtschaftsformen", *AMOS International* 9 (2015), 3–10.

The prominent position of the human being as the image of God (*imago Dei*) is placed in a new and biblical context.

5.1.4 "Environment" and "Sustainability" in *Laudato Si'*

The terms environment and sustainability are mentioned directly as more specific topics. *Laudato Si'*'s contribution to environmental ethics is characterized by a clear concern for the common House, the proposal of house rules for the solidary use of global resources, the recognition of the climate and some basic environmental resources as collective goods of humanity (this corresponds to a further development of Thomas Aquinas' theory of property), and the extension of the common good obligation of property to the climate (*Laudato Si'*, no. 23–25).

In concrete terms, this means that in *Laudato Si'* the climate is conceived as a collective good, which has far-reaching consequences for state and societal obligations to protect the climate. The water and food crisis, which is closely linked to climate change, is called a central challenge. Both virtue and norm ethics are presented here. A total of 55 times, a renewal of lifestyle is mentioned, calling for an "ecological conversion". The issue is a public one for Pope Francis. The cultural change in relation to nature creates a gain in quality of life, economic rationality, and social community (*Laudato Si'*, no. 191).

The concept of sustainability is treated less strongly than the term environment. However, it is used as a conceptual basis.

5.1.5 Criticism on *Laudato Si'*

Criticism can also be levelled at the encyclical. The impact of market-based mechanisms is underestimated, especially regarding emission certificates, for example. Personal virtues and moral concepts are also solely appellative, but not sufficiently structurally conceived and demanded. There is a primarily ethically motivated guideline and no concrete conclusions from it. A sufficiency strategy is pursued that focuses solely on the level of the individual actor. Population growth is also not sufficiently considered.[112]

---

[112] See for example Möhring-Hesse, Matthias, "Gelobt seist Du, nicht aber die 'jetzige Wirtschaft': zur Wirtschaftskritik in Franziskus' Öko–Sozial–Enzyklika", *AMOS International* 9.4 (2015), 26–27, 30–35.

Criticism, therefore, can be found mainly in matters of detail and less in the basic duct. One such point of criticism, for example, is that in the search for causes, overall blame is assigned to the financial markets, consumerism, and the technocratic paradigm. The argumentation of *Laudato Si'* enables a differentiated view of the constellation of responsibility in consumption. Attributions of responsibility do not only depend on causal attributions, but form a persistent structural question.

Recommendations for action that result from *Laudato Si'* can be found on the level of politics, such as the demand for a privileged participation of the population (*Laudato Si'*, no. 183) in the economy or companies, an internalization of negative external effects (*Laudato Si'*, no. 195) and, across the board, in the introduction of obligatory environmental impact assessments. Marianne Heimbach-Steins and Nils Stockmann[113] draw attention to the role of the churches as agents of change. The aim is to understand *Laudato Si'* as an encouragement for ecological conversion. It is inductively carrying out a three-step process: Perceiving the social challenge ("seeing"), analyzing and evaluating it against the background of the faith, more precisely, the theological tradition ("discerning") and orienting it towards an altered practice ("acting").

5.1.6 *Laudato Si'* in the Context of the Global South and Interreligious Studies

Following on from the Apostolic publication, *Evangelii gaudium*, Pope Francis draws attention to the great debt of the affluent countries to the poor of the global South. The universal common good loses credibility in comparison to particular interests. The key message of the encyclical follows the pattern of Old Testament prophecy: The prophetic gesture is found (for example in comparison with Hos 5:12f.) not only in the prophetic accusation, but also in following the call and invitation to conversion (compare Hos 6:1–6), given that the addressees are interested in the knowledge of the Lord (Hos 6:3).

Pope Francis expresses his concern about building alliances that are as broad as possible. In the banner of his "option for the poor", to which he also counts the earth itself, he sends clear ecumenical and interreligious impulses, for example, the appreciation of the creation-theological position of Patriarch

---

[113] Cf. Heimbach-Steins, Marianne / Stockmann, Nils, "Ein Impuls zur 'ökologischen Umkehr' – Die Enzyklika Laudato si' und die Rolle der Kirche als Change Agent", in: Heimbach-Steins, Marianne / Schlacke, Sabine (eds.), *Die Enzyklika Laudato si'. Ein interdisziplinärer Nachhaltigkeitsansatz?*, Baden-Baden: Nomos, 2019, 11–54.

Bartholomew (*Laudato Si'*, no. 8f.), or the quotation of a Muslim mystic as a crown witness of a creation spirituality. Compared to previous papal publications, this strategy of citation and simultaneous opening to a broad spectrum of the world church is new. This also includes the fact that not only Church representatives were present at the presentation of the encyclical in Rome, but also the Greek Orthodox Metropolitan, Johannis Zizioulas, the climate researcher, and then deputy director of the Potsdam Institute for Climate Impact Research, Hans Joachim Schellnhuber, and the American economist, Caroline Woo.[114]

5.1.7 Pope Francis' Ecophilosophy: Krausism

In sum, one might state that Pope Francis develops an Ecophilosophy, based intellectually on the following predecessor. Karl Christian Friedrich Krause (1781–1832), a student of Friedrich Wilhelm Joseph Schelling (1775–1854), elaborates an ecophilosophy that criticizes the anthropocentrism of idealistic subject philosophy. He is considered the namesake of so-called Krausismo (a panentheistic cosmology), which Pope Francis also takes up. Aside from Schelling, Krause never comprehensively joined his other teacher, Johann Gottlieb Fichte (1762–1814). Krause's criticism of Fichte's anthropocentrism refers to the free act on the world. According to him, Fichte erred in assuming a world to which one freely relates. Rather, the world exists only through processing by human freedom. Without such, it has no meaning and intrinsic value. A dualism arises between the realm of the rational (freedom) and one of the irrational realms (necessity of nature). Thus, free action of man is always in opposition to nature.[115]

Krause speaks philosophically of man as the guardian and caretaker of nature; despite an earthly primacy of man, his prerogatives are linked to a duty of care and concern. Theologically speaking, human beings are gardeners in God's garden. One is allowed to enjoy environment and nature; destroying them is not allowed.

Pope Francis, in a similar fashion to Krause's philosophy, assumes an intrinsic value of plants and animals (*Laudato Si'*, no. 33). Against a sharp contrast between man and nature, he speaks of "human beings who, as part of the world, have the duty to cultivate their abilities in order to protect it and develop

---

114 Cf. Gabriel, Ingeborg, "Die Enzyklika 'Laudato Si'". Ein Meilenstein in der lehramtlichen Sozialverkündigung", *Internationale katholische Zeitschrift Communio* 44.6 (2015), 639–646, here: 639.
115 Cf. Dierksmeier, Claus, *Umwelt als Mitwelt. Die päpstliche Enzyklika Laudato si' und der argentinische krausismo*, Kirche und Gesellschaft 428, Köln: J.P. Bachem Medien, 2016, 7.

its potential" (*Laudato Si'*, no. 78). According to Krausism, *Laudato Si'* says: "By virtue of our unique dignity and our gift of intelligence, we are called to respect creation and its inherent laws" (*Laudato Si'*, 69). In the treatment of other living beings, a human moral witness is revealed (*Laudato Si'*, no. 92).[116]

5.2 Amazon Synod

The topic of environment has also been actively addressed at the so-called Amazon Synod of October 2019. It resulted in a Holy See publication entitled: *Post-Synodal Apostolic Exhortation Querida Amazonia of Pope Francis to the People of God and to All People of Good Will*, dated 2 February 2020, which looks at the region of Amazonia, in "its splendour, its tragedy and its mystery" (no. 1), to which the Synod in Rome, from 6 to 27 October 2019, was dedicated. The Synod concluded in the document *Amazonia: New Directions for the Church and for a Holistic Ecology.*

The post-synodal apostolic exhortation calls for indignation just as Moses in Ex 11:8 and Jesus in Mark 3:5 *indignated* (compare likewise God's wrath in Am 2:4–8; 5:7–12 and Ps 106:40). The social conscience should not allow itself to be numbed, but should be alert to the evil and dangers that farmers and indigenous people in Amazonia are exposed to (no. 15).

At the same time, it conveys an ecological vision that assumes that life in a cultural landscape like Amazonia, where nature and human beings are in a close relationship with each other, always has a cosmic dimension. Supporting and helping the people of Amazonia is an expression of opening one's heart to a God who, in addition to his creation, has given himself to us in Jesus Christ (no. 41).

Care for people and the ecosystem in which they live must be accepted as inseparable. The forest can be seen as a being that must be respected and protected in its existence just as we humans do. Respectful and careful treatment of the Amazonian region avoids any abuse and secures the future of our common coexistence (no. 42).

A poet of the Amazonian natives describes Amazonia as follows:

The world suffers from the transformation of the feet into rubber, the legs into leather, the body into cloth and the head into steel [...]. The world suffers from the transformation of the spade into a gun, the plough into a war tank, the image of the sower sowing into a robot

---

[116] Cf. Dierksmeier, *Umwelt*, 13.

with its flamethrower, from whose seed sprout deserts. Only poetry, with the humility of its voice, will be able to save this world. (no. 46[117])

In addition to the large forests in Congo and Borneo, the rainforest in Amazonia also plays a crucial role as a carbon dioxide filter in order to maintain the balance of the planet. The rainy seasons and a great diversity of living creatures on earth also depend on it. It is crucial to know that, when the forest is cut down, it will not grow back as it was before. The area will become desert-like and devoid of vegetation (no. 48).

Protecting and caring for the region also includes using today's technical knowledge and processes. This must always be done while respecting the lifestyle and value system of the inhabitants (no. 51). No information should be withheld from them.

A holistic ecology, as it is necessary for the protection of the region, also goes hand in hand with corresponding educational aspects, which cannot be ignored alongside political, technical, legal, and social aspects. Unfortunately, a lifestyle characterized by consumerism has also spread in the Amazon regions. Making people aware of a fraternal approach to the environment and educating them in their behavior in the sense of a healthy and sustainable ecology is also part of the great ecological vision (no. 58).

With the Amazon Synod in Rome in October 2019, Roman Catholic environmental ethics has attracted special attention from the Universal Church. The Amazon basin is considered a treasure trove of the world's biodiversity and carries global significance for the future viability of human civilization. The Roman Catholic Church is, thus, part of an international solidarity movement and makes an appeal to the states for a participatory international environmental policy.

However, the connection between nature conservation and the legal protection of local indigenous peoples from Latin America (pachammam, buenvivir) is dwelled upon. Gerhard Kruip relates Pope Francis' Latin American background to his appreciation of indigenous wisdom, with reference to the "cry of the poor" and the "cry of Mother Earth." The link to the socio-ecological concept of the good life ("buen vivir") also emanates from his Latin American background. Pope Francis, thus, ties in the new and growth-critical model of the "good life" that originated there.[118]

---

117 Following: De Moraes, Vinicius, *Para vivir un gran amor*, Buenos Aires: Ediciones de la Flor, 2013, 166.
118 Cf. Kruip, Gerhard, "Buen Vivir – Gut leben im Einklang mit Mutter Erde", *AMOS International* 9.4 (2015), 11.

The so-called Rio Conference refers to a UN conference on environment and development that took place in Rio de Janeiro in 1992. Environmental protection and poverty reduction go hand in hand: The concept of sustainable development was coined at the conference and it combines both, environmental protection and poverty reduction. Leonardo Boff, as an exemplary representative, stands for numerous liberation theologians who contributed. He drew on indigenous ideas in his contributions and used, for example, the concept of "Mother Earth"[119]. This denotes the worship of an all-powerful goddess, for example, "Pacha mama" in Andean religions, which is common in many Native American cultures. The concept of a "good life" is part of the constitutions of Ecuador (2008) and Bolivia (2009) initiated by various indigenous peoples. Evo Morales (Bolivia) and Rafael Correa (Ecuador) had previously been opposition forces coming to power under left-leaning presidents who were also supported by indigenous peoples.[120]

According to Pope Francis, a conception of the good life means the demand for a dignified life, the meaning of which must be struggled for. It is worth fighting to be able to live well and in dignity.[121] Moreover, indigenous peoples take a lead role for all other people on earth when it comes to a conversation of biodiversity.[122] A paradigm of holistic ecology with a close interconnectedness of human beings and nature is presented. The diversity and beauty of nature in the Amazon basin are expressed through creation-theological and poetic texts.

Particularly the environmental spirituality is pushed forward, which was, from a theological point of view, introduced years before the Amazon synod. See as an example Karl Bopp.

5.3 Ecological Pastoral Ministry and Creation Spirituality

Karl Bopp proposes a program of ecological pastoral ministry in which he distinguishes between an external dimension of the Church – which means: witnessing to the faith of creation in dialogue with the world – and an internal dimension of the Church – which means: confessing faith in creation in dialogue with God. God and his truth of salvation must be witnessed on the one side, in the world through the proclamation of the Gospel (in the form of the Creator

---

119 Cf. Boff, Leonardo, *Die Erde ist uns anvertraut. Eine ökologische Spiritualität*, Kevelaer: Butzon & Bercker, 2010.
120 Cf. Kruip, *Buen Vivir*, 13.
121 Cf. Kruip, *Buen Vivir*, 16.
122 Cf. Vogt, *Christliche Umweltethik*, 228.

God), diakonia (to the threatened creation itself) and prophetic as well as pathic witness (against the destruction of creation). The koinonia of sisters and brothers must confess and celebrate faith on the other side. This is done through the liturgy (prayer and celebration of the sacraments), magisterial confession (creed), and situational confession. In this form of congregational catechesis, each person's own baptismal confession unfolds and is built up into a contemporary spirituality of creation. In the interaction of these two levels with each other, a witnessing and confessing arises in equal measure, which has God as the Creator of the world and of the whole cosmos, connected with the hope of a new heaven and a new earth at its center.[123]

This creation spirituality understands itself as an open search, challenged by questions of the world, for the will of God in the context of the crisis of creation. Its elements and major themes, in the context of the inner-Church creation dialogue, are: the biblical tradition of the covenant between God and his people (including the whole creation), the praise of the Creator God who creates and sustains life, the incarnational faith (in Jesus Christ the Creator God has turned to the earth), the sacramental understanding of creation, the Sabbath order of creation with the specification of a temporal rhythm, and the hope for the Adventus of God as the fulfillment of the whole creation.[124]

The diaconal task of the Church in the context of creation care must be understood as universal solidarity. The Creator God as God of all people is, thus, the basic assumption of an ecological pastoral care. It must, therefore, also be a concern of the Church to preserve humane foundations of life for future generations.[125] The care of creation and the preservation of the living space for all creatures is today an indispensable practice of a Christian faith in creation.[126]

The Church acts as an advocate for creation. This happens explicitly in a 2006 declaration by the German bishops on climate change.[127] There, reference is made to the Christian responsibility for creation to preserve planet Earth as a sustainable home for all creatures. It advocates an image of humanity that also considers the dignity of human beings in relation to their living conditions. An

---

123 Cf. Bopp, Karl, "Nachhaltigkeit als Basis einer Ökologischen Pastoral", *Pastoraltheologische Informationen. Durcharbeiten und Erinnern*, 30.2 (2010), 217–242, here: 238.
124 Cf. Bopp, *Nachhaltigkeit*, 240.
125 Cf. Bopp, *Nachhaltigkeit*, 241.
126 Cf. Vogt, Markus, "Schöpfung. VIII. Schöpfung und Evolution", in: *Lexikon für Theologie und Kirche*, vol. 9, ³2000, 236–239, here: 239.
127 Cf. Die deutschen Bischöfe – Kommission für gesellschaftliche und soziale Fragen/Kommission Weltkirche, *Der Klimawandel: Brennpunkte globaler, intergenerationeller und ökologischer Gerechtigkeit*, Bonn 2006, no. 9.

attitude of global solidarity is demanded, especially in reference to the responsibility as a Universal Church for the poor and excluded. All people are taken into consideration when it comes to a willingness to rethink and act for the preservation and shaping of a creation that is fit for humanity and the environment. The focus is on long-term thinking in terms of intergenerational justice of the kingdom of God and its righteousness, as well as on a spirituality that enables people to dare and peacefully realize jointly lived responsibility for creation.[128]

Rich sources of creation spirituality are found in Franciscan and Benedictine spirituality. Benedictine spirituality includes praise of creation, reverence for things and people, right measure, living in the rhythm of creation, and mindfulness as well as attention. The right measure is particularly emphasized in Benedictine creation spirituality. Life according to God is characterized by the fact that it is immediately a healthy life. Neither consumption nor distraction are to be striven for, according to Benedict. Rather, it is about the right measure and its observance, the attentive contemplation of the moment and the restriction to what is meaningful and moderate. This also corresponds to the order of life. Franciscan spirituality stands out as less balanced and moderate, but rather radical. Poverty and humility are in focus and expressed in the love of nature.[129] Anton Rotzetter[130], who pursued such a spirituality, can be mentioned here as an example.

So far, the Roman Catholic perspective has been presented. In the following, the view is opened for the ecumenical context, which plays a decisive role in the common protection of the environment.

6 Ecumenical Approach: Anthroporelationality

6.1 Roman Catholicism and Protestantism

Ursula Lorenz presents a Protestant-Catholic comparison by relating the positions of both sides to each other.[131] On the Protestant side, she starts with Albert Schweitzer and his biocentric environmental ethics. This is based on his princi-

---

[128] Cf. Bopp, *Nachhaltigkeit*, 241 f.
[129] Cf. Kleyboldt, Ewald, *Nachhaltigkeit braucht Spiritualität. Antworten aus Christentum und Buddhismus als Beitrag der Religionen*, München: oekom, 2019, 25–39.
[130] Cf. Rotzetter, P. Anton, *Die Freigelassenen. Franz von Assisi und die Tiere*, Freiburg: Paulusverlag, 2011.
[131] Cf. Lorenz, Ursula, *Umweltethik – ein evangelisch-katholischer Vergleich*, Göttingen: Vandenhoeck & Ruprecht, 2013.

ple of reverence for life,[132] which was later adopted by Erich Gräßer[133] and Günter Altner[134].

6.1.1 Protestant Perspectives

Two other Protestant representatives of an environmental ethic based on the concept of God are Sigurd Daecke[135] and Jürgen Moltmann.[136] Daecke proceeds from the assumption of the immanence of God and rejects anthropocentrism and any form of a superior position of mankind. God's creation in the form of nature has an intrinsic value with its own rights and is protected by its Creator. It is, therefore, a theocentric approach to environmental ethics, which understands nature as sacred and places human beings right into nature. Moltmann's justification of environmental ethics can be understood as anti-anthropocentric, emphasizing the immanence of God and the special rights of nature. His position could be described as physiocentric, since the equality and significance of nature are emphasized and human beings appear increasingly insignificant in a possible superior role.

The enormous diversity in Protestant justifications of environmental ethics roots in a fundamental issue: the construction of an environmental ethic from the perspective of the doctrine of God or on the basis of anthropology (here more precisely: God's image of man, sinfulness).

---

132 A collection of important writings for Schweitzer's "Ehrfurcht des Lebens" can be found in the second volume of his collected works: Schweitzer, Albert, *Gesammelte Werke*, vol. 2, ed. by Rudolf Grabs, München: C.H. Beck, 1974.
133 Cf. for example Gräßer, Erich, "Ehrfurcht vor dem Leben", in: Röhrig, Eberhard (ed.), *Der Gerechte erbarmt sich seines Viehs. Stimmen zur Mitgeschöpflichkeit*, Neukirchen-Vluyn: Neukirchener, 1992, 92–103.
134 Cf. for example Altner, Günter, *Naturvergessenheit. Grundlagen einer umfassenden Bioethik*, Darmstadt: Wissenschaftliche Buchgesellschaft, 1991.
135 Cf. for example Daecke, Sigurd M., "Säkulare Welt – sakrale Schöpfung – geistige Materie. Vorüberlegungen zu einer trinitarisch begründeten Praktischen und Systematischen Theologie der Natur", *Evangelische Theologie* 45 (1985), 261–276.
136 Cf. for example Moltmann, Jürgen, *Gott in der Schöpfung. Ökologische Schöpfungslehre*, vol. 5, *Werke*, Gütersloh: Gütersloher Verlagshaus, 2016 (1985). Moltmann, Jürgen, *God in creation: Gott in der Schöpfung: an ecological doctrine of creation; the Gifford lectures 1984–1985*, London: SCM Press, 2005.

6.1.2 Roman Catholic Perspectives

On the Roman Catholic side, the starting point is Alfons Auer as a classical and much-cited anthropocentrist.[137] For him, mankind experiences a superior position, especially in relation to animals and the rest of the world surrounding mankind. Sometimes he is read as too rigid, which is why tendencies towards a moderate anthropocentrism or an anthroporelational environmental ethics are becoming more popular in the Roman Catholic discussion. One example of this is Wilhelm Korff, who argues strongly for the dignity of the human being as a person as the only justification for environmental ethics.[138]

Hans J. Münk proposes another Roman Catholic position as a compromise between the various existing approaches: anthroporelationality.[139] In this approach, an explicit superior position is not ascribed to the human being, but it is seen as a responsible subject in relation to what surrounds him or her. This makes clear that human beings, by virtue of their own creatureliness, are part of the whole of creation and equally hold the position of the authorized and entitled governor there. Human activity, as an intervention in the divine creation, must, therefore, always be thought through with its consequences in mind, and the intrinsic value of the non-human – which is to be distinguished from the human – must be respected.

Hans-Joachim Höhn takes a very similar position, regarding human beings as likewise created in the context of nature.[140] He tries to establish two aspects: the great dignity of the human being and the value of the non-human. Following this, he separates the spheres of God and mankind as well as mankind and animals from each other. According to that, relationality refers to all actors in creation.

Thus, on the Roman Catholic side, also with regard to magisterial texts, it can be stated that the homogeneous position is that of a moderate anthropocentrism or anthroporelationality. The human being has a superior position that embeds him or her equally in the environment but does not make him or her abso-

---

137 Cf. Auer, Alfons, *Umweltethik. Ein theologischer Beitrag zur ökologischen Diskussion*, Düsseldorf: Patmos, 1984.
138 Cf. Korff, Wilhelm, "Schöpfungsgerechter Fortschritt. Grundlagen und Perspektiven der Umweltethik", in: *Herder Korrespondenz* 51 (1997), 78–84.
139 Cf. i.a. Münk, Hans J., "Grundzüge einer christlich-theologischen Umweltethik im Kontext heutigen ökologischethischen Denkens", in: Imfeld Stiftung (ed.), *Ethik und Menschenbild* vol. 1, Schriften der Imfeld-Stiftung, Cuxhaven: Junghans, 1992, 65–82.
140 Cf. Höhn, Hans-Joachim, *Ökologische Sozialethik. Grundlagen und Perspektiven*, Paderborn: Ferdinand Schöningh, 2001.

lute. Mankind as an image of God (*imago Dei*) and as a governor, combined with its creatureliness, describes human existence on earth. Responsibility for fellow creatures goes hand in hand with this existence.

In summary, it can be stated that "[a]s far as Christian creation ethics is concerned [...] an anthroporelational approach suggests itself, which refers to the human being as a subject of responsibility, but does not understand this as a contradiction to the recognition of the intrinsic value of animals, plants and ecosystems, but as their epistemic precondition"[141].

6.2 Roman Catholicism and the Orthodox Tradition

The Roman Catholic and Protestant panorama of important theological figures concerning environment has been presented. The focus is now placed on the Orthodox tradition. An important and decisive figure for the Orthodox theology of creation is the so-called "green" Patriarch Bartholomew I.[142] He is the Primate (the honorary head) of a church with more than 250 million believers worldwide. Firstly, he is the bishop of the Orthodox Christians in Constantinople/Istanbul, and secondly, he is the chairman of the Synod of the Patriarchate of Constantinople, which is responsible for all those who are under the canonical jurisdiction of this church. Thirdly, he is the head of the Orthodox bishops and may take initiatives to secure, deepen, or restore unity. He is also responsible for coordinating the work of the 14 autocephalous Orthodox churches worldwide. However, he does not have the jurisdictional powers of the Pope.[143]

---

[141] Vogt, *Christliche Umweltethik*, 54 [translation K.S.F.].
[142] See also: Theokritoff, Elizabeth, "Green Patriarch, Green Patristics: Reclaiming the Deep Ecology of Christian Tradition", *Religions* 8.7 (2017), 116.
[143] Cf. Vlantis, Georgios, "*Der 'grüne' Patriarch Bartholomaios I. Orthodoxe Initiativen zur Bewahrung der Schöpfung*", Lecture on the Symposium Schöpfungs-Verständnis und praktizierte Schöpfungs-Verantwortung verschiedener Religionen/Konfessionen, Zentrum für Umwelt und Kultur (ZUK), monastery Benediktbeuern, on October 21, 2017. He was born in 1940 on the island of Gökceada (Greek: Imbros) and studied theology in Turkey, more precisely in Chalki (Princes Island), in Bossey (Switzerland), Munich and Rome. In Rome, he obtained his doctorate and was ordained deacon in 1961. On October 22, 1991, the Synod of the Patriarchate of Constantinople elected him Ecumenical Patriarch. Among his great merits in 27 years of service were the revival of the synodal structures of Orthodoxy (a highlight being the convening of the Holy and Great Council of Crete in 2016), the promotion of ecumenical and interreligious dialogue (especially Judaism and Islam), and the strengthening of the witness of Christians in global society. He has received countless awards for this (cf. Vlantis, *Patriarch*, 1f.).

6.2.1 A Shared Starting Point for Creation Theology

Starting in the 1970s with Pope Paul VI's letter *Octogesima adveniens,* the tradition of caring about planet Earth was continued by Pope John Paul II, Pope Benedict XVI and Pope Francis (especially in *Laudato Si'*). Nevertheless, Orthodox and Roman Catholic church leaders follow the same common vision in issues related to the future of humanity, which is also demonstrated by the joint meetings they've held in the past years. Ecology is, therefore, an important concern of the Orthodox and Roman Catholic churches. Pope Francis and Patriarch Bartholomew try to contribute through speeches, letters, and works at the same time as they are holding meetings and practical actions for promoting a new lifestyle. The principles of the Bible and the perpetuation of life in a happy and healthy way will be particularly focused upon.[144]

6.2.2 The Orthodox Tradition: Patriarch Bartholomew

He takes his theological approach to the environmental crisis from the traditional Christian doctrine of creation, which functions because of the ontological distinction between the uncreated and the created. This means, that the Orthodox's respectful attitude towards nature does not function out of a pantheistically understood holiness of nature, but through nature being ontologically radically different from the uncreated God. This does not result in a Manichean bipolarity, but in an image of creation arising from God's love. The act of creation is, thus, a gift of God to all creatures. Each creature is a fruit of divine love, care, and wisdom, and, thus, represents an imprint of divine generosity and the object of the Creator's care.[145]

In the Orthodox Church, which, in the tradition of the Greek concept of nature, is less addicted to dualistic-Western conceptions, there are quite different approaches also to ecological questions. It is based on a dynamic concept of nature, which is contrary to the Western tradition. The Western tradition assumes nature as a thing (natura as res, which is disposed of). The high value of liturgy in the Orthodox tradition can also be found in ethical considerations. Vogt suggests speaking of an "ecology of the spirit"[146] and emphasizes the hymnic ap-

---

144 Cf. Morariu, Iuliu-Marius, "Ecology – Main Concern for the Christian Space of the 21st Century? Catholic and Orthodox Perspectives", *Journal for the Study of Religions and Ideologies* 19.56 (2020), 124–135, here: 133.
145 Cf. Vlantis, *Patriarch*, 3.
146 Vogt, *Christliche Umweltethik*, 280 [translation K.S.F.].

proach to an understanding of liturgy that opposes all inner-worldly idolatry of things.[147]

In the Orthodox tradition, there is also criticism of the constant growth of prosperity and unbridled consumption. Natural resources are, thus, not used appropriately. Like man, creation apart from man also experiences the consequences of human sin (compare Rom 8:20–22). The ecological crisis and climatic changes make it the duty of the churches to use their spiritual resources for the preservation of creation. This means further to work against the spiritual impoverishment of mankind through its greed for gratification, but pointing to the belonging of the natural wealth of the earth to God, the Creator. The Orthodox Church is committed to the protection of God's creation, emphasizing man's responsibility towards creation. Reference is made to future generations, who have a right to natural resources from our Creator. To this end, virtues of frugality and abstinence help.[148]

Current for Orthodox theology is the document of a thirteen-member working group of theologians entitled, "For the Life of the World. Towards a Social Ethos of the Orthodox Church". It was published in 2020. It is a document of the ecumenical patriarchate that collects and records in writing topics that have already been discussed and negotiated in public. It deals with the preservation of creation and human rights and the fight against the causes of flight and nationalism.[149]

Patriarch Bartholomew emphasizes the anthropocentrism of creation, that is, man as the crown and goal of all created things. Cosmologically, the focus is on harmony and inner logic, which are liturgical-doxological in nature in the form of anthropocentrism. In this, man is the priest of creation, directing the cosmic doxology of God and bringing it to a climax in the celebration of the Eucharist. Human beings bear responsibility for preserving the integrity of the cosmos, according to Gen 9:1, and do not legitimize the immoderate exploitation of natural resources in the context of self-centered interests. The Bible gives expression to the praise of God through the beauty and harmony of the cos-

---

[147] Cf. Vogt, *Christliche Umweltethik*, 280.
[148] Cf. "Der Auftrag der Orthodoxen Kirche in der heutigen Welt", Translated by Archpriest Radu Constantin Miron, *Orthodoxie Aktuell* 7 (2016), 23–30, quoted from: *Orthodoxes Forum* 31.1+2 (2017), 199–200.
[149] Cf. Elsner, Regina, "Weiterer Schritt auf dem Weg zu einer orthodoxen Sozialethik. For the Life of the World. Towards a Social Ethos of the Orthodox Church. Dokument des Ökumenischen Patriarchats, veröffentlicht durch die Griechisch-Orthodoxe Erzdiözese von Amerika, Fastenzeit 2020", *AMOS International* 14.3 (2020), 42–45.

mos. Violation of this beauty constitutes an interruption of God's cosmic doxology and is contrary to the will of the Creator.[150]

Prayer is a mode of expressing man's relationality and describing the sacrality of the world. Prayer gives strength and inspiration for shaping human life according to the will of God, which is done in harmony with the natural environment.[151]

The Patriarch calls for an apophatic attitude, that is, an attitude characterized by awareness of the limits of knowledge, of language, and of all human capacities. The mystery of God exists prior, to which people bow down and express their admiration through a pious silence. Silence is not understood as sinful passivity, but as an introduction to the awareness of human limits. He speaks of "eco-silence" that allows the cries of nature to be heard. He refers to the words of the Philokalia, a collection of mystical sayings of the Church Fathers: if you find your own self in silence, you will also find God and the whole world.[152]

Patriarch Bartholomew received the title of honorary doctorate on May 16, 2014, from the Ludwig-Maximilians-University in Munich. In the laudation, in addition to his other merits, reference is made to his commitment to the preservation of creation. It is to be appreciated that he recognized early on the inner interconnectedness of ecology, sustainable development, and social justice, and that he also theologically located social and environmental ethical challenges posed by global climate change and addressed them in their repercussions on human existence. He brought this challenge into the scientific-theological discourse in the field of environmental ethics. According to him, ecological awareness, like the transformation of hearts and community, grows out of God's grace and is to be understood as *metanoia*. Humanity must transform its habits and lifestyle.[153] He also highlights the ecological question as a theological one, to be integrated into inner-Christian and interreligious dialogue.[154]

Iuliu-Marius Morariu points out that the Orthodox and Roman Catholic Church try to raise awareness in the public space on ecology through lectures, conferences, and practical actions. However, the Roman Catholic tradition is older in doing so than the Orthodox one.

---

150 Cf. Vlantis, *Patriarch*, 4.
151 Cf. Vlantis, *Patriarch*, 6.
152 Cf. Vlantis, *Patriarch*, 9.
153 Cf. Patriarch Bartholomaios, "Verwandlung erfordert Metanoia. Gedanken zum Thema der 9. ÖRK–Vollversammlung", *Orthodoxie aktuell* 10.3 (2006), 3.
154 Cf. Bischof, Franz Xaver, "Ehrenpromotion des Ökumenischen Patriarchen Bartholomaios Laudatio", *Münchener Theologische Zeitschrift* 66 (2015), 2–10, 5.

6.2.3 The Cooperation of Roman Catholicism and the Orthodox tradition

Kevin Mongrain writes about Pope Francis and the ecumenical Patriarch (of Constantinople), Bartholomew, that both are trying to take up the challenge of re-spiritualizing Christianity in the Anthropocene age. They are in agreement about the support for their members in environmental issues, also across cultural and religious lines. They distinguish cosmocentric theology (pantheism and animism) and theocentric cosmology (monotheism centered on the incarnation of the Trinity in creation) because both believe that the environmental crisis roots in the modern culture's anthropocentric ethos. Pope Francis specifically aims for a retrieval of St. Francis' relationship to the natural world, elaborated by Ignatius of Loyola to a discipline of learning to see God's glory in all created things. In opposition to modern capitalism and its "disciplined avarice in action", the monastic-Franciscan-Ignatian spiritual ethos of "disciplined contemplation in action" is advocated by Bartholomew and Francis.[155]

They met in November 2014 and took a stand on working together in environmental and climate change issues. The cooperation of Eastern and Western churches is essential for this shared ecumenical vision.[156] Bartholomew has published several texts on environmental issues for more than 25 years.[157] He counts as the inspirator of a new subgenre in Orthodox theology and he approves the human-caused climate change.[158]

In comparison to Bartholomew, Pope Francis presents a more philosophical approach to the causes of the looming catastrophe. He ascribes the environmental crisis to our existential disposition in relation to the world around us as it is known from Heideggerian philosophy tinged with Martin Buber's "personalist" theology of I and Thou.[159]

Both of them know in all their claims that, according to Max Weber, "asceticism moved out of the monastic cells and into working life", which means that the world cannot be put back into monastic cells. However, they favor the simplicity of life and its lifestyle. According to Mongrain, "the monks and those who share their theology can leave their cells and steal back the ascetic ethos that

---

155 Cf. Mongrain, Kevin, "The Burden of Guilt and the Imperative of Reform: Pope Francis and Patriarch Bartholomew Take Up the Challenge of Re-Spiritualizing Christianity in the Anthropocene Age", *Horizons* 44 (2017), 80–107, here: 80.
156 Cf. Mongrain, *Burden*, 87.
157 A bibliography and links to the patriarch's publications, speeches, addresses, and other documents can be found at https://www.patriachate.org/publications.
158 Cf. Mongrain, *Burden*, 89 f.
159 Cf. Mongrain, *Burden*, 92.

was plagiarized and perverted by Puritans and their capitalist descendants".[160] The original ascetic ethos signifies a sense of gratitude and the rediscovery of beauty and not a dualism or denial. Gratitude, in Bartholomew's writings, is an interpretation of the sacrament of Eucharist and in this sense understood from its etymological background as gratitude and thankfulness (from the Greek *eukharistia*). As "ascetic" and "eucharistic" belong together, the eucharistic gratitude and the theme of beauty of life on Earth do. This is reflected by Bartholomew in the meaning of the Christian sacrament of Eucharist.[161]

Bartholomew and Francis guide their churches in participation in the wider and global dialogue about climate change in order to stop the environmental destruction. They symbolize the constructive role of organized religion against the coming crisis and try to gain respect for their churches and their message through presenting a credible and sophisticated well-defined position in saving the Earth from the human-made catastrophe. This might convince people of their cosmological message of finding God's beauty in nature. Simple living, repentance, breaking free of obsessive-compulsive consumerism are their proposed options. The message of a "green apocalypse" might be the message the next generation of the earth's inhabitants will be ready and willing to receive. This way of life will be centered on learning to see and participate without reserve in the ongoing process of God's incarnation. This process started with Jesus Christ followed by his disciples and is now called "New Evangelization" by Pope Francis. It roots back to the ancient evangelization of the monastic, Hesychast strand of the Christian tradition as indicated by Bartholomew.[162]

6.2.4 Other Perspectives in the Orthodox Tradition Concerning Environmental Ethics

Apart from Bartholomew, there are other Orthodox designs of an environmental ethic, as well. One example is Elizabeth Theokritoff, who presents an Orthodox Christian ecology as a "theological understanding of humans-in-the-world", a "spiritual ecosystem"[163]. Both, ecu-mene – the inhabited earth, the human community – and eco-system, built the elementary components of the Church's eco-

---

[160] Cf. Mongrain, *Burden*, 97.
[161] Cf. Mongrain, *Burden*, 99.
[162] Cf. Mongrain, *Burden*, 106 f.
[163] Theokritoff, Elizabeth, *Living in God's Creation. Orthodox Perspectives on Ecology*, Foundations Series 4, Crestwood/New York: St. Vladimir's Seminary Press, 2009, 29.

logical vision. According to Theokritoff, the questions that need to be addressed are:

> What does it mean to see the material world as God's creation?
> What is the spiritual significance of the material world, its relation to God?
> In what sense is God apart from the universe, and in what sense is he present in it?
> Is the rest of nature 'fallen' as a result of human sin?
> [...]
> What does it mean to be a material creature, yet fashioned in God's image and likeness?
> What is the role played by other people and other creatures in our relationship with God, and His with us?[164]

Theokritoff answers these questions by estimating the Church's tradition, explicitly the Church Fathers, who lead into an "ethos of 'taking part in the celebration.'"[165] This includes liturgy as well as the Eucharist and ascetics.[166] In addition, Theokritoff rephrases the slogan "think globally, act locally" for the Orthodox Christian tradition to "think cosmically, act personally" and combines this with the process of metanoia.[167] The concept of every human being as a priest of creation, which she refers to, reveals two consequences for the Orthodox Christian ecology: firstly, the understanding of human work on nature together with transformations within nature, while not reducing "human creativity and international action to the level of waters weathering a rock".[168] And secondly, the actual emphasis on the transformation of nature through art and technology, which can be both: used for good or used for ill. Human creativity can, therefore, be an offering for creation.[169]

7 Ecotheology

Subsequently, the question will be answered as to whether an independent ecotheology can be developed based on this great appreciation of the environment in Christianity.

---

164 Theokritoff, *Creation*, 29.
165 Theokritoff, *Creation*, 255.
166 Cf. Theokritoff, *Creation*, 255.
167 Cf. Theokritoff, *Creation*, 256.
168 Cf. Theokritoff, *Creation*, 261.
169 Cf. Theokritoff, *Creation*, 261.

Ecotheology presents itself as a distinct theological approach to the environment. It is understood as creation-theological environmental ethics. It symbolizes today's place, within which the question of God in theology is kept alive.

Four guiding concepts of creation-theological environmental ethics can be found.[170] The first is the image of God. This means that man, as a moral subject, freely determines himself. This results in a special dignity for man, which at the same time leads to a special responsibility. In general, moral subjects are necessary to be able to recognize the value of life and of being human at all.

The second guiding concept is co-creativity. Man is created together with all other creatures by God. At the same time, this prohibits man from seeing his fellow creatures only to an end. Respect for fellow creatures is a necessary consequence of God's love.

The third guiding concept is reverence. More specifically, it is an attitude of reverence that continually rediscovers and protects the integrity and beauty of creation during suffering and conflict. This means that it is not individual norms and rules that are to be practiced, but a basic attitude. Joy and gratitude are key principles for this, as well as respectful regard for the goods and living beings of creation.

The fourth guiding concept is that of the theology of the gift. The goods of creation are gifts of God for all living beings. Thus, they are not to be thought of in terms of scarcity or competition, but in terms of gifts and a logic of giving, sharing, and abundance.

> It follows that basic environmental goods, such as a stable climate compatible with human life, access to clean water, the availability of fertile soil, or biodiversity, are common goods. Accordingly, property rights relevant to these are always subject to the condition that the global and intergenerational dimensions of the common good are not violated when dealing with basic natural goods.[171]

For a new approach in theological terms to Christian environmental ethics, Vogt calls for the four aforementioned guiding concepts to be thought of together. The special dignity of man as the image of God in no way negates his integration into nature. In his creative responsibility and its concrete implementation, man comes to his creative destiny and identity.[172]

---

170 Cf. Vogt, *Christliche Umweltethik*, 211 f.
171 Vogt, *Christliche Umweltethik*, 212 [translation K.S.F.].
172 Cf. Vogt, *Christliche Umweltethik*, 212.

Moreover, Vogt calls for a profound remeasurement of the relationship between human beings, nature, and God.[173] Thereby, it is demarcated against pantheistic concepts, at the same time the diversity of religious views of nature is in focus. There are also similarities between the religions in this respect. Vogt characterizes Jewish ecotheology as a "search for traces of the face of God in the world"[174], whereas Islamic environmental ethics can be clearly seen in a field of tension between radical criticism of modernity and practice-oriented legal principles of an ecological Sharia.[175]

8 Movements and Practical Examples

In addition to these doctrinal statements and theological approaches, the environmental commitment has many practical dimensions, such as environmental movements, initiatives, and practical examples.

Firstly, the World Council of Churches (WCC) is considered a pioneer of the environmental movement among all religions. In the 1970s, it positioned itself on the side of the global environmental movement and used the slogan of a "sustainable society" for the first time at the 1974 WCC conference on "Science and Technology for Humane Development" in Bucharest. This called for a comprehensive orientation of social development and the inclusion of ecological carrying capacities.[176] Other conferences also took place; prominent among these was the conciliar process initiated in Vancouver in 1983, which brought the ecosocial approach with topics such as environmental protection, global justice, and peace into the three catchwords: "justice, peace and integrity of creation".[177] Responsibility for creation, thus, became an essential dimension of the Church's commitment.

There were further assemblies in Dresden (1988 and 1989), also in Stuttgart (1988), but especially in Basel (1989), which initiated a broad and effective church movement.[178] On environmental issues, an inner-Christian ecumenism quickly emerged, recognizing that it was worthwhile and helpful to address the key issues together.

---

173 Cf. Vogt, *Christliche Umweltethik*, 268.
174 Vogt, *Christliche Umweltethik*, 268 [translation K.S.F.].
175 Cf. Vogt, *Christliche Umweltethik*, 268.
176 Cf. Vogt, *Christliche Umweltethik*, 277.
177 Vogt, *Christliche Umweltethik*, 278 [translation K.S.F.].
178 Cf. Rosenberger, Michael, *Was dem Leben dient. Schöpfungsethische Weichenstellungen im konziliaren Prozeß der Jahre 1987–89*, Stuttgart/Berlin/Köln: Kohlhammer, 2001.

Secondly, the so-called Rio-Process of the United Nations is characterizing because of its content and personnel. The ecumenical document "For a Future in Solidarity and Justice", written in 1997, uses the concept of sustainability again, however, linking it neither to the WCC, nor to the Conciliar Process, but to the UN Conference in Rio de Janeiro. This also resulted in the Reformed World Alliance formulating an approach in the 1980s that granted rights to nature as an extension of human rights.[179]

Thirdly and parallel to the United Nations wide processes around the Sustainable Development Goals (SDGs) (to be implemented in 2030), an ecumenical process under the 2017 slogan: "Umkehr zum Leben. Wandel gestalten" ("Conversion to Life. Shaping Change") is taking place. This deals with central topics such as responsibility for creation and sustainability.

Fourthly, on the Protestant side, the Evangelical Church in Germany (EKD) has also set up a chamber for sustainable development, which is centrally concerned with ecotheological issues.

Thus, it can be observed across various denominations that environmental ethical thinking leads to the idea of transformation or conversion. This way of thinking is clearly different from the classical Roman Catholic natural law, which functions as a way of thinking in terms of order. Also cosmically shaped nature ethics, such as in Buddhism or Taoism, express this order thought. An explicit critique of society is expressed, and environmental ethics as an ethic of transformation relates directly to the lifestyles of believers.[180] This is evident not only in church statements and publications, but also in everyday interaction within church congregations and parishes. Church environmental management according to the European EMAS standard (Eco-Management and Audit Scheme) as an ecumenical initiative enjoys great popularity and creates a vital network for the practical implementation of environmental protection on site. More than 1000 church institutions participate in it. Only one other example out of many is the ecumenical network for climate justice[181], which unites church institutions with a special concern for climate justice, ecology, and support for developing countries. Churches, thus, emerge as the largest environmental management group in the non-profit sector in Germany.

---

[179] Cf. Vogt, *Christliche Umweltethik*, 280.
[180] Cf. Vogt, *Christliche Umweltethik*, 280f.
[181] Cf. https://www.kirchen-fuer-klimagerechtigkeit.de/, last access: 2021/06/22.

Conclusion

The question of the environment in Christianity is not a simple one. The most urgent one to ask, is the question of moral psychology: How do we get from ought to willingness and acting?

> The overcoming of static models in the understanding of nature or creation also contributes enormously to the conceptual development of environmental ethics. Here, especially process philosophy and theology in the tradition of Alfred North Whitehead have opened up fundamentally new perspectives that are far from being explored in environmental ethics.[182]

The environment serves as a space, in which theologians can move away from the idea of the burden of the thesis that Christianity is responsible for the exploitation of the environment. Vogt stresses the meaning of the cross and the resurrection as trusting elements for the Christian hope. Human failure that is dependent on mercy and the possibility of a new beginning, puts its future in God's hands to reach the kingdom of God.[183]

For the future, the living conditions that are given must not be assumed to be static. They are subject to constant change. This is also noticeable in the fact that the adherence to an always same order structure does not constitute the creation-appropriate organization of the living conditions. Rather, it is the preservation of future viability for the individual and his fellow human beings as well as for subsequent generations. An ethics based on creation as man's self-interpretation regards the natural foundations of life as particularly worthy of protection. The history of human life always takes the form of a life story that relates to what it finds. The extra-human belongs to the self-understanding and self-interpretation of the individual existence of man just as much as the human and, therefore, becomes the subject of ethics and theology.[184]

In addition, because of the environmental crisis, Christians must change their theological teaching. It is only in this way, that they can actively contribute to an overcoming of the crisis. It is necessary to conceive an anthropology that understands the human being together with and in dependence on his co-creation. Man does not exist detached from his environment, more precisely: the non-human. The being-there and being-so of man goes back to a co-evolutionary process of the human and the non-human and expresses mutual dependence.

---

[182] Vogt, *Christliche Umweltethik*, 54 [translation K.S.F.].
[183] Cf. Vogt, *Christliche Umweltethik*, 158 [translation K.S.F.].
[184] Cf. Anselm, *Schöpfung*, 276 f.

Before any theological interpretation, it is important to realize this as a theologian.[185]

Bibliography

Primary Literature

"Der Auftrag der Orthodoxen Kirche in der heutigen Welt", Translated by Archpriest Radu Constantin Miron, *Orthodoxie Aktuell* 7 (2016), 23–30, quoted from: *Orthodoxes Forum* 31.1+2 (2017), 199–200.

Augustine, *Concerning the City of God against the Pagans*, trans. John O'Meara, London: Penguin Books, 1972.

Augustine, *The Enchiridion: on Faith, Hope, and Love*, trans. J.F. Shaw, Henry Paolucci (ed.), Chicago: Regnery Gateway, 1961.

Augustine, *The Trinity*, trans. Stephen McKenna, Washington, DC: Catholic University of America Press, 1963.

Basil of Caesarea, On the Hexaemeron, in: *Exegetic Homilies*, trans. Sister Agnes Clare Way, Fathers of the Church 46, Washington, DC: Catholic University of America Press, 1963.

Francis of Assisi, Canticle of the Creatures, in: *Early Documents*, vol. 1, New York-London-Manila: New City Press, 1999, 113–114.

Bundesminister für Umwelt, Naturschutz und Reaktorsicherheit (ed.), *Bericht der Bundesregierung über die Konferenz der Vereinten Nationen*, Bonn: Köllen Druck + Verlag GmbH, 1994.

Die deutschen Bischöfe – Kommission für gesellschaftliche und soziale Fragen/Kommission Weltkirche, *Der Klimawandel: Brennpunkte globaler, intergenerationeller und ökologischer Gerechtigkeit*, Bonn 2006.

Encyclical Letter Caritas In Veritate of the Supreme Pontiff Benedict XVI to the Bishops Priests and Deacons Men and Women Religious the Lay Faithful and all People of Good Will on Integral Human Development in Charity and Truth, Rome 2009.

Encyclical Letter Laudato si' of the Holy Father Francis on Care for our Common Home, Rome 2015.

Schweitzer, Albert, *Gesammelte Werke*, vol. 2, Rudolf Grabs (ed.), München: C.H. Beck, 1974.

The ESV® Bible (The Holy Bible, English Standard Version®), adapted from the Revised Standard Version of the Bible, copyright Division of Christian Education of the National Council of the Churches of Christ in the U.S.A.

United Nations, *Convention on Biological Diversity*, 1993, CBD, "Convention Text", https://www.cbd.int/convention/articles/?a=cbd-06, last access: 2021/02/28.

Vlantis, Georgios, *"Der 'grüne' Patriarch Bartholomaios I. Orthodoxe Initiativen zur Bewahrung der Schöpfung"*, Lecture on the Symposium Schöpfungs-Verständnis und

---

[185] Cf. Enxing, Julia, "Und Gott schuf den Erdling", *Herder Korrespondenz* 74.3 (2020), 24–26, here: 26.

praktizierte Schöpfungs-Verantwortung verschiedener Religionen/Konfessionen, Zentrum für Umwelt und Kultur (ZUK), monastery Benediktbeuern, Saturday 2017/10/21.

Secondary Literature

Anselm, Reiner, "Schöpfung als Deutung der Lebenswirklichkeit", in: Schmid, Konrad (ed.), *Schöpfung*, Themen der Theologie 4, Tübingen: Mohr Siebeck, 2012, 225–294.
Auer, Alfons, *Umweltethik. Ein theologischer Beitrag zur ökologischen Diskussion*, Düsseldorf: Patmos, 1984.
Barr, James, "Man and Nature. The Ecological Controversy and the Old Testament", *Bulletin of the John Rylands Library* 55 (1972/73), 1–28.
Bederna, Katrin, *Every Day for Future. Theologie und religiöse Bildung für nachhaltige Entwicklung*, Ostfildern: Matthias Grünewald Verlag, 2019.
Bederna, Katrin / Gärtner, Claudia, "Wo bleibt Gott, wenn die Wälder brennen?", *Herder Korrespondenz* 74.3 (2020), 27–29.
Bischof, Franz Xaver, "Ehrenpromotion des Ökumenischen Patriarchen Bartholomaios Laudatio", *Münchener Theologische Zeitschrift* 66 (2015), 2–10.
Boff, Leonardo, *Die Erde ist uns anvertraut. Eine ökologische Spiritualität*, Kevelaer: Butzon & Bercker, 2010.
Bopp, Karl, "Nachhaltigkeit als Basis einer Ökologischen Pastoral", *Pastoraltheologische Informationen. Durcharbeiten und Erinnern*, 30.2 (2010), 217–242.
Crutzen, Paul, "The Geology of mankind", *Nature* 415 (2002), 23.
da Silva, Jorgiano dos Santos, *Füllet die Erde und macht sie euch untertan! (Gen 1,28). Strukturen einer alttestamentlich begründeten Schöpfungstheologie und deren Konsequenzen für eine biblisch orientierte Umweltethik*, Münster: LIT, 2018.
Daecke, Sigurd M., "Säkulare Welt – sakrale Schöpfung – geistige Materie. Vorüberlegungen zu einer trinitarisch begründeten Praktischen und Systematischen Theologie der Natur", *Evangelische Theologie* 45 (1985), 261–276.
Degen-Ballmer, Stephan, *Gott – Mensch – Welt. Eine Untersuchung über mögliche holistische Denkmodelle in der Prozesstheologie und der ostkirchlich-orthodoxen Theologie als Beitrag für ein ethikrelevantes Natur- und Schöpfungsverständnis*, Frankfurt a. M. et al.: Peter Lang, 2001.
De Moraes, Vinicius, *Para vivir un gran amor*, Buenos Aires: Ediciones de la Flor, 2013.
Dierksmeier, Claus, *Umwelt als Mitwelt. Die päpstliche Enzyklika Laudato si' und der argentinische krausismo*, Kirche und Gesellschaft 428, Köln: J.P. Bachem Medien, 2016.
Ebach, Jürgen, "Bild Gottes und Schrecken der Tiere. Zur Anthropologie der priesterlichen Urgeschichte", in: id., *Ursprung und Ziel. Erinnerte Zukunft und erhoffte Vergangenheit. Biblische Exegesen, Reflexionen, Geschichten*, 16–47, Neukirchen-Vluyn: Neukirchener, 1986.
Elsner, Regina, "Weiterer Schritt auf dem Weg zu einer orthodoxen Sozialethik. For the Life of the World. Towards a Social Ethos of the Orthodox Church. Dokument des Ökumenischen Patriarchats, veröffentlicht durch die Griechisch-Orthodoxe Erzdiözese von Amerika, Fastenzeit 2020", *AMOS International* 14.3 (2020), 42–45.
Enxing, Julia, "Und Gott schuf den Erdling", *Herder Korrespondenz* 74.3 (2020), 24–26.

Ford, Lewis S., *The Lure of God. A Biblical Background for Process Theism*. Fortress Press: Philadelphia 1978.

Gabriel, Ingeborg, "Die Enzyklika 'Laudato Si'". Ein Meilenstein in der lehramtlichen Sozialverkündigung", *Internationale katholische Zeitschrift Communio* 44.6 (2015), 639–646.

Gräßer, Erich, "Ehrfurcht vor dem Leben", in: Röhrig, Eberhard (ed.), *Der Gerechte erbarmt sich seines Viehs. Stimmen zur Mitgeschöpflichkeit*, 92–103, Neukirchen-Vluyn: Neukirchener, 1992.

Hartshorne, Charles, *Beyond Humanism: Essays in the Philosophy of Nature*, Chicago: Willet Clark & Co, 1937.

Heimbach-Steins, Marianne / Stockmann, Nils, "Ein Impuls zur 'ökologischen Umkehr' – Die Enzyklika Laudato si' und die Rolle der Kirche als Change Agent", in: Heimbach-Steins, Marianne / Schlacke, Sabine (eds.), *Die Enzyklika Laudato si'. Ein interdisziplinärer Nachhaltigkeitsansatz?*, 11–54, Baden-Baden: Nomos, 2019.

Höhn, Hans-Joachim, *Ökologische Sozialethik. Grundlagen und Perspektiven*, Paderborn: Ferdinand Schöningh, 2001.

Janowski, Bernd, "Herrschaft über die Tiere. Gen 1,26–28 und die Semantik von רדה", in: id., *Die rettende Gerechtigkeit. Beiträge zur Theologie des Alten Testaments 2*, 33–48, Neukirchen-Vluyn: Neukirchner, 1999.

Kessler, Rainer, "'Eine Grenze hast du gesetzt' (Ps 104,9). Psalm 104 im Horizont globaler Krisen", *Bibel und Kirche* 76.1 (2021), 22–27.

Kleyboldt, Ewald, *Nachhaltigkeit braucht Spiritualität. Antworten aus Christentum und Buddhismus als Beitrag der Religionen*, München: oekom, 2019.

Koch, Klaus, "Gestaltet die Erde, doch hegt das Leben! Einige Klarstellungen zum *dominium terrae* in Genesis 1" (1983), in: id., *Spuren des hebräischen Denkens. Beiträge zur alttestamentlichen Theologie. Gesammelte Aufsätze 1*, Bernd Janowski/Martin Krause (eds.), 223–237, Neukirchen-Vluyn: Neukirchener, 1991.

Korff, Wilhelm, "Schöpfungsgerechter Fortschritt. Grundlagen und Perspektiven der Umweltethik", in: *Herder Korrespondenz* 51 (1997), 78–84.

Kruip, Gerhard, "Buen Vivir – Gut leben im Einklang mit Mutter Erde", *AMOS International* 9.4 (2015), 11–18.

Link, Christian, *Schöpfung. Schöpfungstheologie angesichts der Herausforderungen des 20. Jahrhunderts*, Handbuch Systematischer Theologie 7/2, Gütersloh: Mohn, 1991.

Lohfink, Norbert, "'Macht euch die Erde untertan'?" (1974), in: id., *Studien zum Pentateuch*, SBAB 4, 11–28, Stuttgart: Verlag katholisches Bibelwerk, 1988.

Lohfink, Norbert, "Die Priesterschrift und die Grenzen des Wachstums", in: id., *Unsere großen Wörter. Das Alte Testament zu Themen dieser Jahre*, 156–171, Freiburg et al.: Herder, 1977.

Lorenz, Ursula, *Umweltethik – ein evangelisch-katholischer Vergleich*, Göttingen: Vandenhoeck & Ruprecht, 2013.

Marlow, Hilary, *Biblical Prophets and Contemporary Environmental Ethics. Re-Reading Amos, Hosea, and First Isaiah*, Oxford: Oxford University Press, 2009.

Maurer, Reinhart, "Ökologische Ethik als Problem", in: Bayertz, Kurt (ed.), *Ökologische Ethik*, 11–30, München/Zürich: Schnell & Steiner, 1988.

Möhring-Hesse, Matthias: "Gelobt seist Du, nicht aber die 'jetzige Wirtschaft': zur Wirtschaftskritik in Franziskus' Öko-Sozial-Enzyklika", *AMOS International* 9.4 (2015), 26–27.30–35.
Moltmann, Jürgen, *God in creation: Gott in der Schöpfung: an ecological doctrine of creation; the Gifford lectures 1984–1985*, London: SCM Press, 2005.
Moltmann, Jürgen, *Gott in der Schöpfung. Ökologische Schöpfungslehre*, vol. 5, *Werke*, Gütersloh: Gütersloher Verlagshaus, 2016 (1985).
Mongrain, Kevin, "The Burden of Guilt and the Imperative of Reform: Pope Francis and Patriarch Bartholomew Take Up the Challenge of Re-Spiritualizing Christianity in the Anthropocene Age", *Horizons* 44 (2017), 80–107.
Morariu, Iuliu-Marius, "Ecology – Main Concern for the Christian Space of the 21st Century? Catholic and Orthodox Perspectives", *Journal for the Study of Religions and Ideologies*, 19.56 (2020), 124–135.
Münk, Hans J., "Grundzüge einer christlich-theologischen Umweltethik im Kontext heutigen ökologischethischen Denkens", in: Imfeld Stiftung (ed.), *Ethik und Menschenbild* vol. 1, 65–82, Schriften der Imfeld-Stiftung, Cuxhaven: Junghans, 1992.
Norwich, Julian of, *Showings*, trans. Edmund Colledge/James Walsh, New York: Paulist Press, 1978.
Ott, Konrad / Dierks, Jan / Voegt-Kleschin, Lieske (eds.), *Handbuch Umweltethik*, Stuttgart: J.B. Metzler Verlag, 2016.
Patriarch Bartholomaios, "Verwandlung erfordert Metanoia. Gedanken zum Thema der 9. ÖRK-Vollversammlung", *Orthodoxie aktuell* 10.3 (2006).
Reder, Michael et al., *Umweltethik. Eine Einführung in globaler Perspektive*, Stuttgart: Verlag W. Kohlhammer, 2019.
Reitz, Helga, "Was ist Prozess-Theologie?", *Kerygma und Dogma* 16.2 (1970), 78–103.
Riede, Peter, "Mensch und Welt in der Sicht des Alten Testaments. Am Beispiel von Psalm 104", in: id., *Schöpfung und Lebenswelt. Studien zur Theologie und Anthropologie des Alten Testaments*, Leipzig: Evangelische Verlagsanstalt 2009, 101–117.
Rosenberger, Michael, *Was dem Leben dient. Schöpfungsethische Weichenstellungen im konziliaren Prozeß der Jahre 1987–89*, Stuttgart/Berlin/Köln: Kohlhammer, 2001.
Rotzetter, P. Anton, *Die Freigelassenen. Franz von Assisi und die Tiere*, Freiburg: Paulusverlag, 2011.
Schaefer, Jame, *Theological Foundations for Environmental Ethics. Reconstruction Patristic and Medieval Concepts*, Washington: Georgetown University Press, 2009.
Sander, Hans-Joachim, *Natur und Schöpfung – die Realität im Prozess: A.N. Whiteheads Philosophie als Paradigma einer Fundamentaltheologie kreativer Existenz*, Frankfurt a. M. et al: Peter Lang, 1991.
Schmitz, Barbara, "Der Mensch als 'Krone der Schöpfung'. Anthropologische Konzepte im Spannungsfeld von alttestamentlicher Theologie und moderner Rezeption", *Kirche und Israel* 27.1 (2012), 18–32.
Schlögl-Flierl, Kerstin, "Papst Franziskus als Akteur für Nachhaltigkeit", in: Tögel, Jonas / Zierer, Klaus (eds.), *Nachhaltigkeit ins Zentrum rücken: ein interdisziplinärer Zugang zu den wichtigsten Fragen unserer Zeit*, 156–163, Baltmannsweiler: Schneider Verlag Hohengehren, 2020.
Theokritoff, Elizabeth, "Green Patriarch, Green Patristics: Reclaiming the Deep Ecology of Christian Tradition", *Religions* 8.7 (2017), 116.

Theokritoff, Elizabeth, *Living in God's Creation. Orthodox Perspectives on Ecology*, Foundations Series 4, Crestwood/New York: St. Vladimir's Seminary Press, 2009.
Uehlinger, Christoph, "Vom dominium terrae zu einem Ethos der Selbstbeschränkung? Alttestamentliche Einsprüche gegen einen tyrannischen Umgang mit der Schöpfung", *Bibel und Liturgie* 64 (1991), 59–74.
Vogt, Markus, "Schöpfung. VIII. Schöpfung und Evolution", in: *Lexikon für Theologie und Kirche*, vol. 9, ³2000, 236–239.
Vogt, Markus, "Ein neues Kapitel der katholischen Soziallehre. Ganzheitliche Ökologie – Eine Frage radikal veränderter Lebensstile und Wirtschaftsformen", *AMOS International* 9 (2015), 3–10.
Vogt, Markus, *Christliche Umweltethik. Grundlagen und zentrale Herausforderungen*, Freiburg et al.: Herder, 2021.
Vollenweider, Samuel, "Wahrnehmungen der Schöpfung im Neuen Testament", *Zeitschrift für Pädagogik und Theologie* 55 (2003), 246–253.
Zenger, Erich, *Gottes Bogen in den Wolken. Untersuchungen zu Komposition und Theologie der priesterschriftlichen Urgeschichte*, SBS 112, Stuttgart: Verlag katholisches Bibelwerk ²1987.

Suggestions for further reading

Deane-Drummond, Celia / Artinian-Kaiser, Rebecca (eds.), *Theology and Ecology Across the Disciplines: One Care for Our Common Home*, London: International Clark, 2018.
Deane-Drummond, Celia / Bergmann, Sigurd / Vogt, Markus (eds.), *Religion in the Anthropocene*, London: The Lutterworth Press, 2018.
Northcott, Michael S., *Place, Ecology, and the Sacred. The Moral Geography of Sustainable Communities*, London: Bloomsbury, 2015.
Rosenberger, Michael, *Eingebunden in den Beutel des Lebens. Christliche Schöpfungsethik*, Münster: Aschendorff Verlag, 2021.
Steck, Christopher W., *All God's Animals. A Catholic theological framework for animal ethics*, Washington D.C.: Georgetown University Press, 2019.

Yasin Dutton
The Concept of Environment in Islam

Introduction

As is frequent now, and for good reason, we start with the verse in Sūrat ar-Rūm (Qur'ān, 30:41), as do many writers and speakers on environmental matters:

"Corruption (*fasād*) has appeared on the land and the sea because of what people's own hands have brought about, to give them a taste of what they have done, that hopefully they will return."

Fasād is not an easy word to translate. Many people suggest "corruption", but that suggests a moral element, which is not necessarily present. I prefer to think of "messed-up-ness", even if it is not so mellifluous. You can for example, mess up some cooking, or anything else that you can spoil, and *fasād* would be an appropriate word to use for the concept. "Despoliation" is perhaps along the right lines, although it may seem a little too strong for such everyday purposes. Also, I am assuming a meaning of messing up the environment; it may be that the idea of *fasād* does in fact relate to a quality in our actions, and thus our being, and not just the result in the world around us. But the environmental meaning is definitely there.

Whatever a good translation might be, there is no doubt that we are spoiling our environment. We are polluting the land and the sea, including the earth and the soil beneath us, the rivers and the lakes around us, and even the air we breathe. Our inner cities may be obviously polluted, but so too is our countryside and farmland, including the very soil we use to grow our crops, and therefore to feed our cattle and, directly or indirectly, ourselves. And the run-off from the fields, with all its pesticide and/or fertilizer residues, goes into our rivers and eventually the sea.

The above verse – "Corruption (*fasād*) has appeared on the land and the sea because of what men's hands have done" – indicates firstly the concept of the environment, referred to here as "the land and the sea". It also indicates that "the land and the sea" is the arena for man's actions. So what is it that we have done? And how might one be able to counteract it? In other words, is there a diagnosis and, if so, what is the cure?

Before we consider this broader question, let us look first at the basic terminology and the sources for the concept of the environment in the textual sources of the Qur'ān and the *ḥadīṯ*.

1 The Basic Terminology of the Concept in Arabic

Firstly, we note that, although both the Qur'ān and the ḥadīṯ are in Classical Arabic, there is no word in Classical Arabic for "the environment". There is a word in Modern Arabic, and that word is *"bī'a"*. If you look at the classical dictionaries, they tell you that the verb *bā'a, yabī'u* means "to come back to", and that the word *bī'a* means "home, dwelling, inn" (Hava's Dictionary). This allows us to say that our environment is, quite literally, our "home", and the place we "come back to." It is of note that the prefix "eco" in words such as "economics" and "ecology" refers to the Greek word *oikos*, meaning "household", "home" or "place to live", thus bearing a very similar meaning to the classical Arabic word *bī'a*. Applying this to the above verse, it is clear that we have, basically, messed up our home.

Secondly, one has to remember that man is part of the picture. There is no boundary between man and his environment; one blends seamlessly into the other. Expanding the focus a little further, one can mention the Sufi understanding that man is the universe writ small, and the universe is man writ large.

This understanding of a unity to existence is part of what the Muslims understand by *tawḥīd*, or affirmation of oneness – meaning, to understand a oneness and connectedness to the world. From this point of view, we can understand that whatever we do to the environment, we are in fact doing to ourselves.

1.1 The Environment in the Qur'ān

There are many verses in the Qur'ān that have a bearing on the concept of the environment in Islam. As a start-point, we shall consider the following five examples.

Example 1. Sūrat an-Naḥl, "The Chapter of the Bees", (Q. 16:3–17):

> 3. He created the heavens and the earth with truth. He is exalted above anything they associate with Him.
>
> 4. He created man from a drop of sperm and yet he is an open challenger!
>
> 5. And He created livestock. There is warmth for you in them, and various uses, and some you eat.
>
> 6. And there is beauty in them for you, in the evening when you bring them home, and in the morning when you drive them out to graze.
>
> 7. They carry your loads to lands you would never reach except with great difficulty. Your Lord is All-Gentle, Most Merciful.

8. And horses, mules and donkeys, both to ride and for adornment. And He creates other things you do not know.

9. The Way should lead to Allah, but there are those who deviate from it. If He wished He could have guided every one of you.

10. It is He who sends down water from the sky. From it you drink and from it come the shrubs among which you graze your herds.

11. And by it He makes crops grow for you and olives and dates and grapes and fruit of every kind. There is certainly a Sign in that for people who reflect.

12. He has made night and day subservient to you, and the sun and moon and stars, all subject to His command. There are certainly Signs in that for people who use their intellect.

13. And also the things of varying colours He has created for you in the earth. There is certainly a Sign in that for people who pay heed.

14. It is He who made the sea subservient to you so that you can eat fresh flesh from it, and bring out from it ornaments to wear. And you see ships cleaving through it so that you can seek His bounty, and so that hopefully you will show thanks.

15. He cast firmly embedded mountains on the earth so it would not move under you, and rivers and pathways so that hopefully you would be guided,

16. And landmarks. And they are guided by the stars.

17. Is He who creates like him who does not create? So will you not pay heed?

Later in the same chapter we read:

65. Allah sends down water from the sky and by it brings the dead earth back to life. There is certainly a Sign in that for people who hear.

66. There is instruction for you in cattle. From the contents of their bellies, from between the dung and the blood, We give you pure milk to drink, easy for drinkers to swallow.

67. And from the fruit of the date-palm and the grape-vine you derive both intoxicants and wholesome provision. There is certainly a Sign in that for people who use their intellect.

68. Your Lord revealed to the bees: "Build dwellings in the mountains and the trees, and also in the structures which men erect.

69. "Then eat from every kind of fruit, and travel the paths of your Lord, which have been made easy for you to follow." From inside them comes a drink of varying colours, containing healing for mankind. There is certainly a Sign in that for people who reflect.

...

79. Do they not see the birds suspended in mid-air up in the sky? Nothing holds them there except Allah. There are certainly Signs in that for people who have belief.

80. Allah has made your houses places of rest for you and made houses for you out of cattle hides, which are light for you to carry, both when you are travelling and when you are stay-

ing in one place; and from their wool and fur and hair you obtain clothing and carpets and household utensils for a time.

81. Allah has made shaded places for you in what He has created, and He has made shelters for you in the mountains, and He has made shirts for you to protect you from the heat and shirts to protect you from each other's violence. In that way He perfects His blessing on you so that hopefully you will submit.

These, and similar verses (see further below), indicate that things on the earth have been created for us, but that we are also responsible for what we do with them and how we use them. Above all else we should recognize the source of these gifts (vv.11, 12,13) and express our gratitude for them (v.14). Most of us may not be involved in taking grazing animals out to pasture in the morning (v.6) or diving for pearls or coral in the sea (v.14), but it is still the case that we rely on rain for our water (v. 10), on the sea for most of our fish (v.14), on livestock for our meat (vv.5–6), and on various plants for our food (v.11). Nor should we forget the clothing that we derive from animals (v.6).

Example 2: Sūrat an-Naml, "The Chapter of the Ants", Q.27:61–63

61. Say: 'Praise be to Allah, and peace be upon His slaves whom He has chosen.' Is Allah better, or what you associate with Him?

62. He who created the heavens and the earth and sends down water for you from the sky, by which He makes luxuriant gardens grow – you could never make their trees grow. Is there another god besides Allah? No, indeed, but they are people who equate others with Him!

63. He who made the earth a stable dwelling place and appointed rivers flowing through its midst and placed firmly embedded mountains on it and set a barrier between the two seas. Is there any god besides Allah? No, indeed, but most of them do not know it!

Example 3: Sūrat Ibrāhīm, "The Chapter of Ibrahim", Q.14:34–36

34. Allah is He who created the heavens and the earth and sends down water from the sky and by it brings forth fruit as provision for you. He has made the ships subservient to you to run upon the sea by His command, and He has made the rivers subservient to you.

35. And He has made the sun and moon subservient to you, holding steady to their courses, and He has made the night and day subservient to you.

36. He has given you everything you have asked Him for. If you tried to number Allah's blessings you could never count them. Man is indeed wrongdoing, ungrateful.

Example 4: Sūrat al-Jāthiya, "Kneeling", Q.45:2–4, 11–12

2. In the heavens and the earth, there are certainly Signs for the believers.

3. In your creation and all the creatures He has spread about, there are Signs for people who have certainty.

4. In the alternation of day and night and the provision Allah sends down from the sky, bringing the earth to life by it after it has died, and the varying direction of the winds, there are Signs for people who use their intellect.

...

11. It is Allah who has made the sea subservient to you so that the ships sail on it at His command, enabling you to seek His bounty, so that hopefully you will be thankful.

12. And He has made everything in the heavens and everything on the earth subservient to you. It is all from Him. There are certainly Signs in that for people who reflect.

Example 5: Sūrat ar-Raḥmān, "The Merciful", Q.55:1–25

1. The All-Merciful taught the Qur'ān.

2. He created man and taught him clear expression.

3. The sun and the moon both run with precision.

4. The stars and the trees all bow down in prostration.

5. He erected heaven and established the balance,

6. so that you would not transgress the balance.

7. Give just weight – do not skimp in the balance.

8. He laid out the earth for all living creatures.

9. In it are fruits and date-palms with covered spathes,

10. and grains on leafy stems and fragrant herbs.

11. *So which of your Lord's blessings do you both deny?*

12. He created man from dry earth liked baked clay,

13. And He created the jinn from a fusion of fire.

14. *So which of your Lord's blessings do you both deny?*

15. The Lord of the two Easts and the Lord of the two Wests.

16. *So which of your Lord's blessings do you both deny?*

17. He has let loose the two seas, converging together,

18. with a barrier between which they do not break through.

19. *So which of your Lord's blessings do you both deny?*

20. From out of them come glistening pearls and coral.

21. *So which of your Lord's blessings do you both deny?*

22. His, too, are the ships sailing like mountain peaks on the sea.

23. *So which of your Lord's blessings do you both deny?*

24. Everyone on it will pass away,

25. But the Face of your Lord will remain,

26. Master of Majesty and Generosity.

We note especially here v. 8: "He laid out the earth for all living creatures." As with many of the examples above, this indicates that it is all "for us", and thus available for us to use. But, at the same time, we are responsible for what we do.

On a more general level, we note also the following two verses in the Qur'ān: (i) Sūrat Fuṣṣilat (Q.41:54): "He [Allah] encompasses all things"; and (ii) Sūrat al-Baqara (Q.2:115): "Wherever you turn, there is the Face of Allah." Thus one could say that the environment as a whole exhibits Allah, or, more correctly, the Face of Allah. More importantly, how we are with what is around us – our environment – is how we are with Allah.

1.2 The Environment in the Ḥadīṯ

Just as there are many verses in the Qur'ān that have a bearing on the environment, so too are there many ḥadīṯs which help us to understand the Islamic concept of the environment, of which the following are examples:

1. It is related in the *Muwaṭṭa'* of Imam Mālik (d. 795/179) – which is a traditional source accepted by all Muslims – that three people once came to the mosque of the Prophet in Madina. One of them turned away and left; one of them found a space toward the front and sat down; the third sat down at the back. Then the Prophet said: "Shall I tell you about the three people? One came, looking for a place with Allah, and Allah gave him a place. One was shy, and so Allah was shy of him. The third turned away, and so Allah turned away from him."[1] So, we see that, as their feelings were, so was their experience. And, as just indicated, this is mainstream Islam and not some fringe understanding.

2. A ḥadīṯ of similar import is the *ḥadīṯ qudusī* (a category of ḥadīṯ where Allah is the main speaker but which is not Qur'ān), which is reported by all the

---

[1] Mālik ibn Anas, *al-Muwaṭṭa'*, 2 vols, Cairo: Maṭba'at al-Ḥalabī wa-awlāduh, 1349/1930 [hereinafter *Muw.*] 2:238–9.

main collectors of ḥadīt̠, to the effect that: "Allah says: I am in My slave's expectation of Me. I am with him if he remembers Me. If he remembers Me in his self, I remember him in My self. And if he remembers Me in a group, I remember him in a group which is better than that."[2] So it is important how we approach things and how we think about the world, as our thinking will affect the outcome. As the common saying goes, "Be careful about what you wish for, and don't be surprised if it happens."

3. It is reported in the ḥadīt̠ literature that the Prophet, may Allah bless him and grant him peace, said: "This world is a green and pleasant [place]. Allah puts you in charge of it (*mustakhlifukum fīhā*) and looks at how you behave."[3] So we can use it, but we are responsible for how we do so. We are accountable for what we do, and will be asked about it.

4. There is another well-known ḥadīt̠ which says: "All of you are shepherds, and will be asked about your flock", i.e. are responsible for your flock, whatever it may be.[4] In other words, we are accountable for what we do, and will be brought to account for it. This, again, as with the previous ḥadīt̠, is the idea of stewardship.

5. There is an important ḥadīt̠ which indicates our collective, social responsibility. It is related that the Prophet said: "The likeness of those who uphold the limits laid down by Allah and those who transgress them is like that of a group of people who draw lots on a boat [as to who should go where]. Some of them get the upper deck while some of them get the lower. When the people on the lower deck want to get water, they have to pass by those who are above them, so they say, 'Let's make a hole in our part of the boat and then we won't be inconveniencing those above us.' If the others let them do this, they will all perish; but if they stop them, they will not only save themselves, but all the others as well."[5]

These last three ḥadīt̠s are also a reminder that we are social animals. We live in communities and, as communities, we need leaders. Furthermore, as communities, we need to transact with one another. The idea of leadership leads us to politics, while the idea of transactions leads us to economics. A basic understanding of both politics and economics is critical for any understanding of environmental

---

[2] Cf., for example, Sunnah.com, *Riyāḍ aṣ-Ṣāliḥīn*, *Kitāb al-Adhkār*, Book 15, Ḥadīt̠ 28.
[3] Sunnah.com: *Ṣaḥīḥ Muslim*, *Kitāb ar-Riqāq*, Book 49, Ḥadīt̠ 12; *Riyāḍ aṣ-Ṣāliḥīn*, Introduction, Ḥadīt̠ 70; etc.
[4] Sunnah.com: *Ṣaḥīḥ al-Bukhārī*, *Kitāb an-Nikāḥ*, Book 67, Ḥadīt̠ 122, and elsewhere; *Ṣaḥīḥ Muslim*, *Kitāb al-Imāra*, Book 33, Ḥadīt̠ 24.
[5] Sunnah.com: *Ṣaḥīḥ al-Bukhārī*, *Kitāb ash-Shahādāt*, Book 52, Ḥadīt̠ 47.

matters today. At the same time, as I once heard it put, "If they talk to you politics, talk back to them economics; and, if they talk to you economics, talk back to them politics." In other words, see the economic reality behind seemingly political decisions, and see the political reality behind the movement of money, and the economic forces of the world. We shall return to this issue further below.

2 Theological and Philosophical Principles of the Concept in Islam

As we have seen above, the basic position as outlined in the Qur'ān and ḥadīṯ is that people are allowed to use whatever is available to them ("He has subjugated for you what is in the heavens and the earth") but with responsibility ("He has left you in charge of the earth, and looks at how you behave"), meaning that people are accountable and answerable for what they do. This, as noted above, is the well-known idea of stewardship. Being accountable also presupposes that there is a measure by which one can be judged, which, for the Muslim, is effectively what is known as "Islamic law". Islamic law is based on "Qur'ān and Sunna", with Sunna, or the normative practice of the Prophet, in turn being understood by most people to be equivalent to Ḥadīṯ. Thus we have a scriptural understanding of authority, represented by the two textual sources of the Qur'ān and the Ḥadīṯ. Thus it is that, in seeking to find out the Islamic legal position on any matter, most scholars will start with a consideration of what is to be found in these two textual sources. This, in theory, provides the "answer" to whatever problem is being addressed.

However, most Muslims nowadays, and certainly most policy-makers among them, while respecting these two textual sources, will also be conscious of the possibility of – indeed, the desirability of – a "scientific" solution to the problems of today, including those of an environmental nature. There is thus a potential conflict between scriptural and scientific authority. In effect we have two world-views: one that, in putting scriptural authority uppermost, seems to be declaring its allegiance to a God-centred view of the world, and one that, in putting scientific authority uppermost, seems to be declaring its allegiance to a human-centred view of the world.

In fact, of course, the two overlap. There is a well-known ḥadīṯ in which we are told that the Prophet was once passing by some people who were pollinating their palm-trees (a practice which is necessary to ensure effective pollination of the palms). As he saw them doing this, he expressed his surprise at this being of benefit and suggested that it might perhaps be better if they did not do so. It is said that the people stopped doing it that year and that, as a result, the palms produced very sub-standard fruit that year. When the people complained about this to the Prophet, he said, "I am just a human being. Do what is of benefit to yourselves." In another version of the report, the Prophet said, "It was merely a thought that I had, and thoughts can be right or wrong [or, in another version, 'so do not take me to task for such thoughts']. But if I tell you something about Allah, accept it from me, because I will never say what is untrue about Allah."[6]

We can conclude from this that there is no intrinsic conflict in Islam, and therefore in Islamic law, between "religious" and "scientific" knowledge. On the contrary, the two are seen as complementary, and even very traditional text-based scholars will accept the validity of both. Commenting on the above-mentioned ḥadīṯ about the palm trees, Ibn Rushd the Grandfather (the grandfather of the famous scholar and philosopher of the same name known in the West as Averroes) says:

> Allah is the One who causes harm (al-mufsid) and the One who causes benefit (al-muṣliḥ) since He is the Doer of everything. However, He – may He be exalted – has made it part of the way things are (al-ʿāda, "custom") that He causes harm and benefit by means of other things. This is known by people who have direct experience of this and have found this custom (ʿāda) to be constant, such as doctors, who know which drugs cause benefit and which cause harm because of their experience and the experience of others before them, whereas others who do not have this experience do not know what is safe in this respect. It is the same with pollinating date-palms. Those with long experience of date-palms know that this practice is useful, whereas the Prophet, may Allah bless him and grant him peace, did not know this because of his lack of experience of date-palms, which is why he said what he said, as mentioned in the various ḥadīṯ reports.
>
> When I say "such as doctors, who know which drugs cause benefit and which cause harm", I am allowing myself some liberty of expression, since in reality drugs neither cause benefit nor harm in themselves. Rather the causer of benefit and the causer of harm is Allah, the Lord of all the worlds.[7]

This position is systematized in classical Islam into a three-way division of "facts" (aḥkām), in the sense of what one can posit and/or say about the world and "the way things are". These three categories are:
1. Facts which can only be known about through the Sharīʿa (aḥkām sharʾiyya), such as the knowledge that fasting the month of Ramadan is obligatory, or

---

6 Cf. Ibn Rushd al-Jadd, al-Bayān wa-t-taḥṣīl wa-sh-sharḥ wa-t-tawjīh wa-t-taʿlīl fī masāʾil al-Mustakhraja, ed. Muḥammad Ḥajjī et al, Beirut: Dār al-Gharb al-Islāmī, 1404–7/1984–7. 17:236.
7 Ibn Rushd al-Jadd, Bayān, 17:237.

that fasting the Day of 'Ashura (10th Muharram) is not obligatory. This type of fact forms the main legal judgements of Islamic law.
2. Facts which are arrived at purely by intellectual means (*aḥkām ʿaqliyya*), such as that ten is an even number, or that three times ten is thirty.
3. Facts which are arrived at by everyday experience of the world around us (*aḥkām ʿādiyya*), such as that fire burns, or that knives cut, or that certain foods are difficult to digest.[8] It is this category which includes "scientific" judgements, although such laws may be broken by "miracles", such as fire being made cool for Abraham, or his knife being made blunt when he tried to sacrifice his son following a divine directive to do so (see Qur'ān 21:69 ("We said, 'Fire, be coolness and peace for Ibrahim!'"); and Q. 37:107 ("We ransomed him with a mighty sacrifice")).

Nevertheless, in terms of the environment and the environmental crisis of our time, it is this third category that people most often look to for solutions to environmental problems. However, judgements arrived at by such means must never over-rule judgements arrived at by the Sharīʿa. Indeed, the assumption is that the Sharīʿa will provide the best parameters for the use of the human intellect.

We might also mention that taking scripture as an authority and guide implies a certain approach and attitude. As the Qur'ān says:

> That is the Book: there is no doubt. In it is guidance for the God-fearing, those who believe in the Unseen and establish the prayer and spend out from what We have provided them with; those who believe in what has been sent down to you, and what was sent down before you, and who have certainty about the Next World. Those are guided by their Lord, and those are the prosperous. (Q.2:1–4)

So it is only those who are God-fearing, who believe "in the Unseen" and thus their accountability after death, and who exhibit the other characteristics mentioned, who will accept and respect these scriptural commands. For those who do not believe, there is necessarily only the humanly-arrived-at scientific solution.

We referred above to the concept of stewardship and how this is reflected in Qur'ānic language by using the term *khalīfa*, or caliph. In the Qur'ān, Allah says about Adam: "I am going to put a caliph (*khalīfa*) on the earth" (Q.2:30). Thus all

---

[8] Muḥammad ibn Aḥmad Mayyāra, *al-Durr al-thamīn wa-l-mawrid al-maʿīn, sharḥ "al-Murshid al-muʿīn"* Beirut: Dār al-Fikr, n.d., 15; Ibn Ḥamdūn, *Ḥāshiyat Ibn Ḥamdūn ʿalā sharḥ Mayyāra li-manẓūmat Ibn ʿĀshir al-musammāt bi-"al-Murshid al-muʿīn"*, 2nd ed. Beirut: Dār al-Fikr, 1392/1972. 1:18.

mankind, as the children of Adam, share this attribute of *khalīfa*-dom, of being like Allah's representative, or deputy, in the (seeming) absence of the ever-present Lord.

This, then, is the position of people on the earth. As we saw earlier, Allah has created everything that is on the earth for people ("He created for you everything that is on the earth" [Q.2:29]), as He also subjugated the sun and the moon, day and night, the rivers and the sea, and indeed "everything", for people, and He looks at how people behave with these gifts. We can thus say that it is not people that subdue the earth, but Allah that subdues the earth for people. Nor do people have complete freedom to do with the earth what they like. People are neither equal to all other living beings, nor are they the masters of creation. Rather, people are in the middle of a two-way relationship: people are *khalīfa*, that is, in charge of and therefore responsible for what is below, but are *'abd*, that is, slave, to what is above; people must look after what is below because of their answerability to what is above. Indeed, people have to be *khalīfa* precisely because they are *'abd:* Allah has appointed people as *khalīfa*, and it is part of their *'abd*-ness that they be *khalīfa*, since the chief characteristic of slavehood is obedience to the master. Thus people, in their *khalīfa*-dom, are free to use the good things of the earth, but, in their *'abd*-ness, are bound by the laws of Allah.

3 Islamic Law and the Environment

What, then, are the laws of Allah with respect to the environment? One might think immediately of those laws that apply to land and water usage, or to the treatment of animals. There are many such laws, but the main principle behind them is summed up in the ḥadīṯ that says that there should be "No harm or reciprocation of harm".[9] In other words, the prime consideration in all instances is to protect the rights of access to land and water and the benefits that accrue from them, and to ensure that these rights are exercised equitably, whether this is in the public or private domain. With regard to animals, the main concern is that they be treated with kindness – the ḥadīṯ says that "There is a reward in every moist liver",[10] i.e. every living animal – and that, if animals are to be killed, for food or other purposes, this should be done – as the ḥadīṯ literature also tells us – with correctness (*iḥsān*), and due respect for the animal.[11]

---

9 *Muw.* 2:122.
10 *Muw.* 2:223–4.
11 Cf., for example, al-Nawawī, *Forty Hadith*, Ḥadīṯ No. 17.

But in a situation where there are many laws, and many issues that need addressing, the task is to successfully prioritize.

From an Islamic point of view, one might then ask, what is the most serious wrong action in Islam? The first answer has to be, as in Biblical terms, "Thou shalt have no other gods before Me" (Exod 20:3 KJV). This, in Muslim terms of right and wrong action, is the idea of *shirk*, or associating anyone or anything with Allah as Creator and Sole Power in the universe. It says in the Qur'ān: "Allah does not forgive anything being associated with Him, but He forgives whoever He wills for anything less than that" (Q.4:48 and 116). In other words, to worship other-than-Allah and have the wrong inner picture of the nature of existence and to willfully deny Allah is the greatest wrong action that anyone can be guilty of.

But if *shirk* is the most serious wrong action, then what might be the next most serious one? In modern media-swayed terms one might think of apostasy, with its possible penalty of execution, or of *zinā* (illicit sexual intercourse), with its possible penalty of being stoned to death, or of stealing, with its possible penalty of having the hand cut off. However, although these are obviously serious offences against God's law – indeed, in every religious law, one might add[12] – there is one wrong action which is described as being 36 times worse than illicit sexual intercourse, and also as consisting of 70, or 99, types of wrong action, the least of which is like that of a man having intercourse with his mother.[13] This wrong action is the taking of usury (*ribā*), which refers to the taking of money at interest, however great or small in amount, and various associated practices.

---

12 Sīdī 'Abdallāh al-Shinqīṭī (d. AH 1152 [1814 or 1815]) says, in his didactic poem Marāqī l-Suʿūd:

Dīnun fa-nafsun thumma ʿaqlun nasabu
  mālun ilā ḍarūratin tantasibu
Wa-rattiban wa-l-taʾtifan musāwiyā
  ʿIrḍan maʾa l-māli takun muwāfiyā
Fa-ḥifẓuhā ḥatmun ʿala l-insāni
  Fī kulli shirʿatin min al-adyāni
   *

"Religion, life, then intellect, lineage,
  Wealth, are connected to [the category of] necessity.
 Keep them in that order, and then add, equating [the two],
  Honour with wealth, and you will be fulfilling [the task].
 Protecting these is essential for mankind,
  In every religious law."

13 Cf. al-Qurṭubī, *Tafsīr* [= *al-Jāmiʿ li-aḥkām al-Qurʾān*], Cairo: Dār al-Kitāb al-ʿArabī, 1387/1967. 3:364 (36 times; 99 types); Ibn Mājah, *Sunan*, (= *Kitāb at-Tijārāt: Bāb at-taghlīẓ fī l-ribā*), Muḥammad Fuʾād ʿAbd al-Bāqī (ed.), Beirut: Dār Iḥyāʾ al-Turāth al-ʿArabī, n.d. 2:764 (70 types).

We are therefore entitled to affirm that the prohibition against usury is an extremely important judgement. The Qur'ān (Q.2:275–9) tells us:

> Those who consume usury will not rise up [that is, out of their graves] except as one who has been made mad by Satan. This is because they say that trade is like usury, whereas Allah has permitted trade and forbidden usury [...] Allah wipes out usury and makes charity grow, and Allah does not love every unbelieving wrong-doer. Those who believe and act correctly, who establish the prayer and pay the zakāt, will have their reward with their Lord. There will be no fear on them, nor will they grieve. O you who believe, have fear of Allah and leave what remains of usury if you are truly believers; and if you do not, then be informed of a war from Allah and His Messenger. If you repent, you may have your capital, without you either wronging or being wronged.

There is thus the possibility of war from Allah and His Messenger, which must be taken as a very serious threat.

4 The Concept of Usury and Its Development

The prohibition against usury, of course, is not just a Qur'ānic, and therefore an Islamic, prohibition. It is of course – or was – part of canon law, deriving from the Biblical passage in Deuteronomy:

> Thou shalt not lend upon usury to thy brother; usury of money, usury of victuals, usury of any thing that is lent upon usury: Unto a stranger thou mayest lend upon usury; but unto thy brother thou shalt not lend upon usury: that the Lord thy God may bless thee in all that thou settest thine hand to in the land whither thou goest to possess it. (Deut 23:19–20 KJV)

This Biblical passage resulted in the severe condemnation of usury in the pre-modern period. The Third Lateran Council (1179) and the Second Council of Lyon (1274) both roundly condemned the practice, but the Fifth Lateran Council of 1517 said that usurers "ought not to be punished in any way." For many the question was how to understand the words "brother" and "foreigner" in the passage, with the two words being understood by both Jews and Christians to refer to members of their own faith community ("brothers") or those who were not ("foreigners"). As a result, Jews could not "lend upon usury" to Jews, but could do so to non-Jews, and Christians could not "lend upon usury" to Christians, but could do so to non-Christians.[14]

---

14 Cf., for example, Caridi, Cathy, "What Does the Church Say About Usury?", available at

Nevertheless, despite this biblical condemnation, these strictures were gradually relaxed – especially, it seems, at the time of the Reformation when John Calvin (1509–64) accepted usury at 5%.[15] By way of justification, Calvin said, echoing the view that we have seen explicitly condemned in the Qur'ān: "Many such cases exist in which, as far as equity is concerned, usury is not worse than purchase."[16] We recall that in the Qur'ān it says: "They say that trade is like usury, but Allah has permitted trade and forbidden usury." (Q.2:275).

It should be noted that in the traditional Islamic understanding, usury – which includes any amount of interest, and not just what might be termed "exorbitant" – is prohibited whatever the circumstances. In Malik's *Muwaṭṭa'*, for example, one of the earliest books of Islamic law, it is stated clearly that any amount of usury is forbidden. In the Book of *Qirāḍ* (a type of commenda partnership) in the chapter on "What is not permissible in *qirāḍ*", Malik says: "Some transactions may be allowed if the transaction has gone ahead and it is difficult to annul, but usury in a transaction automatically annuls it. Neither a little nor a lot of it is allowed, nor is there the same leeway with regard to it as there is for other types of transaction, because Allah, the Blessed and Exalted, says in His Book: 'And if you repent, you may have your capital back, without either wronging or being wronged'".[17] Elsewhere in the *Muwaṭṭa'*, in the Book of Business Transactions, Malik affirms the judgement of the Companion Ibn Mas'ūd (d. c. 32 AH/650) as having said: "If anyone makes a loan, they should not stipulate better than it. Even if it is a handful of fodder, that is usury."[18]

It is thus clear that there was a development of the concept of usury within the Christian tradition in particular, as reflected in the statements of the various

---

https://canonlawmadeeasy.com/2014/09/04/what-does-the-church-say-about-usury/ (accessed 17 March 2021).
15 For Calvin accepting usury at 5%, cf. Calvin, John, *Sermons on Deuteronomy*, trans. A. Golding. London, 1583. 824; and Sutherland, John K. (ed.), *The Library of Christian Classics XXII. Calvin: Theological Treatises*, trans. John Reid, London, SCM Press, 1954. 81. For the change in thought on usury at this time, cf., for example, George, Charles H., "English Calvinist Opinion on Usury, 1600–1640", *Journal of the History of Ideas* 18,4 (1957), 455–474, especially p. 455, where the author says: "nearly all modern writers on usury are agreed that the change in opinion was associated with Calvin and Calvinism and with co-ordinated capitalistic economic and social developments".
16 Calvin, John, *Commentaries on the Last Four Books of Moses*, trans. C.W. Bingham, Edinburgh: Calvin Transmission Society, 1854, III, 131.
17 *Muw.* 2:89 (citing Q.2:279).
18 *Muw.* 2:85.

Church Councils mentioned above, with an acceptance of 5% by Calvin.[19] For Muslims, however, there is no controversy among jurists from all schools of law in this regard, the only "developments" being a pragmatic acceptance of modern financial realities to allow some kind of compromise on the matter of usury.[20] Indeed, so-called "Islamic banking" seems little more than an attempt to find some way of accommodating the necessity of usurious payments for loans in a global financial framework. We will see that the global financial system has a strong grip which is extremely hard to avoid, if that is even possible.

As this is an essential part of understanding our situation, we shall look briefly at politics and economics in their environmental context from a Muslim point of view.

5 Politics in an Environmental Context

With regard to politics, I would simply say – at the risk of being over-simplistic – that we must not expect the government – any government – to do much, or to be able to do much (and the exception proves the rule). I remember a British TV programme that was broadcast at the end of 1994 called "Undercurrents of 1994". In it, there was a short, but very revealing interview with Sir Fred Atkinson (1918–2018), a former UK Chief Economic Advisor (1977–79) who had spent most of his life advising governments of both major political parties in Britain, i.e. Conservatives and Labour, on economic policy. He had this to say about who is in control of a nation's economic policy:

> A government has very little control, because it needs the approval, so to speak, of world financial centres, otherwise the money will be taken out and the exchange rate will fall. So it has to play the game according to the opinions of international banks, you might say, which means it has to have its interest rates at what the world thinks is a correct level for a country in that position. It has to keep its budget within limits that people think are reasonable. So it is under a discipline not from an international authority, but from all the money-men of the world, all the banks of the world.

Now that is quite a statement, but it needs to be understood if we are to understand where the pressures on the environment are really coming from, and what we might be able to do to change them.

---

19 For an overview of this change, cf., for example, George, Charles H., "English Calvinist Opinion on Usury, 1600–1640", *Journal of the History of Ideas* 18, 4 (1957), 455–474.
20 Cf., for example, Ansari-pour, M. A., "Interest in International Transactions under Shiite Jurisprudence", *Arab Law Quarterly* 9, 2 (1994), 158–170, 158.

The narrator of the programme went on to refer to the "real places of power, the board-rooms of Britain" – or anywhere – "and the trading floors of international banks" which, he said, are "home to the new masters of the universe, the bond and currency dealers, who make and break governments' economic policies and the careers of politicians with them". He went on to conclude:

> This is the reality of the forces of global integration. A national politician has about as much power in the world economy as a village has in a national economy. 1994 was the year in which one of President Clinton's advisers said if he believed in reincarnation, he would come back not as the President or the Pope, but as the world bond-markets. As he said, 'You can intimidate anybody.'[21]

This was over 25 years ago, but the situation is, if anything, worse now than it was then. The key point to remember is that power is being exercised by "all the money-men of the world, all the banks of the world."

This understanding was confirmed in a lecture given by Jack Straw (former UK Foreign Secretary, 2001–2006) entitled "Foreign Policy in a Fracturing World", in which he reminded his audience of "the US's iron grip on the world banking system".[22] One might be tempted to re-phrase this as "the iron grip of the world banking system", regardless of which country is involved, as in this respect the US is really no different from any other polity.

In this context, it is important to be aware of the reality of politics and some of the myths surrounding it, especially the question of democracy. Most people in Europe and the US, and many people in many other parts of the world, believe that they are living in a democracy. Democracy is generally understood as "a system of government by the whole population or all the eligible members of a state, typically through elected representatives" (Oxford Dictionary), or "a system of government in which power is vested in the people and exercised by them directly or through freely elected representatives" (britannica.com). However, to what extent is this the case? An article written by two American academics, Martin Gilens, Professor of Politics at Princeton University, and Benjamin Page, Professor of Decision Making at Northwestern University, contains a useful critique of how people normally think of democracy. Their article is entitled "Testing Theories of American Politics: Elites, Interest Groups, and Average Citizens".[23] They

---

21 BBC 2, *Undercurrents of 1994* (television programme broadcast 31 December 1994); cf. also Yasin Dutton, "The Politics of Usury or the Politics of Zakāt? Reflections on the future of Islam in Britain", *Journal of Islamic Law and Culture* 13, 2–3 (2011), 226–241, 229–230.
22 Lecture given at the Oxford Centre for Islamic Studies, 5 March 2020.
23 Gilens, Martin / Page, Benjamin, "Testing Theories of American Politics: Elites, Interest Groups, and Average Citizens", *Perspectives on Politics* 12, 3 (2014), 564–581.

start the article by asking the following questions: Who governs? Who really rules? To what extent is the broad body of U.S. citizens sovereign, or largely powerless? They then say:

> We have been able to produce some striking findings. One is the nearly total failure of 'median voter' and other Majoritarian Electoral Democracy theories. When the preferences of economic elites and the stands of organized interest groups are controlled for, the preferences of the average American appear to have only a miniscule, near-zero, statistically non-significant impact upon public policy.
>
> What do our findings say about democracy in America? They certainly constitute troubling news for advocates of "populistic" democracy, who want governments to respond primarily or exclusively to the policy preferences of their citizens. In the United States, our findings indicate, the majority does not rule – at least in the causal sense of actually determining political outcomes. When a majority of citizens disagrees with economic elites or with organized interests, they generally lose.

From this, they find themselves suggesting that most of the American public actually have little influence over the policies that their government adopts. As summarized in the article's abstract: "Multivariate analysis indicates that economic elites and organized groups representing business interests have substantial independent impacts on U.S. government policy, while average citizens and mass-based interest groups have little or no independent influence."

They try to sweeten the pill, but it remains bitter:

> Americans do enjoy many features central to democratic governance, such as regular elections, freedom of speech and association, and a wide-spread (if still contested) franchise. But we believe that if policymaking is dominated by powerful business organizations and a small number of affluent Americans, then America's claims to being a democratic society are seriously threatened.

Furthermore, if America is seen by a large portion of the world as the bastion of democracy, then it seems that the reality of this claim is in fact very different from what most people have been led to believe.

What we notice is that this claim of the power of "economic elites and organized groups representing business interests" is very similar to what Jack Straw alluded to in his talk and what Sir Fred Atkinson pointed out in his interview. But it is not new. Jeffrey Mark, for instance, in his book *The Modern Idolatry* (1934) states the same idea very blatantly:

> Of the absolute authority of Finance today there can be no question. To those who still cling to an illusion that politicians, bishops, military authorities, judges and educators, or some combination of any two, three, four or all five of them, have the fate of nations and the world in their hands, it should be unnecessary to submit evidence to the contrary [...] See-

ing that all things are produced through the agency of money, and that all money now comes into existence as a debt to the banking systems of the world, this simply means [...] that our internationally organized moneylenders 'are the actual or potential owners of everything produced in the world'.[24]

This takes us back to a deeper understanding of the phrase referred to above: "if they talk to you politics, talk back to them economics, and if they talk to you economics, talk back to them politics."

6 Economics in an Environmental Context

With regard to economics, the best inroad is a specific example. Sharon Blackie, in her 2016 book *If Women Rose Rooted*, refers to the issue of the so-called "tar sands" of Alberta, Canada, where an expansive programme of oil and gas exploration, which has been endorsed by the Canadian government, has left vast toxic scars across an otherwise unspoiled environment. The "tar sands" contain a combination of clay, sand, water and bitumen, and it is this bitumen – a heavy black viscous oil – which, when extracted and processed, is a much-desired source of fuel. But bitumen cannot be pumped from the ground in its natural state; instead it must be mined. Once this "tar sand" has been dug out of the ground, it is taken to an extraction plant where it is mixed with hot water and chemicals to liberate the oil and then release it into pipelines, or into tankers, to be transported to refineries. But not all the water that it used during the extraction process can be recycled, and what remains is a thick liquid waste which is toxic to aquatic organisms and mammals. This is held in open man-made 'ponds', pollutants from which are known to migrate through groundwater into the surrounding soil and surface water, into the Athabasca River, and thence into the ocean. They are also released into the air. The result is an increase in major health issues in the local people living in the area. The result is, as Blackie points out, that "we are left with one of the bleakest and most devastating scenes of man-made destruction on the planet", and yet "development in tar sands continues to expand and to be actively encouraged by the Canadian government." [25] (Another source describes tar sands mining and drilling in Canada's Boreal Forest as "the largest and most destructive project on earth.")[26]

---

24 Mark, Jeffrey, *The Modern Idolatry*. London: Chatto & Windus, 1934, 70.
25 Blackie, Sharon, *If Women Rose Rooted*, Tewkesbury: September Publishing, 2019, 46–47.
26 https://www.nationalgeographic.com/environment/article/alberta-canadas-tar-sands-is-growing-but-indigenous-people-fight-back

"Man-made destruction". Does this not remind us of the verse we referred to at the beginning of our enquiry: "Corruption has appeared on the land and the sea because of what men's hands have done"?

Another particularly invidious example is that which has been highlighted recently by the publication of Shanna Swan's *Count Down*, which points at the deleterious effects of the chemicals known as PFAS (Per- and Polyfluoroalkyl Substances) – which are found "everywhere and in everything", and which have resulted in, amongst other things, "plummeting sperm counts and shrinking penises" and other threats to human reproductive health.[27] This, of course, is in the tradition of Rachel Carson's 1962 book, *Silent Spring*, which documented the adverse environmental effects of the indiscriminate use of pesticides, particularly DDT, and is considered by many to be one of the forerunners of the environmental movement.[28]

These are just two of many, many examples of environmental destruction being wrought on the earth.[29]

What is it that we have done? And how might we be able to counteract it? In other words, is there a diagnosis, and, if so, what is the cure?

It seems that greed, and a subsequent insatiability, is a big part of the picture. People want more and, when they get it, they want even more. There is a ḥadīt recorded in the Ṣaḥīḥ of al-Bukhārī to the effect that the Prophet, may Allah bless him and grant him peace, said: "If the son of Adam were to have two valleys of wealth, he would want a third. But the only thing that will fill the belly of the son of Adam is earth."[30]

In business terms, this is understood as growth, and growth is understood as "a good thing". But never-ending growth is unsustainable. And infinite growth in a finite environment – i.e. our world – is a false dream. It is not possible.

There is also an element of selfishness: people want what is good for them, or what they think is good for them, even if it is at the expense of what is good

---

[27] Swan, Shanna, *Count Down: How Our Modern World Is Threatening Sperm Counts, Altering Male and Female Reproductive Development, and Imperilling the Future of the Human Race*. New York: Simon and Schuster, 2021. Cf. also, for example, Brockovich, Erin "Plummeting sperm counts, shrinking penises: toxic chemicals threaten humanity", https://www.theguardian.com/commentisfree/2021/mar/18/toxic-chemicals-health-humanity-erin-brockovich; https://theintercept.com/2021/01/24/toxic-chemicals-human-sexuality-shanna-swan/
[28] Cf., for example, Griswold, Eliza, "How 'Silent Spring' Ignited the Environmental Movement", *The New York Times Magazine*, September 21, 2012.
[29] For a particularly comprehensive view of the main categories of destruction, cf. https://www.stopecocide.earth/what-is-ecocide (mentioning the oceans, deforestation, land and water contamination and air pollution, and numerous sub-categories).
[30] Sunnah.com: *Ṣaḥīḥ al-Bukhārī, Kitāb al-riqāq*, Book 81, Ḥadīt 25.

for other people. And they often see the near, and forget, or are unaware of, the far. So clothes may be bought, or food may be eaten, that has involved the abuse of people and abuse of the environment in "faraway" places such as, for example, India or Indonesia – far enough away, that is, for it not to be noticed by the average consumer who lives elsewhere.

But where does the responsibility lie? It is often next to impossible to identify individual people, especially now that "legal" ownership seems to have moved from individuals to corporations, who now constitute entities that are so surrounded by legal loopholes that it is very difficult, if not almost impossible, to hold anyone to account for "what they have done".

But behind every decision, there is a decider: a person who has made that decision. And that decider is one of us.

Polly Higgins (1968–2019) was a lawyer who used the word "ecocide" to describe what humans are doing to the planet and who spent the last part of her life fighting to make ecocide an international criminal offence. She pointed out that at the moment, the law instructs a company to put its shareholders' interests first, which means maximizing profits. A law of ecocide would shift those priorities. Rather, it would say: first and foremost, do no harm, and then think about making profits. (We recall the Prophetic ḥadīṯ we mentioned earlier: "No harm or reciprocation of harm.") Higgins asks: "Can you imagine a world in which the law would prevent corporations from investing in business practices that cause harm to people and the planet? [...] no matter how we look at it, commoditizing the planet and destroying it for short-term profit makes no sense."[31]

Firstly, and I think this would be accepted by everybody, Muslim and non-Muslim, we have to accept that it is we who have caused this mess. It is anthropogenic, to use the modern term. We are all in it, and of it, whether directly or indirectly. We, as consumers, may be sitting comfortably in front of our TV screens – or smart-phone screens – but how did these TVs and phones come into being? What are the chemicals and minerals that were used and how were they accessed and acquired? What clothes are we wearing and how and where and by whom did they get produced? What are we eating, and how and where and by whom did it get produced?

---

[31] Blackie, *If Women Rose Rooted*, 51. For more about ecocide law, see https://ecocidelaw.com and, especially, www.stopecocide.earth/what-is-ecocide

7 Ways Forward?

Kate Raworth, in her book *Doughnut Economics* (2017), refers to "the ingenious twentieth-century inventor" Buckminster Fuller (1895–1983) as saying: "You never change things by fighting the existing reality. To change something, build a new model that makes the existing model obsolete".[32]

Raworth also notes, in a section entitled "Avoiding collapse":

> We have transgressed at least four planetary boundaries (climate change, chemical pollution, ocean acidification and biodiversity loss), billions of people still face extreme deprivation, and the richest 1% own half of the world's financial wealth. These are ideal conditions for driving ourselves towards collapse. If we are to avoid such a fate for our global civilization, we clearly need a transformation and it can be summed up like this:
>
> "Today's economy is divisive and degenerative by default. Tomorrow's economy must be distributive and regenerative by design."[33]

In other words, we need to look at the situation in a different way.

We cannot expect to be able to change the divisive and degenerative banking system and its chimera of constant growth. Let Allah do that: "Be informed of a war from Allah and His Messenger." But it is possible to offer something else on the economic front: regenerative halal trade, i.e. trade without usury, and distributive zakāt, especially correctly collected and distributed zakāt. For zakāt in particular, this should not be online, but hand to hand, and not international, or even national, but local, as it was initially in the time of the first Muslims, who would collect it and then distribute it in the place where they had collected it. This then allows the possibility of bringing local communities to life without having to rely on impersonal, centralized institutions who do not know what the situation is on the ground. An organization called *The Local Zakāt Initiative* has recently been established along these lines in Britain,[34] but the possibility exists wherever zakāt is seen as a means of revivifying local communities. In the environmental context there are many such activities throughout the world where people try to do the best with zakāt despite the circumstances we are all obliged to live in.[35]

---

32 Raworth, Kate, *Doughnut Economics: Seven Ways to Think Like a 21st-Century Economist*, New York: Random House, 2017, 4.
33 Raworth, *Doughnut Economics*, 155–156.
34 Cf, for example, *The Local Zakāt Initiative*, https://localzakat.co.uk.
35 One example that highlights the importance of decentralizing and de-politicizing the collection of zakāt is documented in: Machado, Anna Carolina / Bilo, Charlotte / Helmy, Imane, "The

Let us conclude with the assessment of Ibn Khaldūn (1332–1406), six times appointed judge in the law courts, where he outlines the social dimension of the Islamic identity. Alongside, and as important as the acts of worship – ritual prayers, Ramadan, zakāt and hajj – Ibn Khaldun considers that the doctrine which charters the social and political nature of a Muslim society is that which defines what man is in Islam. He calls this *istikhlāf* (being appointed "caliph" / taking on stewardship). As Ian Dallas puts it:

> This means that man is the guardian of the world.
> Allah, the Creator of the Universe, has set man on earth to worship Him and to be the guardian of the world.
> To man is given the task of defending the earth, the ocean and the sky, from destruction, pollution and over-exploitation.
> He has to answer for the usage of what is on the earth, and under it.
> Man's charge is that he must abolish usury – even to a blade of grass.[36]

We must also recognize that, as indicated earlier, the inward and the outward are necessarily connected, and the one is not healthy unless the other is. To further emphasize this meaning, we note the words of Shaykh Abd al-Qadir as-Sufi in his introduction to the translation of Shaykh ʿAlī al-Jamal's (d. 1780) *The Meaning of Man*, where he says:

> We live in an age where the meaning of man itself is in danger, therefore man is in danger, therefore his environment, this Earth is in danger. We live in a society that is determined to destroy man and make him the servant of the lowest aspects of himself, instead of the master of the highest aspects of himself.[37]

We saw before that how we are with the world is how the world is with us. And we saw that it is important for us to think well about the world, and to have a good opinion of Allah.

To end on a positive note, and to encourage us to realign our inward with our outward, and to indicate a path that leads us to the highest rather than the lowest aspects of ourselves, we finish with a poem about the environment by one of the most influential Sufi shaykhs of the 20th century, Shaykh Muḥam-

---

Role of Zakāt in the Provision of Social Protection: A Comparison between Jordan, Palestine and Sudan", *Working Paper, No. 168*, Brasilia: International Policy Centre for Inclusive Growth (IPC-IG), 2018.

36 Dallas, Ian, *The Time of the Bedouin*, Cape Town: Budgate Press, 2006, 302–303.

37 as-Sufi, Abd al-Qadir, *Introduction*, in: Shaykh ʿAlī al-Jamal, *The Meaning of Man: The Foundations of the Science of Knowledge*, 5, Norwich: Diwan Press, 1977.

mad ibn al-Ḥabīb (1876–1972). The poem is entitled "Reflection", and is a reminder to reflect on the majesty and beauty of creation, and thus the Majesty and Beauty of the Creator:

> Reflect upon the beauty of the workmanship with which the land and the sea are made,
>   And openly and secretly busy yourself with the attributes of Allah.
> In the self and on the horizon is the greatest witness
>   To the limitless perfections of Allah.
> If you were to concern yourself with the physical bodies and their perfection of form
>   And their inner connection, like a string of pearls;
> If you were to concern yourself with the secrets of the tongue and its articulation,
>   And its expression of what you conceal in your breast;
> If you were to concern yourself with the secrets of all the limbs
>   And the ease with which they obey the heart;
> If you were to concern yourself with the turning of the hearts to obedience,
>   And how they sometimes move to disobedience;
> If you were to concern yourself with the earth and the variety of its plants
>   And the great expanse of smooth and rugged land that it contains;
> If you were to concern yourself with the secrets of the seas and the fish in them,
>   And the endless waves held back by an unconquerable barrier;
> If you were to concern yourself with the secrets of the winds, and how
>   They bring mists and clouds which bring down rain;
> And if you were to concern yourself with the secrets of all the heavens
>   And the Throne and the Footstool and the spirit of the Command,
> Then you would believe in *tawḥīd* with a firm belief
>   And would turn from illusions, doubt and the other.
> You would say: "My God, You are my desire and my goal
>   And my fortress against evils, injustice and deceit.
> You are my hope in providing for my needs
>   And You are the One who rescues us from evil and wickedness.
> You are the Compassionate, the Answerer to whoever calls upon You.
>   And you are the One who makes up for the poverty of the poor.
> To you, Oh Exalted, I have raised my pleas,
>   So hasten the Opening and the Secret, Oh my God,
> By the rank of the one who is hoped for on the day of grief and distress,
>   And the day when people come to the Place of Gathering.
> May the blessings of Allah be upon him as long as there is a gnostic
>   Who concerns himself with the lights of His Essence in every manifestation,
> And upon his family and Companions and every one who follows
>   His glorious sunna in prohibition and command.[38]

---

38 Shaykh Muḥammad ibn al-Ḥabīb, *Dīwān*, Beirut: Dār Ṣādir, 2001/1422, 54; for the translation, cf.: *The Diwans of the Darqawa*, trans. 'Aisha 'Abd ar-Rahman at-Tarjumana, 65–66, Norwich: Diwan Press, 1980.

Finally, we recall two ḥadīts which point to our common future:
1. "No time comes upon you but that the one coming after it is worse than it."³⁹
2. "If the Day of Rising comes and you are planting a palm tree, continue planting it."⁴⁰

Sources

al-Nawawi, *Forty Ḥadīt*
Sunnah.com, *Riyāḍ aṣ-Ṣāliḥīn, Kitāb al-Adhkār*, Book 15, Ḥadīt 28
Sunnah.com: *Sahih Muslim, Kitab al-Riqaq*, Book 49, Ḥadīt 12; *Riyad as-Salihin*, Introduction, Ḥadīt 70; etc.
Sunnah.com: *Ṣaḥīḥ al-Bukhārī, Kitāb an-Nikāḥ*, Book 67, Ḥadīt 122, and elsewhere; *Sahih Muslim, Kitab al-Imara*, Book 33, Ḥadīt 24.
Sunnah.com: *Ṣaḥīḥ al-Bukhārī, Kitāb ash-Shahādāt*, Book 52, Ḥadīt 47.
Sunnah.com: *Ṣaḥīḥ al-Bukhārī, Kitāb ar-Riqāq*, Book 81, Ḥadīt 25.
BBC 2, *Undercurrents of 1994* (television programme broadcast 31 December 1994)
https://www.nationalgeographic.com/environment/article/alberta-canadas-tar-sands-is-growing-but-indigenous-people-fight-back
https://www.stopecocide.earth/what-is-ecocide
https://localzakāt.co.uk
Sunnah.com: *Ṣaḥīḥ al-Bukhārī, Kitāb al-Fitan*, Book 92, Ḥadīt 19.
Sunnah.com: *Al-Adab al-mufrad, Kitāb al-I'tinā' bi-d-dunyā*, Book 27, Ḥadīt 479.
https://theintercept.com/2021/01/24/toxic-chemicals-human-sexuality-shanna-swan/

Bibliography

Ibn Anas, Malik, *al-Muwaṭṭa'*, 2 vols, Cairo: Matba'at al-Ḥalabī wa-awlāduh, 1349/1930.
Ansari-Pour, M. A., "Interest in International Transactions under Shiite Jurisprudence", *Arab Law Quarterly* 9, 2 (1994), 158–170.
Blackie, Sharon, *If Women Rose Rooted*, Tewkesbury: September Publishing, 2019.
Brockovich, Erin, "Plummeting sperm counts, shrinking penises: toxic chemicals threaten humanity", https://www.theguardian.com/commentisfree/2021/mar/18/toxic-chemicals-health-humanity-erin-brockovich
Calvin, John, *Sermons on Deuteronomy*, trans. A. Golding, London, 1583.
Calvin, John, *Commentaries on the Last Four Books of Moses*, trans. C.W. Bingham, Edinburgh: Calvin Transmission Society, 1854.
Caridi, Cathy, "What Does the Church Say About Usury?", https://canonlawmadeeasy.com/2014/09/04/what-does-the-church-say-about-usury/ (accessed 17 March 2021).
Dallas, Ian, *The Time of the Bedouin*, Cape Town: Budgate Press, 2006.

---

39 Sunnah.com: *Ṣaḥīḥ al-Bukhārī, Kitāb al-Fitan*, Book 92, Ḥadīt 19.
40 Sunnah.com: *Al-Adab al-mufrad, Kitāb al-I'tinā' bi-l-dunyā*, Book 27, Ḥadīt 479.

Dutton, Yasin, "The Politics of Usury or the Politics of Zakāt? Reflections on the future of Islam in Britain", *Journal of Islamic Law and Culture* 13, 2–3 (2011), 226–241.
George, Charles H., "English Calvinist Opinion on Usury, 1600–1640", *Journal of the History of Ideas* 18, 4 (1957), 455–474.
Gilens, Martin / Page, Benjamin, "Testing Theories of American Politics: Elites, Interest Groups, and Average Citizens", *Perspectives on Politics* 12, 3 (18 September 2014), 564–581.
Griswold, Eliza, "How 'Silent Spring' Ignited the Environmental Movement", *The New York Times Magazine*, September 21, 2012.
ibn al-Habib, Shaykh Muhammad, *Diwan*, Beirut: Dar Sadir, 2001/1422.
ibn al-Habib, Shaykh Muhammad et al. (eds.), *The Diwans of the Darqawa*, trans. 'Aisha 'Abd ar-Rahman at-Tarjumana, Norwich: Diwan Press, 1980.
Ibn Ḥamdūn, *Ḥāshiyat Ibn Ḥamdūn 'alā sharḥ Mayyāra li-manẓūmat Ibn 'Āshir al-musammāt bi-"al-Murshid al-mu'īn"*, 2nd ed. Beirut: Dār al-Fikr, 1392/1972.
Machado, Anna Carolina / Bilo, Charlotte / Helmy, Imane, "The Role of Zakāt in the Provision of Social Protection: A Comparison between Jordan, Palestine and Sudan", *Working Paper, No. 168*, Brasilia: International Policy Centre for Inclusive Growth (IPC-IG), 2018.
Ibn Mājah, *Sunan*, (= *Kitāb at-Tijārāt: Bāb at-taghlīẓ fī l-ribā*), Muḥammad Fu'ād 'Abd al-Bāqī (ed.), Beirut: Dār Iḥyā' al-Turāth al-'Arabī, n.d.
Mark, Jeffrey, *The Modern Idolatry*, London: Chatto & Windus, 1934.
Mayyāra, Muhammad ibn Ahmad, *ad-Durr ath-thamin wa-l-mawrid al-ma'in, sharh "al-Murshid al-mu'in"*, Beirut: Dar al-Fikr, n.d.
al-Qurṭubī, *Tafsīr* [= *al-Jāmi' li-aḥkām al-Qur'ān*], Cairo: Dār al-Kitāb al-'Arabī, 1387/1967.
Raworth, Kate, *Doughnut Economics: Seven Ways to Think Like a 21st-Century Economist*, New York: Random House, 2017.
Ibn Rushd al-Jadd, *al-Bayān wa-t-taḥṣīl wa-sh-sharḥ wa-t-tawjīh wa-t-ta'līl fī masā'il al-Mustakhraja*, Muḥammad Ḥajjī et al (eds.), Beirut: Dār al-Gharb al-Islāmī, 1404–1407/1984–1987.
as-Sufi, Abd al-Qadir, *Introduction*, in: Shaykh Ali al-Jamal, *The Meaning of Man: The Foundations of the Science of Knowledge*, Norwich: Diwan Press, 1977.
Sutherland, John K. (ed.), *The Library of Christian Classics XXII. Calvin: Theological Treatises*, trans. John Reid, London, SCM Press, 1954.
Swan, Shanna, *Count Down: How Our Modern World Is Threatening Sperm Counts, Altering Male and Female Reproductive Development, and Imperilling the Future of the Human Race*, New York: Simon and Schuster, 2021.
ibn al-Habib, Shaykh Muhammad et al. (eds.), *The Diwans of the Darqawa*, trans. 'Aisha 'Abd ar-Rahman at-Tarjumana, Norwich: Diwan Press, 1980.

Suggestions for Further Reading

Abdel Haleem, Harfiyah (ed.), *Islam and the Environment*, London: Ta-Ha Publishers 1998.
Dien, Mawil Izzi, *The Environmental Dimensions of Islam*, Cambridge: The Lutterworth Press, 2000.

Foltz, Richard / Denny, Frederick M. / Baharuddin, Azizan (eds.), *Islam and Ecology: A Bestowed Trust*, Cambridge: Harvard University Press for the Center for the Study of World Religions, 2003.
Khalid, Fazlun M., *Signs on the Earth: Islam, Modernity and the Climate Crisis*, Markfield: Kube, 2019.

Christoph Böttigheimer and Wenzel M. Widenka
Epilogue

Introduction

As multifarious as God's creation are the ways of investigating this concept. The articles that are assembled in this volume thus present very different approaches to the idea of "Environment" in the three faiths. Rabbi Yonatan Neril's and Rabbi Leo Dee's essay on "The Concept of Environment in Judaism" presents an investigation and a very rabbinic approach based on the Holy Scriptures, on rabbinic teaching, on religious contemplation. It is more than a mere scholarly text and this is the basis of its fascination. Kerstin Schlögl-Flier's strictly systematical investigation in the understanding of environment from a Christian perspective encompasses both the historical development of the concept, approaches of systematical theology and current challenges. Yasin Dutton's starting point is the Qur'ān but his essay focuses on current ecological challenges and the possible answers Islamic thinking can give to them. Whatever the approach, none of the three faiths can ignore that a fundamental entity as the environment points towards a greater concept, read: it is creation that surrounds the believer in his and her everyday life. It is thus legit to rather speak of environment as a part of speaking of creation. The term "creation" is a theological one, whereas "environment" represents a secular approach. What is more, "nature" refers only to a certain environment on a single planet, not to the whole of all the created universe. It is thus stunning that all three religions denote this tension between a theological and a secular thinking when speaking of environment. Dealing with environment is more than keeping care of nature. It is the challenging handling of the complex relation between creator, creation and its most delicate creature, man.

The Concept of Environment from a Jewish Perspective

Judaism is not a religion of systematised doctrines, but rather a lively, ongoing debate by means of religious law (halacha) and textual approaches (agada). Therefore we should not be surprised that Jewish approaches to ecology and environment are a many-voiced choir of explorations into text and tradition that, however, enable to draw a broad picture of Judaism's main thoughts and concerns about the created world. The Garden of Eden, the origin of human encounter with creation, is threatened. Judaism sees the ecological crisis of our days not merely as a current event, but addresses it in the light of creation itself, as a question of metaphysical dimension. Focal is the Torah, the five books of Moses. Its teachings, though seemingly cryptic, are of fundamental value for the treatment of recent questions. The elaborated method of rabbinic commenting on the Bible's teaching enables a current "updating" of a wisdom a thousand years old, that was never meant to be static. Thus, it seems clear for Judaism that the ecological crisis has spiritual roots. The aim is not to draw an apocalyptic vision of creation collapsing but to offer a perspective of hope and repentance. Man is responsible for God's creation, including his fellow beings. The idea of stewardship is crucial for the Jewish understanding of the concept of environment. Man is set into the garden to take care of it and to work it. The question is not individual concern, but collective responsibility, as Judaism normally thinks in terms of standing as a people before God and not as an individual believer. Man is bound to God's plan for this earth and is part of the constant struggle for upholding the structure and balance of creation. The creation could not bring forth life if there were not man to till the ground and harvest its fruits. Man, being formed of soil, is part of creation. Here, the words "creation" and "environment" fall into each other and are used equally and nearly interchangeably. Focal is one thought that combines all attempts towards creation and environment: God's creation is "very good", there is no failure or evil spark. It is wholly accepted and loved by its creator. This positive approach towards the created world is fundamental and a sharp contrast to any gnostic idea of an ill-natured matter.

The Book of Genesis is the starting point of all endeavours to highlight the special features of the Jewish concept of environment, resp. creation. The latter is a both divine and ongoing process wherein man is an integrative part of. God initiated a perfect creation man has to maintain. This divine order links man's acting within creation to a spiritual act. The rabbis believe that this world may not be the first world ever created. God had created several other worlds, which he rejected and destroyed. The last one is the perfect creation, which must not be damaged by man's agency. Yet the famous dominion order of Gen 1:28 remains. This task to dominate is however based on the well-behaviour of mankind. If man does not merit dominion, the mandate can be withdrawn and he may be overthrown. This unworthiness can occur by pillaging the environment or the unnecessary killing of animals. The first humans in the Garden of Eden are believed to having had a vegetarian diet and having lived in a state of comprehensive harmony. This lost harmony is a state man yearns to re-establish. Thus, the above mentioned dominion mandate is a moral one. For the garden and the entire creation belong to the creator, God, and man is set into it to uphold the beauty of all created things, to take care of creation and to guarantee the historical continuity of the created world as God's steward.

The first point of comparison similar to the current crisis is the story of Noah and the ark. Like today, the lack of spiritual pleasure caused a materialistic, hedonistic substitute to emerge. God granted a time of warning before unleashing the flood, for man is capable of self-restraint, a feature he oftentimes lacks. Since man did not respond, the catastrophe occurred. Today's ecological crisis has not yet developed that far and Judaism still sees man as being capable of avoiding the crash, if he sticks to the fundamental key principles of Jewish ecological thinking. These are the commandment not to waste or destroy, the Oneness of God's creation, the keeping of the Sabbat, esp. the idea of the fallow year, and the commandments regarding the ethical treatment of animals. Animals possess a special relationship towards man. The biblical story of Adam's naming of every animal reflects a wisdom on both sides: it is by heart that Adam knows the nature of the animal and the animal serves as a teacher of human behaviour. Creation is thus connected part by part. This is a reflection of the initial state of creation before eating the forbidden fruit, where everything was linked and whereby man is responsible for creation and all creatures, a status that cannot be ignored and leads back to the steward paradigm. The very material man is formed of, dust, reveals this connectedness with the soil. If man forgets this, he follows the example of Cain who was forced to wander the earth. On the positive side, the example of Noah shows a man who lives in a harmonious and productive relation with nature even under the direst of circumstances. God's symbol to Noah, the rainbow, spans a new canopy above mankind to preserve him from divine wrath. But the ark is not completed, man has the freedom to destroy creation again.

Yet this new established order is prone to pride. The story of the tower of babel reflects the human misconception of an order being solely man-made and independent from God, where man puts his faith in technology rather than in the creator. This leads to disaster. The palace of creation is on fire and man is held responsible for it.

Judaism, being a religion with a deep devotion to the land that God gave to Israel, sees a deep interconnectedness of man with the soil. Hence finding God in nature is a recurrent topic of religious story and thought. The interdependence of man and nature leads to the ideal of leading a modest lifestyle that will not harm others, including animals, and that takes a strong interest in charity, lifting up the poor and executing justice towards the other. Man is made of clay and dust, thus he is part of nature and can find peace and serenity therein. Nature is also a place where man can encounter God. The Hebrew words for soil (adama) and man (adam) stem from the same root, a definite sign of their strong nexus. Even eating becomes a holy agency when it is done with awareness and a spiritual mind-set. The Hebrew Bible strongly refuses any waste of food or wanton water destruction.

The Bible knows two great catastrophes in the Book of Genesis: the flood and the fiery rain over Sodom. The latter was once a lush place full of blossoming vegetation which was turned into the desolate void which is known today. All this because of man's inability to take care of the other and of nature. The overall attitude of Judaism towards nature is thus a conservative one, where man is obliged to plan diligently for the future, not just rejoice in the delights of the present. This means more than just taking care for the environment. The other is also part of this environment, so taking care of nature and promoting peace and justice are deeply connected. Sustainability means both an ecological and a political level. The will for peace is signified by the act of planting a tree. Peace and sustainability are active purposes. Judaism's attitude towards the concept of environment may be a conservative one, but it is under no means passive. It forces man to act.

The Concept of Environment from a Christian Perspective

Christianity's central sacred text, the Bible, offers a primal approach to what "Environment" means in Christian terms. The central theme is the story of the creation and man's place in paradise. The tragic yet inevitable dispel from paradise is not only a catastrophe for mankind but also puts man in a special place and responsibility for the creation. Man, as he is forced to bear the burdens of birth and the need to till the soil, becomes an active co-worker in the process of creation. With participation comes responsibility. It is upon man to preserve God's creation, a creation he should not dominate, as the famous creation imperative or dominion order in Gen 1 is often interpreted, but rather maintain as a faithful steward or royal agent of the Creator God. It is here that we first encounter the famous narrative of the good shepherd who cares for his flock that was later used to describe Christ's work an earth. However, for the most time of church history the dominion order was seen as it classically sounded: as an imperative for the "crown of creation" to rule and subdue. It is only in recent history that the focus falls on the cooperation between man and creation. Man has a special place in creation and God puts him in place to give names to the created animals (for man is the only creature that knows these names), but man is also created by the same decree and the same words as are the animals. Therefore, there is no ontological separation between creation and man.

The book of psalms praises God's creation and treats man as a king installed to rule by gentle hands. A responsible, ideal king, caring for his fellow beings, only slightly inferior to his creator, because only the latter can have access to the kingdom of animals, a world concealed to man. Creation is a dialogue between creator and the created, everything and everyone has its place therein and it is this creation where God reveals himself as a healer and saviour.

In comparison to the book shared to the greatest part by both Jews and Christians, the Hebrew Bible resp. Old Testament, the books of the New Testament offer a relatively minuscule amount of passages dealing with creation. Creation here becomes soteriological, cosmic rather than environmental. In Jesus Christ, creation happens anew and Christ himself becomes a mediator of creation. If the two scriptures are read together, they build up a framework of creational work, a lasting command to protect and preserve creation and a fair warning not to trespass against it, which will only cause harm.

Catholic tradition, Church Fathers like Augustine or Thomas Aquinas in the West and Basil of Caesarea in the East, values the goodness of creation, a creation God made perfect and in which everything has a single value and an undeniable beauty, thus leaving an impact for today's appreciation of nature. Yet this beauty surpasses mere immanent nature, it is in itself of sacramental character, a means of divine communication and a representation of God's unending wisdom and mercy. It is not surprising that medieval conceptions of nature and creation conceive the creational structure as a static, geocentric design with man as the "crown of creation" standing in the middle or on top. Others, like Francis of Assisi, focused more on the loving-kindness towards the fellow being and the overwhelming joy humans experience in embracing nature. All these approaches plus several mystical ones maintained a lasting impact and a message for today's environmental problems.

Systematically, the question of man and the environment is both a question of relationship and of responsibility. Most Christian concepts of the relation between man and nature focus on an anthropocentric view that enables more or less normative moral restrictions for other beings. Current systematical approaches, like process theology, try to establish a holistic view of the abovementioned relationship to distinguish it from a strict dualism that sees man outside of nature. Nature is creation and is thus oriented towards the creator, i.e. God. It has a value of its own.

To apply these thoughts to recent problems that long for a solution, biodiversity and sustainability can be mentioned. Man is called to maintain creation since he did not create it in the first place. He himself is a creature and thus limited and obliged to adore creation, not to exploit and destroy it. One of the most striking examples of current Catholic environmental thinking is Pope Francis' encyclical *Laudato Si'*. The encyclical captures both ecology, economy and ecumenism. It pictures an illustrative image of our mutual "house", which is creation, and what man has done to her. The "Gospel of Creation" that Francis formulates here opts for a holistic ecology in both a practical and a spiritual sense. The cry of God's creation is linked to the cry of the poor and to injustice in an ever-colder world. The Pope, who's akin to liberation theology approaches, turns the focus from an anthropocentric to a biocentric view and places man again in a biblical context. On the practical side, *Laudato Si'* defines climate and nature as collective goods and stresses the responsibility of all people for the common house as well as a mandatory change of lifestyle. Man is again the gardener in Paradise. The encyclical is contentious and not valuated by everyone, same as the so-called Amazon-Synod, which once again proved the close bonds between spiritual renewal and political action that underlines the fraternal approach to environment and the idea of dignity and justice for all people that *Laudato Si'* focused on. This is based on a long history of long-term-thinking within the Christian churches, deriving, among others, from monastic spirituality and the idea of asceticism. Catholic teaching sees man in a superior, yet relative position with the other fields of creation. As a result, man is responsible for his fellow creatures. A close ally of Pope Francis is the "Green Patriarch" Bartholomew I., speaking for the Orthodox side. Orthodoxy distinguishes sharply between the Creator and the created and holds creation as a gift of divine love. This gift must not be wasted and man plays a crucial role in preserving the gift. He is seen not only as the crown of creation, but as creation's high priest; a creation that constantly praises its creator. Thus, the human responsibility for creation has a dimension concerning the whole cosmos, man sustains creation in a way that surpasses mere questions of consume or political questions. It is a mystical approach that however forms direct practical outcomes. As with Pope Francis, a change might not come with a change of mind but of spirit.

What unites all of Christianity's approaches to the concept of environment is the high adoration Christianity holds for creation. From this adoration stems the special dignity of man, as the image of God and as a result, the special responsibility man upholds for the created world. He is more than a mere creature; he is the co-creator and has to have a deep respect for his fellow beings. At the same time, he is not separated from nature. Man is an integral part of creation, there is no dualism that would place man outside or against nature.

The Concept of Environment in Islam

A comprehensive illustration of the main ideas of Islamic treatment of "environment" must be based on the holy scripture of Islam, the Qur'ān. Here we meet the disturbing fact that neither the Qur'ān nor the classical Arabic language has a word for "environment". The modern "bi'a" refers to "home, dwelling" which can be linked to the Greek *oikos*, which is the stem room of ecology. The image of creation as a house wherein man lives and is thus responsible for is crucial to Islamic ecological understanding. This house has been built by God for man to dwell in, like everything that was created was created for man. Since God not only creates everything, but encompasses everything, creation is not just the house man lives in, but the very face of God himself. That means man's connection to his environment and thus to creation is a direct image of man's relation to God.

In qur'ānic understanding man upholds a position as a steward, or to speak in Arabic terms, as *khalif*. Man is therefore responsible for the state of creation and held accountable on it. This is not just in individual forms but always in terms of man as a part of a social body, as a community of created beings, of believers. All within this body are subject to Islamic law, to scripture and *hadith*. But by relating on these scriptures to evaluate the accountability of man, a rift of potential authority could open up: are today's environmental problems to be solved by tradition, scripture and the ways of Islamic law or should the believer rely on modern science? Islamic tradition handles this problem by assigning that its proper topics complement each other and by thus making no real difference (and therefore creating no conflict) between religious and scientific knowledge. At least theoretically. Benefit and harm both stem from the same root, which is always God. And God's law, the *sharia*, is unsurpassable and is treated as holding the best possible solutions for whatever problem, be it current or historical. The faithful believer is in the lucky situation to be able to have both religious and scientific knowledge, whereas the unbeliever can only rely on unstable science.

Coming back to the idea of stewardship, it can be stated that, due to his position, man has no absolute freedom to do whatever he wants to creation. God, not man, is the master of creation and man might be the *khalifa* enjoying the pleasures of creation, but always remains a slave to the almighty. And to the almighty he owes allegiance. God's laws concerning the environment are bound up in the principle of "No harm or reciprocation of harm", which means that every creature must be able to take benefit from creation. It is a striking fact that the second most serious sin in Islamic thought, next to the famous ban on associating anything else to God and far more serious than the sin against the blood, is the taking of usury which is laid out much stricter than in Jewish, let alone Christian thought. Yet corruption that flourishes economically has also an ecological imprint, for both are seen as corruption against creation. Human greed that sustains economic and ecological corruption is trespassing against God's laws who told his creature to look after his "house", i.e. creation and not to waste and pollute it.

Islamic thought imagines man as co-worker and steward in God's ongoing creation-process. Thus, it is able to share the burden of mandatory change of behaviour. God will do his part in changing an unjust reality whereas man is obliged to do his share. This happens in keeping the commandments; especially the above mentioned two most important ones. Since man is the guardian of the world and at the same instant part of the world, he must realise that every harm that is done to creation causes harm against man himself. If this fact is ignored, man acting against creation is culpable of the sin of ignoring or insulting God's rightful decision to create.

Common features and differences

If an inquiry is made about the understanding of the key concept of "environment" in Judaism, Christianity and Islam, not only does the concept of creation immediately arise, but there is also a lot in common in the religious convictions. This is due to the fact that all three religions assume that man's environment, like the whole of reality, is not the ultimate but only the penultimate, insofar as it does not carry the reason for its being in itself but was created. In its being created, it refers to something greater, God. In addition to this fundamental agreement on the religious dimensions of the environment, a closer look reveals differences between Judaism, Christianity and Islam in their religious attitudes towards the environment. In conclusion, the commonalities and differences are to be named in an overview.

As already mentioned, all three major revelatory religions assume that the reality of the world owes its existence to a divine cause and that, because it always originates from God, it is on the one hand fundamentally good and on the other hand characterised by a revelatory character. Because no anti-divine principle is involved in the process of creation, a dualism therefore fundamentally excluded, creation not only has nothing negative to offer, but is also characterised by beauty and orderliness, wherefore it is appreciated and religiously revered by man. Because it was originally created good, the ambivalence of the world does not come from God, but from man.

In a religious context, when we speak of the environment, we are speaking of the special relationship of human beings to divine creation. According to the theology of creation in Judaism, Christianity and Islam, human beings were first created as part of creation, i.e. as God's creature to communicate with. Thus he is integrated into creation together with all other co-creatures. The relationship to creation, his bodily integration into the environment is essential for man. He can neither distance nor detach himself from it; he does not stand outside the world that surrounds him. Despite the mutual reference to the world, man differs from other creatures in that he is the one to whom this creation has been entrusted. Thus, in all three religions, man has a special position, which has sometimes led to anthropocentrism in Jewish, Christian and Islamic theology. Analogous to the task and function of the gardener, man is given responsibility for God's creation, the Garden of Eden, so that he may work and cultivate it, nurture and care for it. The relationship between man and his environment is thus described in all three monotheistic religions not, as is often misunderstood, in terms of domination and exploitation, but rather in the image of stewardship. The care for the created world is given to man as a steward; he is to live in peace and harmony with it, but this does not exclude exploration of nature and interventions in it. Based on man's creation mandate and his co-creative action, environmental protection and animal welfare, sustainability and justice etc. are fundamentally inscribed in Judaism, Christianity and Islam, although this does not mean that they have always been seen and implemented in this way.

Even if the original state of creation could not be preserved, Judaism, Christianity and Islam assume that the paradisiacal state is also the object of divine promise. The idea of paradise therefore does not only have a backward-looking meaning, but rather a salvific future is promised to creation; creation and creatures will not perish into nothingness.

Judaism, Christianity and Islam not only share the conviction that the world was well created by God and entrusted to human beings, but all three religions also share the insight that human beings have failed to live up to their responsibility for creation. The paradise narrative combined with the expulsion from paradise is found in all three monotheistic religions. The consequence is a manifold deformation of the environment, which is reflected in the ecological or socio-ecological crisis of our days, which is interpreted in all three religions as a failure of man with regard to his mission of creation. Today, the ecological crisis affects the three great religions of revelation in equal measure, and together they have a common responsibility before God with regard to the preservation of creation.

At this point, however, the differences also become clear. Although Judaism, Christianity and Islam agree on the paradise narrative, they differ in their understanding of the expulsion from paradise. While this is understood by Christians as the fall of man and is linked to a so-called doctrine of original sin, such an idea is foreign to both Judaism and Islam. Instead, both religions assume that there is a tendency towards both good and evil in human beings and that people are responsible for their actions in their freedom. God's instructions enable him to orientate himself towards the good, for the benefit of his own life, his fellow human beings, fellow creatures and the environment.

With regard to the idea of freedom, another difference can be identified in the fact that according to the Christian understanding, a far greater distinction is made between the Creator God and creation than in Islam. According to the Muslim view, God is always present in his creation, he sustains and causes everything. While this view is shared in principle in the Christian faith, on the Christian side not only man but also the whole of creation is granted a certain autonomy – the differentiation between God as the first cause and the laws of nature as the second causes has become classical in Western theology. This difference is also continued with regard to the future, insofar as, according to Islamic understanding, there will be a community of people among themselves in the gardens of paradise, but not, as assumed in Christianity, a community with God. The paradisiacal gardens of the Koran are not the kingdom of God or heaven, but this world in its ideal state.

If we attempt to draw a conclusion regarding the religious classification of man in his environment, knowing full well that Judaism, Christianity and Islam do not exist in this form and that genetic statements are always problematic, we can nevertheless say that with regard to the key concept of "environment", the common ground between the three great religions of revelation is greater than the differences.

List of Contributors and Editors

Yonatan Neril is a Jerusalem-based interfaith environmental advocate, NGO director and rabbi. He is an international speaker on religion and ecology and co-author of "Eco Bible: An Ecological Commentary on Genesis and Exodus" (with Rabbi Leo Dee, 2020). He is also lead author and general editor of "Uplifting People and Planet: 18 Essential Jewish Teachings on the Environment" (Canfei Nesharim, 2013). He is founder and director of the international Interfaith Center for Sustainable Development (ICSD) in Jerusalem. His numerous lectures, reports for ICSD and organised conferences have led him to many places in Israel, North America and Europe. He writes frequently on religion and ecology for international newspapers.

Leo Dee received a Master's in Engineering from Cambridge University, a Master's in Public Health from Hebrew University, and rabbinical ordination in Israel. A trip around the least affluent countries in Asia and South America woke him up to the tremendous poverty that exists in the world. Encountering people who owned not much more than the clothes on their back, he began to understand the huge impact of lack of food, water and power suffered by half of humanity. So, following six years as a community Rabbi in the United Kingdom, he moved to Israel where he has developed a passion for changing hearts and minds in order to encourage sustainable development – initially among the Israeli financial community, and then within the field of Responsible Investment. He served as director of programs at The Interfaith Center for Sustainable Development. He lives near Jerusalem with his wife, Lucy, and their five children.

Kerstin Schlögl-Flierl has been Professor of Moral Theology at the University of Augsburg since 2015. She studied Catholic theology and German linguistics and literature at the University of Regensburg and Catholic theology at the Pontifical Gregorian University in Rome. After completing her doctorate and habilitation at the University of Regensburg with research stays in Boston (USA), Ljubljana (Slovenia) and Vienna (Austria), she has been offered a chair at Augsburg, where she now is also coordinator of the Master's programme in Environmental Ethics. In the field of bioethics, her research interests focus on issues at the beginning of life (genome editing, reproductive medicine) as well as issues at the end of life. Integrated into the Centre for Interdisciplinary Health Research at the University of Augsburg, issues such as the question of compulsory vaccination are also part of her research. In the area of relationship ethics, she deals with questions such as fidelity and a deeper understanding of a personal relationship ethic. In the area of fundamental morality, it is the ethical judgement formation of young people and the instruments of epics that she focusses on. Kerstin Schlögl-Flierl has been inter alia member of the German Ethics Council since 2020, member of the Ethics Commitee of the University Hospital Augsburg and advisor to the Episcopal Sub-Commission "Bioethics" of the Faith Commission (I) of the German Bishops' Conference.

Yasin Dutton is Professor Emeritus of Arabic Studies at the University of Cape Town, South Africa, and Senior Research Fellow at the Oxford Centre for Islamic Studies. He studied Arabic and Oriental Studies at the University of Oxford (D.Phil 1993) and taught at the University of Oxford before being appointed to posts in the Universities of Edinburgh and Cape Town. He is the author of The Origins of Islamic Law: The Qur'an, the Muwatta' and Madinan 'Amal

(Curzon Press, 1999), and Original Islam: Malik and the Madhhab of Madina (Routledge, 2007), and many articles. His research continues to focus on early Islamic law, early Qur'an manuscripts, and Islamic law in the modern world, particularly with regard to economic and environmental issues.

Christoph Böttigheimer has held the Chair of Fundamental Theology at the Catholic University of Eichstätt-Ingolstadt since 2002. He studied Catholic Theology at the universities of Tübingen and Innsbruck, Austria, and obtained his doctorate at the University of Munich in 1993. He is the author of "Lehrbuch der Fundamentaltheologie", one of the most well-received and influential textbooks in the field of fundamental theology in the German-speaking world. His works in the ongoing legacy of the Second Vatican Council, on supplicatory prayer and core questions of faith have been translated into several languages. His most recent publication, besides a new and revised edition of the famous "Lehrbuch", is "Die Reich-Gottes-Botschaft Jesu. Verlorene Mitte christlichen Glaubens" (Herder, 2020) on Jesus' teaching on the Kingdom of God. He is member of many academic research and working committees, especially in the field of ecumenical dialogue and cooperation.

Wenzel Maximilian Widenka studied History, Catholic Theology and Interreligious Studies at the Universities of Bamberg and Vienna. He received his PhD in Jewish Studies at the University of Bamberg in 2019 with a study about the struggle for religious emancipation of 19th century Jews on the countryside. He was research assistant at the Chair of Fundamental Theology at the Catholic University of Eichstätt-Ingolstadt and is currently working for a German publishing house specialized in the fields of religion and theology. His most recent publications are *"'Sehet, da kommen Schakale, den Weinberg zu zerstören, den Weinberg Israels.' Emanzipation und Konfessionalisierung im fränkischen Landjudentum in der ersten Hälfte des 19. Jahrhunderts"* (University of Bamberg Press, 2019), as well as "Seinen Namen heiligen, um das Volk zu retten", in: Bruns, Peter / Kremer, Thomas / Weckwerth, Andreas (Eds.): *Sterben & Töten für Gott? Das Martyrium in Spätantike und frühem Mittelalter* (Koinonia – Oriens), Münster 2022.

Index of Persons

Abel   23, 27 f.
Abraham   39–43, 45–48, 51–54, 63 f., 144
Adam   11, 18 f., 21–26, 31, 83, 144 f., 163
al-Jamal, Ali   156
Altner, Günter   117
Amos   82
Aquinas, Thomas   89, 109, 165
Arrhenius, Svante   7 f.
as-Sufi, Abd al-Qadir   156
Athanasius   91
Atkinson, Fred   149, 151
Auer, Alfons   118
Augustine   89, 92 f., 165

bar Yochai, Shimon   5
Barr, James   80
Bartholomew (Patriarch)   111, 119–124, 166
Basil of Caesarea   90–92, 165
ben Aderet, Shlomo   3
ben Asher, Jacob   13
ben Elieser, Israel (Ba'al Shem Tov)   6
ben Gamliel, Shimon   3
ben Lakish, Shimon   33, 62
ben Moshe ibn Attar, Chayim   24
ben Nachman, Mosche   19 f., 33–35
ben Yechiel Michel, Meir Leibush   32
ben Yitzchak, Schlomo   16, 18 f., 25 f., 29, 36, 42, 45, 51, 56 f., 64
Benedict of Nursia   116
Benedict XVI. (Pope)   77, 94, 120
Ber Soloveitchik, Joseph   27
Berezovsky, Sholom   12
Berkowitz, Dov   3
Blackie, Sharon   152
Boff, Leonardo   114
Bolsonaro, Jair   85
Bonaventure   94
Bopp, Karl   114–116
Buber, Martin   23, 54, 123

Cain   27 f., 163
Calvin, John   148 f.
Carson, Rachel   153

Chanina   15
Chrysostom   89
Clement of Alexandria   91
Clinton, Bill   150
Cobb, John B.   98
Correa, Rafael   114
Crutzen, Paul   78

da Silva, Jorgiano dos Santos   79
Daecke, Sigurd   117
David   83
Degen-Ballmer, Stephan   97 f., 100
Descartes, René   98
Diamond, Jared   38 f.

Eiger, Shlomo   11
Eisenberg, Evan   36 f.
Ephrem the Syrian   91
Esau   57–64, 66 f.
Eve   21–26, 32

Fichte, Johann Gottlieb   111
Ford, Lewis S.   100
Francis of Assisi   94, 106 f., 165
Francis (Pope)   105, 107, 109–114, 120, 123 f., 166
Freedman, Harry   16

Gerstenfeld, Manfred   37
Gräßer, Erich   117
Gregorios, Paulos   98
Gregory of Nazianzus   90
Gregory of Nyssa   98

HaKohen, Tzadok   24, 61 f.
Hartshorne, Charles   98
Heimbach-Steins, Marianne   110
Higgins, Polly   154
Himes, Kenneth R.   94
Himes, Michael J.   94
Hirsch, Samson Raphael   2, 7, 11, 20, 22, 34, 41, 61
Höhn, Hans-Joachim   118

Homer 90
Hosea 23, 82

ibn Anas, Malik 140, 148
Ibn Khaldun 156
ibn Rushd, Abū l-Walīd Muhammad ibn Ahmad (Averroes) 143
Ibn Rushd al-Jadd 143
Ignatius of Loyola 123
Isaac 39f., 43, 55–57, 60, 63–67
Isaiah (Prophet) 19, 86

Jacob 39f., 43, 57–61, 63f., 66f.
Janowski, Bernd 79–81
Jesus Christ 86f., 112, 115, 124, 165
John 87
John Paul II. (Pope) 120
Judah the Prince 58
Julian of Norwich 95

Karo, Isaac 15
Kessler, Rainer 85
Kimchi, David 14, 30, 48
Koch, Klaus 80
Kohn, Daniel 3, 19
Kook, Abraham Isaac 3, 17f., 20
Krause, Karl Christian Friedrich 111
Kruip, Gerhard 113

Lohfink, Norbert 80
Lorenz, Ursula 116
Luke 87

Malbim See ben Yechiel Michel, Meir Leibush
Manemann, Jürgen 87
Mark, Jeffrey 151
Marks, Gil 15
Marlow, Hilary 82
Maurer, Reinhart 97
Meland, Bernard Eugene 98
Mendel, Menachem 11
Moltmann, Jürgen 117
Mongrain, Kevin 123
Morales, Evo 114
Morariu, Iuliu-Marius 122

Moses 1, 3, 112, 162
Münk, Hans J. 118

Nachmanides See ben Nachman, Mosche
Newton, Isaac 98
Noah 6–8, 29–34, 36, 49, 163

Or HaChayim See ben Moshe ibn Attar, Chayim

Page, Benjamin 150
Pannenberg, Wolfhart 100
Paul 86f.
Paul VI. (Pope) 120
Pittenger, William Norman 98

Radak See Kimchi, David
Rashi See ben Yitzchak, Schlomo
Raworth, Kate 155
Reish Lakish See ben Lakish, Shimon
Reitz, Helga 100
Riede, Peter 85
Riskin, Shlomo 27, 35
Rosen, David 11
Rotzetter, Anton 116

Sacks, Jonathan 1, 5, 20, 40
Samet, Elchanan 18
Schaefer, Jame 88–95
Schelling, Friedrich Wilhelm Joseph 111
Schellnhuber, Hans Joachim 111
Schneider, Sarah Yehudit 24
Schweitzer, Albert 116
Sears, David 17
Seidenberg, David 23, 64
Simon, Maurice 16
Sittler, Joseph 94
Stockmann, Nils 110
Straw, Jack 150f.
Swan, Shanna 153

Temple, William 98
Theokritoff, Elizabeth 124f.
Thunberg, Greta 55
Trump, Donald 85

Vogt, Markus 78, 103–105, 108, 120, 126f., 129

Wadler, Maya 8
Waskow, Arthur 22
Whitehead, Alfred North 98f., 129
Wieman, Henry Nelson 98

Wiesel, Elie 46
Wilson, Edward O. 5
Williams, Daniel Day 98
Woo, Caroline 111

Zenger, Erich 80
Zizioulas, Johannis 111

Index of Subjects

acid rain 48f., 51
adama 19, 54, 163
Amazon Synod 112–114, 166
Amazonia 94, 112–114
Anthropocene 8, 34, 78, 123
anthropocentrism 82, 84, 86, 96, 108, 111, 117f., 121, 142, 165f., 169
Ark 3, 7, 28f., 30–34, 36, 163

ba'al tashḥit 66
Babel 36–38, 163
bī'a 136, 167
biocentrism 96, 108, 116, 166
biodiversity 2, 9, 39, 101–103, 113f., 126, 155, 165
biophilia 94

chaos 2, 79, 84
Chicago School 98
climate change 6–8, 13, 16, 21, 28, 34f., 41, 43, 47, 55, 60, 63, 66, 94, 115, 122–124, 155
CO2 6, 35
Constantinople 119, 123
covenant 30, 34, 78, 115
COVID-19 (Corona) 2, 16, 28, 31, 77
creation 1f., 4, 8–12, 14, 17–22, 25, 33–36, 39, 50f., 53f., 59, 79–94, 97–101, 105, 108, 110–112, 114–123, 125–129, 139, 145, 157, 161–170

Dead Sea 42–44
democracy 104, 150f.
Deuteronomy 2, 147
dominion mandate 16, 21–23, 81, 87, 162, 164

earth 1, 6, 10, 13–15, 17–23, 27f., 30f., 33f., 48, 53f., 57, 60, 64, 81, 83–85, 87, 89f., 93–96, 102, 106–108, 110, 113–115, 119f., 124, 135–140, 142, 144f., 152f., 156f.
eating 10, 14, 19, 21, 24, 26, 61–63, 163f.

ecology 1, 3f., 6, 9f., 25, 31, 39, 42f., 49, 77, 87f., 100, 102–105, 107–110, 112–115, 120, 122, 124f., 136, 161–164, 166–169
economy 103–105, 107, 110, 136, 141f., 149–152, 155, 166, 168
ecosystem 2, 25, 34, 90, 96, 102, 119, 124
ecotheology 125–127
ecumenical dialogue 98
ecumenism 116, 127f.
Eden 1, 11, 19–22, 25–27, 42f., 161f., 169
Egypt 40, 42f.
enosh 83
environment 1f., 4f., 9–11, 41f., 50, 77f., 82, 88, 95f., 105, 108f., 112–114, 125–127, 129, 135f., 140, 144f., 149, 153, 156, 161–169
eukharistia 124
Evangelii gaudium 110
Exodus 2

famine 40f.
fasād 135
flood 7f., 21, 31, 49
fracking 64

Genesis 10–15, 17–22, 24–28, 30, 32–34, 36–43, 45–49, 51–58, 60f., 63–65, 67, 79–82, 87, 92, 121, 162, 164
Gomorrah 43f., 48f.
Greenland 38

ḥamas 7
Hebrew Bible 1–3, 5, 164f.
home 136, 167
house 77, 107–109, 136, 166–168

imago Dei 81, 109, 119
inculturation 108
Israel 9f., 35, 40, 42f., 52f., 58, 66, 68, 84

Jerusalem 53f.

Index of Subjects

Kerala 36
khalifa 144 f., 167
Krausism 111 f.
Krausismo See Krausism

Latin America 28, 107, 113
Laudato Si' 78, 106–112, 120, 166
Leviticus 2
liberation theology 107 f., 114, 166
liturgy 115, 120 f., 125

Madina 140
manicheans 89, 120
Midrash 2, 11 f., 15 f., 19, 21, 23, 25, 29, 31, 36, 39 f., 45, 48, 54, 61, 64
Muwaṭṭa' 140, 148

nature 1 f., 8, 16, 20 f., 28, 30, 36 f., 40, 42 f., 57, 77, 84–86, 91–100, 103–105, 108 f., 111–114, 117 f., 120, 124–128, 161, 163–166, 169
nefesh ḥaya 23
New Testament 86
Numbers (Book of) 2

Octogesima adveniens 120
oikos 107, 136, 167
Old Testament 82, 86, 110, 165
ownership 52, 103, 154

paradise 19 f., 79, 87, 164, 166, 169 f.
Paris Climate Agreement 107
Patriarchate of Constantinople 119, 121
process theology 97–100, 165

quantum theory 107
Querida Amazonia See Amazon Synod

rainbow 32, 34 f., 163
Ramadan 143, 156
recycling 9 f., 29, 66
Reformation 148
religion 3–5, 124

riba 146
Rio Conference 103, 114, 128
Roman Catholic Church 105, 113, 116, 118–120, 122

Sabbath 9, 115
science 5, 99, 108, 167
Shabbat 22, 25
Shari'a 127, 143 f.
shepherd 80, 141, 164
shirk 146
Sinai 2 f.
Slow Food Movement 63
Sodom 42–46, 48–51, 164
stewardship 1 f., 6, 17, 20–22, 28, 30, 37, 141 f., 144, 156, 162–164, 167–169
suffering 94, 96, 100 f.
Sufi 54, 136, 156
sustainability 9, 11 f., 41, 55, 58, 66 f., 90, 103–105, 109, 128, 164 f.

Talmud 4, 7, 17, 29, 31, 33, 40, 54–58, 62
tar sand 43–45, 152
tawḥīd 136
theory of evolution 107
theory of relativity 107
Titanic 7 f.
Tree of Knowledge 22, 24
Tree of Life 24

United Nations (UN) 7, 41, 55, 128
usury 146–149, 155 f., 168

violence 79

war 35, 65 f., 80, 147, 155
water 12 f., 29, 42 f., 55 f., 64–66
West Nile Virus 16
World Council of Churches 127 f.

zakāt 147, 155 f.
Zika Virus 16
zina 146

www.ingramcontent.com/pod-product-compliance
Lightning Source LLC
Chambersburg PA
CBHW030625230426

43661CB00053B/2142